Dont forget it's mine
Le Roy T. Harkness

PUBLIC SERVICE COMMISSION FOR THE FIRST DISTRICT

INVITATION TO CONTRACTORS, FORM OF CONTRACT, BONDS, SCHEDULES AND CONTRACTOR'S PROPOSAL

FOR

CONSTRUCTION, EQUIPMENT, MAINTENANCE AND OPERATION

OF

Tri-Borough Rapid Transit Railroad

COMPRISING

PORTIONS OF

Lexington Avenue Route, River Avenue Route, Jerome Avenue Elevated Route, Southern Boulevard and Whitlock Avenue Route, Southern Boulevard and Westchester Avenue Route, Canal Street Route, Manhattan Bridge Route, Revised, Fourth Avenue Route, Bensonhurst, Bath Beach and Coney Island Route, Brooklyn, Manhattan and Long Island City Route and Brooklyn and Manhattan Loop Lines

---

Form finally adopted by the Commission September 1, 1910, and approved as to form by the Corporation Counsel and filed on Commencement of Advertisement of Invitation to Contractors

PUBLIC SERVICE COMMISSION FOR THE FIRST DISTRICT

CONTRACT

FOR

THE CONSTRUCTION, EQUIPMENT, MAINTENANCE AND OPERATION

OF

Tri-Borough Rapid Transit Railroad

Approved as to form this 1st *day of September,* 1910.

ARCHIBALD R. WATSON,

CORPORATION COUNSEL

OF THE CITY OF NEW YORK.

MARTIN B. BROWN
PRESS
49 57
PARK
PLACE
NEW YORK

TABLE OF CONTENTS.

INVITATION TO CONTRACTORS

The City of New York (hereinafter called the " City "), acting by the Public Service Commission for the First District (hereinafter called the " Commission "), hereby invites proposals to construct in part, to equip, and thereafter to use, maintain and operate for a term of years a Rapid Transit Railroad in the City of New York, known as the Tri-Borough Rapid Transit Railroad and hereinafter in this Invitation referred to for convenience as " the Railroad." The points within the City between which the several parts of the Railroad to be constructed by the Contractor are to run and the route or routes to be followed are briefly as follows: One part begins at a point under Battery Park, near the water-front, in the Borough of Manhattan, and runs thence as a subsurface railroad along and under Greenwich street, Church street, and Broadway (with a connecting line running east and west under Canal street) and under Irving place and Lexington avenue, passing under other streets and private property; thence under the Harlem River and private property to One Hundred and Thirty-fifth street and Park avenue, in the Borough of The Bronx, where the line divides. The east side branch extends under Park avenue and private property to One Hundred and Thirty-eighth street, thence under One Hundred and Thirty-eighth street, the Southern Boulevard, and Whitlock avenue to a point in private property south of Westchester avenue, where the line emerges and becomes an elevated railroad, thence continuing along Whitlock avenue and Westchester avenue to Pelham Bay Park. The west side branch, beginning at One Hundred and Thirty-fifth street and Park avenue, extends thence under private property, Mott avenue, Franz Sigel Park, crossing under other streets and private property to a point in private property near River avenue and One Hundred and Fifty-seventh street, where the line emerges and becomes an elevated railroad, thence continuing along River avenue and Jerome avenue to Woodlawn road. The connecting line in the Borough of Manhattan under Canal street begins near Chrystie street and extends westerly as a sub-surface railroad under Canal street and Watts street to West street. In the Borough of Brooklyn, the Railroad consists of several portions. One portion, which begins in Fourth avenue near Forty-third street, runs thence as a sub-surface railroad under Fourth avenue to Fort Hamilton, and another portion beginning in Fourth avenue near Fortieth street runs thence as a sub-surface railroad under Fortieth street, New Utrecht avenue and Eighty-sixth street to a point between Twenty-third and Twenty-fourth avenues, where it emerges from the ground and becomes an elevated railroad, thence continuing over Eighty-sixth street and Stillwell avenue to Coney Island. The other portion of the Railroad in Brooklyn consists of two branches. One branch begins at the Brooklyn Terminal of the Williamsburg Bridge and runs as a sub-surface railroad under the plaza of Williamsburg Bridge, private property and Broadway to a point between Greene avenue and Lexington avenue. The other branch begins under Fulton street near Ashland place and runs also as a sub-surface railroad under Fulton street, Lafayette avenue and Kossuth place to Bushwick avenue.

The general plan of construction of the Railroad calls for two tracks between Battery Park and Chambers street in Manhattan and four tracks from Chambers street in Manhattan to One Hundred and Thirty-fifth street and Park avenue in The Bronx, with the branches in The Bronx having in the main three tracks each. The branch under Canal street in Manhattan will have two tracks.

In Brooklyn the portion of the Railroad beginning in Fourth avenue and extending to Fort Hamilton will have two tracks, and the other portion, extending to Coney Island, will have three tracks for the subway part and four tracks for the elevated part; the portion consisting of two branches, one running under Broadway from Williamsburg Bridge to Greene avenue, and the other, under Fulton street and Lafayette avenue from Ashland place to Bushwick avenue, will have two tracks for each branch. Turn-outs, cross-overs, connections, sidings, loops, etc., will be constructed, all of which are more particularly indicated on the contract drawings.

The work of constructing the Railroad will include the construction of all necessary sewers and connections along the line of the Railroad; also the necessary support, maintenance, readjustment and reconstruction of vaults adjacent to buildings, pipes, tubes, conduits, subways or other sub-surface structures, the support and care, including underpinning where necessary, of all buildings, monuments, surface, sub-surface, and elevated railroads, and other surface or sub-surface structures, etc., affected by or interfered with during the construction of the work; also the restoration of street surfaces, including pavements.

The method of construction will be partly

trench excavation (under cover unless otherwise provided in the form of contract or permitted by the Commission) and partly tunnel, as set forth in the form of contract.

For the tunnel tubes under the Harlem River two plans, designated Type H and Type K, respectively, have been prepared. Type H is for cast-iron tubes enclosed in concrete. Type K is for riveted steel tubes enclosed in concrete. Bidders for the contract for construction, equipment and operation may select the type they prefer, and shall state their selection in the proposal.

Bidders must examine the form of contract, specifications, maps and plans, must visit the location of the work and inform themselves of the present conditions along the line thereof and make their own estimates of the facilities and difficulties attending the execution of the proposed work.

In addition to the construction, equipment, maintenance and operation of the portion of the

Railroad above referred to, the Contractor shall equip, and thereafter use, maintain and operate as a component part of the Railroad the parts of the Fourth Avenue Route, the Manhattan Bridge Route, Revised, and the Brooklyn and Manhattan Loop Lines now constructed or under construction by the City. The points within the City between which the several parts of the Railroad so constructed or under construction by the City, are to run and the route or routes to be followed are briefly as follows:

> (a) Beginning at a point in the Borough of Manhattan contiguous to the Brooklyn Bridge and extending thence northerly under Centre street to a point at or near Broome street, thence curving easterly into Delancey street; and thence easterly under Delancey street to and over the Williamsburg Bridge to the Brooklyn terminal of such bridge.
>
> (b) Beginning at a point in the line just described at or near White street, in the Borough of Manhattan, and curving thence easterly into Walker street; and thence easterly under Walker street and Canal street

to and over the Manhattan Bridge to a point in Flatbush avenue extension, in the Borough of Brooklyn; thence southerly under Flatbush avenue extension and private property to Fulton street; thence southeasterly under Fulton street and private property to Ashland place; and thence under Ashland place and private property to Hanson place; and thence under Hanson place, private property, Flatbush avenue and Atlantic avenue to Fourth avenue; and thence in a general southerly direction under Fourth avenue to a point therein at or near the intersection of Fourth avenue and Forty-third street.

The maximum fare which will be charged a single passenger for a continuous ride over the whole or any part of the Railroad shall not exceed five cents, unless the Commission shall consent to a higher rate of fare as provided in the form of contract.

Bidders may state in their proposals what transportation facilities connecting or to connect with the Railroad, the Contractor will assure to the

City, specifying separately in List A forming part of the proposal the connecting lines over which the Contractor will assure to any passenger a continuous trip for a single fare not exceeding five cents without change of cars; in List B forming part of the proposal the connecting lines over which the Contractor will assure to any passenger a continuous trip for a single fare not exceeding five cents with or without change of cars at the option of the Contractor; and in List C forming part of the proposal the connecting lines over which the Contractor will assure to any passenger a continuous trip with or without change of cars at the option of the Contractor for fares exceeding five cents per trip, but within limitations to be specified.

A fuller description of the work to be done is set forth and other requirements, provisions, details and specifications are stated in the printed form of contract and in the contract drawings therein referred to. Printed copies of the form of contract, forms of bonds and form of contractor's proposal may be had on application at the office of the Commission, No. 154 Nassau street, Borough of Manhattan, New York City. The contract drawings for the Railroad may be inspected at the same office. The printed form of contract and the contract drawings therein referred to are to be deemed a part of this Invitation.

The Contractor will be required to begin actual work within sixty (60) days after the execution of the contract, and to complete the construction and equipment of the portions of the Railroad to be constructed by him and the equipment of the portions of the Railroad constructed or under construction by the City so that the Railroad shall be ready for immediate, full and continuous operation within four (4) years from the date of the delivery of the contract.

Sealed bids or proposals will be received at the office of the Commission at No. 154 Nassau Street, Borough of Manhattan, City of New York, until the 20th day of October, 1910, at twelve (12) o'clock noon, at which time or at a later date to be fixed by the Commission, the proposals will be publicly opened.

Proposals must be in the form prescribed by the Commission, copies of which may be obtained at the office of the Commission.

The Contractor shall at his or its own expense construct and equip the portion of the Railroad to be constructed by him and shall at his or its own expense equip the portion of the Railroad constructed or under construction by the City except as noted in the form of contract, and shall thereafter put the Railroad into operation, and use, maintain and operate the same for the term of years to be specified in the proposal. The Contractor shall amortize the cost of constructing the portion of the Railroad to be constructed by him and upon the expiration of such amortization period which will be equivalent to the term for the operation of the Railroad the Contractor shall surrender possession of the Railroad (including both the portion constructed by him and the portion constructed by the City) to the City, without compensation to the Contractor, except for the remainder of the cost of additions to and changes in the Railroad that at the rate specified in the contract should remain unamortized and except that the City shall purchase the equipment of the Railroad suitable to and used for the purposes of the contract as therein provided.

The City will provide all real estate or interests therein necessary for the equipment and operation of the Railroad as provided in the form of contract.

The City shall have the right to terminate the contract for the equipment, maintenance and operation of the Railroad at any time after the expiration of ten years from the date when operation of any part of the Railroad shall actually begin, in which event the City shall purchase the equipment of the Railroad suitable to and used for the purposes of the contract and shall pay an amount for the Contractor's investment in the construction of the portion of the Railroad constructed by him which shall not exceed the actual cost to the Contractor plus fifteen per cent. (15%) thereof, all as provided in the form of contract.

Bidders must specify in their proposals as follows:

(1) The term of years during which the Contractor shall have the right to use, maintain and operate the Railroad subject, however, to termination by the City.

(2) The percentage of the cost of construction, of the portion of the Railroad to be constructed by the Contractor, which the Contractor shall set aside annually in quarterly installments as an amortization fund.

(3) The annual rate of interest, to be compounded semi-annually, upon such percentage to be set aside as an amortization fund.

(4) The rate of interest (not to exceed six (6%) per centum per annum) desired upon the cost of constructing and equipping the portion of the Railroad to be constructed and equipped by the Contractor and the cost of equipping the portion of the Railroad constructed or under construction by the City.

The Contractor will be required to pay to the City interest upon the investment of the City in the portion of the Railroad constructed or under construction by it as provided in the form of contract.

Any and all income and increase derived by the Contractor or on his behalf in any manner from the enterprise of constructing, equipping, maintaining and operating the Railroad, shall, after deducting operating expenses, taxes, payments to reserve and amortization and interest upon the investment of the Contractor and the City in the construction and equipment of the Railroad, all as in the form of contract provided, be divided share and share alike between the Contractor and the City.

Each proposal must, when submitted, be enclosed in a sealed envelope endorsed "Proposal for Construction, Equipment, Maintenance and Operation of Tri-Borough Rapid Transit Railroad" and must be delivered to the Commission or to the Secretary of the Commission and in the presence of the person offering the proposal, the proposal will be deposited in a sealed box in which all proposals will be deposited. No proposal will be received or deposited unless accompanied by a certified check drawn upon a national or state bank or trust company, having its principal office in the City of New York, and satisfactory to the Commission, payable to the order of the Comptroller of The City of New York for the amount of one hundred thousand dollars $100,000). Such check must not be enclosed in the envelope containing the proposal.

No proposal will be allowed to be withdrawn for any reason whatever after it shall have been deposited with the Commission.

The award of the contract will be made by the Commission as soon as practicable after the opening of the proposals.

Bidders must state in their proposals the names and places of business of their proposed sureties and a description of the securities they propose depositing. Bidders whose proposals are otherwise satisfactory may, in case the sureties or securities named by them are not approved by the Commission, substitute in their proposals other sureties or securities approved by the Commission, but such substitution must be made within five days after notice of disapproval, unless this period is extended by the Commission.

The bidder whose proposal shall be accepted shall in person or by duly authorized representative attend at the said office of the Commission within ten days after the delivery of a notice by the Commission that his proposal is accepted and that the contract is consented to by the Board of Estimate and Apportionment and such bidder shall then deliver a contract in the form referred to duly executed and with its execution duly proved.

At the time of the delivery of the contract the Contractor will be required to give security to the City as follows: (1) By deposit of two million dollars ($2,000,000) in cash or securities of the character of securities in which savings banks of this State may invest their funds and which securities shall be approved by the Commission, (2) By bond for construction and equipment for two million dollars ($2,000,000), and (3) By bond for construction, equipment, maintenance and operation for three million dollars ($3,000,000). The Contractor's bonds must be in the forms annexed to the form of contract.

In case of failure or neglect to execute and deliver the contract or to make the required deposit or to execute and deliver the required bonds such bidder will, at the option of the Commission, be deemed either to have made the contract or to have abandoned the contract. In the latter case the Commission will give notice thereof to the defaulting bidder and the Commission may thereupon proceed to make another contract with such, if any, of the original bidders as in the opinion of the Commission it will be to the best interests of the City to contract with, or may by new advertisement invite further proposals. The defaulting bidder shall thereupon be liable to the City for all loss and damage by it sustained.

If the Commission shall give notice to any bidder that his or its proposal is accepted and that the contract is consented to by the Board of Estimate and Apportionment and if the bidder shall fail within ten days thereafter or within such further period, if any, as may be prescribed by the Commission, to execute and deliver the contract and to make the required deposit and to execute and deliver the bonds with sureties, then this Invitation to Contractors and proposal accepted as aforesaid shall be a contract binding the bidder to pay to the City the damage by it sustained by reason of such failure, and in such case the bidder shall by the terms of the proposal absolutely assign to the City the ownership of the check accompanying his or its proposal as a payment on account of such damages.

All certified checks deposited by bidders whose proposals shall not be accepted by the Commission will be returned to the person or persons depositing the same within five days after the contract shall be executed and delivered. The check of the successful bidder will be returned when the contract is executed and its provisions as to security are complied with.

The right to reject any and all bids is reserved.

New York, September 1, 1910.

PUBLIC SERVICE COMMISSION FOR THE FIRST DISTRICT,

By WILLIAM R. WILLCOX,
Chairman.

TRAVIS H. WHITNEY,
Secretary.

TRI-BOROUGH RAPID TRANSIT RAILROAD

CONTRACT

Agreement, made this day of , 1910, between THE CITY OF NEW YORK, hereinafter called the City, acting by the PUBLIC SERVICE COMMISSION FOR THE FIRST DISTRICT, hereinafter called the Commission, party of the first part, and

of

hereinafter called the Contractor, party of the second part.

WHEREAS, the Commission, in behalf of the City, by due advertisement pursuant to law, has invited contractors to submit to the Commission proposals for making this contract; and

WHEREAS, the Contractor has thereupon duly submitted to the Commission a proposal which has been accepted; and

WHEREAS the Board of Estimate and Apportionment of The City of New York has consented to this contract;

Now, therefore, in consideration of the mutual stipulations and covenants hereinafter contained, and under the authority of chapter 4 of the laws of 1891, entitled, "An Act to Provide for "Rapid Transit Railways in Cities of over One "Million Inhabitants," and of the various acts amending the same, the parties hereby do, the City for itself and its successors and the Contractor for*

and assigns

Agree each with the other as follows:

*Here insert, if a corporation, *itself, its successors;* if a single individual, *himself, his executors, administrators;* if several individuals, *themselves jointly and severally, and their and each of their executors, administrators.*

Chapter I

GENERAL PROVISIONS

Article I The Contractor agrees with the City to construct the portion of the rapid transit railroad hereinafter described wholly at his own cost and to do all incidental work in connection therewith as hereinafter provided, to equip such portion and the portion of such rapid transit railroad hereinafter described which is constructed or under construction by the City and put the same in operation and thereafter to use, maintain and operate the same in accordance with the Operation Provisions hereof; but the City shall have the right as hereinafter provided to terminate the contract for the equipment, maintenance and operation of the Railroad at any time after the expiration of ten years from the date when operation of any part of the Railroad shall actually begin, in which event the City shall purchase the equipment of the Railroad suitable to and used for the purposes of this contract and shall pay an amount for the Contractor's investment in the construction of the Railroad, which shall not exceed the actual cost to the Contractor, plus fifteen per cent. thereof, and shall decrease under the provisions hereof as the term continues, all as hereinafter provided.

Returns under the Operation Provisions

ARTICLE II Any and all income and increase derived by the Contractor or on his behalf in any manner from or in connection with the enterprise of constructing, equipping, maintaining and operating the Railroad shall, after deducting operating expenses, taxes, payments to reserve and amortization funds and interest upon the actual cost to the City and the Contractor of the construction and equipment of the Railroad as hereinafter provided, be divided share and share alike between the Contractor and the City as provided in Chapter III hereof.

Portion to be built by Contractor

Article III (a) The Rapid Transit Railroad System embraced in this contract comprises parts of several projected rapid transit railroads, some of which are to be constructed, equipped, maintained and operated by the Contractor while others, which are either already constructed by the City or under construction by it, are to be equipped, maintained and operated by the Contractor. The routes and general plans of such projected railroads to be constructed, as well as equipped, maintained and operated by the Contractor (which routes and general plans shall be deemed to be incorporated in this contract), were adopted and approved or consented to as follows:

Lexington Avenue Route

Adopted by the Board of Rapid Transit Railroad Commissioners for The City of New York on the 12th day of May, 1905, approved by the

Board of Estimate and Apportionment of the City on the 14th day of July, 1905, by the Mayor of the City on the 28th day of July, 1905, and by the Appellate Division of the Supreme Court in and for the First Judicial Department by an order entered in the office of its clerk on the 19th day of October, 1906. MODIFIED by the Commission by resolutions adopted on February 4, 1908, and April 29, 1908, respectively, which modifications were approved by the said Board of Estimate and Apportionment on the 13th day of March, 1908, and the 8th day of May, 1908, respectively, by the said Mayor on the 18th day of March, 1908, and the 12th day of May, 1908, respectively, and by the said Court by an order entered in the office of its clerk on the 4th day of January, 1909. FURTHER MODIFIED by the Commission by resolutions adopted on the 21st day of May, 1909, which modification was approved by the said Board of Estimate and Apportionment on the 4th day of June, 1909, by the said Mayor on the 8th day of June, 1909, and by the said Court by an order entered in the office of its clerk on the 24th day of February, 1910.

The portion of such route to be constructed under this contract is as follows:

> Beginning at a point under Battery Park near the water front, and running thence under Greenwich street, Trinity place and Church street and private property to Vesey street, under Vesey street and private property to Broadway, northerly under Broadway to a point near East Ninth street where it leaves Broadway and continues under private property and the several cross streets to Irving place and Fourteenth street; thence northerly under Irving place, Gramercy Park and Lexington avenue to and under the Harlem River to the Borough of The Bronx at about Park avenue, thence northerly under private property and Park avenue to about East One Hundred and Thirty-fifth street and Park avenue where it divides into two branches; the east branch extending un-

der Park avenue, private property and East One Hundred and Thirty-eighth street to a point near Third avenue where a connection can conveniently be made with the Southern Boulevard and Westchester Avenue Route; the west branch extending under private property and Mott avenue to about One Hundred and Fiftieth street where a connection can conveniently be made with the River Avenue Route.

This route is entirely in subway and in general there are to be two tracks from the Battery to Chambers street, four tracks from Chambers street to One Hundred and Thirty-fifth street and Park avenue, thence three tracks on each branch, with necessary switches, connections and sidings as permitted by the general plan of construction.

As a part of this contract and in conjunction with this route there is to be constructed a portion of the Seventh and Eighth Avenue Route, which was authorized by the Board of Rapid Transit Railroad Commissioners for The City of New York on the 12th day of May, 1905, approved by the Board of Estimate and Apportionment of the City on the 14th day of July, 1905, by the

Mayor on the 28th day of July, 1905, and by the said Appellate Division by an order entered in the office of its clerk on the 19th day of October, 1906. Such portion of such route may be described as follows:

> All that portion of the subway and terminal, west of the centre line thereof, from a point on the centre line of the subway in Greenwich Street produced about fifteen (15) feet north of Morris Street to the end of the terminal under Battery Park.

River Avenue Elevated Route

Adopted by the Commission on the 16th day of June, 1908, approved by the said Board of Estimate and Apportionment on the 26th day of June, 1908, by the said Mayor on the 30th day of June, 1908, and by the said Court by an order entered in the office of its clerk on the 13th day of July, 1909.

The portion of such route to be constructed under this contract is as follows:

Beginning at a point in Mott avenue near One Hundred and Fiftieth street where a connection can conveniently be made with the Lexington Avenue Route; thence extending northwesterly under Mott avenue, Franz Sigel Park, private property and the several cross streets and emerging from the ground to an elevated structure at a point near the intersection of East One Hundred and Fifty-seventh street and River avenue; thence continuing northerly as an elevated structure along River avenue to a connection with the Jerome Avenue Elevated Route at about Clark place and Jerome avenue.

There are to be three tracks on this route, together with a loop and necessary switches, connections and sidings as permitted by the general plan of construction.

Jerome Avenue Elevated Route

Adopted by the Board of Rapid Transit Railroad Commissioners for The City of New York on the 1st day of June, 1905, approved by the said Board of Estimate and Apportionment on the 14th day of July, 1905, by the Mayor on the

28th day of July, 1905, and consented to by the owners of more than one-half in value of property abutting upon the line of such route. MODIFIED by the Commission by resolution adopted on the 26th day of May, 1910, which modification was approved by the said Board of Estimate and Apportionment on the 24th day of June, 1910, and by the Mayor on the 5th day of July, 1910.

The portion of such route to be constructed under this contract is as follows:

> Beginning at a point in Jerome avenue, near Clark place, where a connection can conveniently be made with the River Avenue Elevated Route, and extending thence northerly over Jerome avenue and over a portion of the Jerome Park Reservoir property to Woodlawn road.
>
> This road is entirely an elevated structure excepting the portion crossing Jerome Park Reservoir property, which is partly elevated and partly in open cut, and there are to be three tracks, with necessary switches, connections and sidings as permitted by the general plan of construction.

Southern Boulevard and Whitlock Avenue Route

Adopted by the Commission on the 6th day of August, 1909, approved by the said Board of Estimate and Apportionment on the 10th day of December, 1909, by the said Mayor on the 13th day of December, 1909, and consented to by the owners of more than one-half in value of property abutting upon the line of such route.

The portion of such route to be constructed under this contract is as follows:

> Beginning at a point under East One Hundred and Thirty-eighth street, near Cypress avenue, where a connection can conveniently be made with the Southern Boulevard and Westchester Avenue Route, and continuing thence as a subway under East One Hundred and Thirty-eighth street to a point near Robbins avenue; thence curving into the Southern Boulevard and continuing under the Southern Boulevard to a point near Hunt's Point road where it curves to and under Whitlock avenue and extends thence under Whitlock avenue and private property to a point in private property on the west side of Whitlock avenue, between Aldus street and Bancroft street, at which point it emerges from the ground to an elevated structure and continues thence as an elevated structure over private property, Whitlock avenue and Westchester avenue to a point

near Edgewater road, where a connection can conveniently be made with the Southern Boulevard and Westchester Avenue Route.

This route is both subway and elevated, and there are to be three tracks, with necessary switches, connections and sidings as permitted by the general plan of construction.

Southern Boulevard and Westchester Avenue Route

Adopted by the Board of Rapid Transit Railroad Commissioners for The City of New York on the 17th day of May, 1906, approved by the said Board of Estimate and Apportionment on the 8th day of June, 1906, by the said Mayor on the 14th day of June, 1906, and consented to by the owners of more than one-half in value of property abutting upon the line of such route.

The portion of such route to be constructed under this contract is as follows:

One portion thereof begins at a point under East One Hundred and Thirty-eighth street, near Third avenue, where a connection can conveniently be made with the Lexington Avenue Route and extends easterly under

East One Hundred and Thirty-eighth street to a point near Cypress avenue, where a connection can conveniently be made with the Southern Boulevard and Whitlock Avenue Route. The other portion thereof begins on Westchester avenue near Edgewater road, where a connection can conveniently be made with the Southern Boulevard and Whitlock Avenue Route and extends thence easterly over Westchester avenue to the terminus thereof at Pelham Bay Park.

The portion of the route on East One Hundred and Thirty-eighth street is in subway and on Westchester avenue is an elevated structure.

There are to be three tracks throughout, with necessary switches, connections and sidings as permitted by the general plan of construction.

Canal Street Route

Adopted by the Commission on the 4th day of February, 1908, approved by the said Board of Estimate and Apportionment on the 13th day of March, 1908, by the said Mayor on the 18th day of March, 1908, and by the said Court by an order entered in the office of its clerk on the 13th day of July, 1909.

The portion of such route to be constructed under this contract is as follows:

> Beginning at a point in the Borough of Manhattan near the intersection of Canal street and Centre street at which a connection can conveniently be made with the Manhattan Bridge Route, Revised, and thence extending westerly under Canal street and Watts street to a point near West street.
>
> There are to be two tracks throughout with necessary switches, connections and sidings as permitted by the general plan of construction.

Manhattan Bridge Route, Revised

Adopted by the Board of Rapid Transit Railroad Commissioners for The City of New York on the 18th day of April, 1907, approved by the said Board of Estimate and Apportionment on the 26th day of April, 1907, by the said Mayor on the 1st day of May, 1907, and as to the portion in the Borough of Manhattan by the said Court by an order entered in the office of its clerk on the 13th day of July, 1909, and as to the portion in the Borough of Brooklyn, by the owners of one-half in value of the property abutting upon such portion of the route.

The portion of such route to be constructed under this contract is as follows:

> Beginning at a point in the Borough of Manhattan near the intersection of Canal street and Centre street at which a connection can conveniently be made with the Canal Street Route and thence extending easterly under Canal street to the Manhattan Bridge.
>
> There are to be two tracks throughout, with necessary switches, connections and sidings as permitted by the general plan of construction.

Brooklyn and Manhattan Loop Lines

Adopted by the Board of Rapid Transit Railroad Commissioners for The City of New York on the 25th day of May, 1905, approved by the said Board of Estimate and Apportionment on the 14th day of July, 1905, by the said Mayor on the

28th day of July, 1905, by the Appellate Division of the Supreme Court in and for the First Judicial Department by an order entered in the office of its clerk on the 12th day of March, 1907, and by the Appellate Division of the Supreme Court in and for the Second Judicial Department by an order entered in the office of its clerk on the 25th day of January, 1907.

The portion of such route to be constructed under this contract is as follows:

> The portion of this route to be constructed hereunder is divided into two branches, the Broadway branch and the Lafayette avenue branch.
>
> The Broadway branch begins at the Brooklyn terminal of the Williamsburg Bridge, at or near Driggs avenue, and extends thence under the plaza of the Williamsburg Bridge and private property to Broadway at a point near Marcy avenue; thence under Broadway to a point about midway between Greene avenue and Lexington avenue.
>
> The Lafayette avenue branch begins under Fulton street at a point near Ashland place

where a connection can be made with a section of a subway now under construction, known as Section 9-C-1; thence extending easterly under Fulton street to the intersection of Fulton street and Lafayette avenue; thence extending easterly under Lafayette avenue to a point at or near Stuyvesant avenue where a connection can conveniently be made with the Brooklyn, Manhattan and Long Island City Route.

This route is a two track subway, the two tracks on the Broadway branch being built on the southerly side of the street so that two tracks may be built on the northerly side at a future date. There are also switches, connections and sidings as permitted by the general plan of construction.

The Broadway branch may be extended in the future under Broadway.

Brooklyn, Manhattan and Long Island City Route

Adopted by the Board of Rapid Transit Railroad Commissioners for The City of New York on the 25th day of May, 1905, approved by the said Board of Estimate and Apportionment on the 14th day of July, 1905, by the said Mayor on the 28th day of May, 1905, and by the Appellate Division of the Supreme Court in and for the Second Judicial District by an order entered in the office of its clerk on the 15th day of March, 1907.

The portion of such route to be constructed under this contract is as follows:

> Beginning at a point near the intersection of Lafayette avenue and Stuyvesant avenue where a connection can conveniently be made with the Lafayette avenue portion of the Brooklyn Sections of the Brooklyn and Manhattan loop lines and extending thence easterly under Lafayette avenue to Broadway, crossing under the Broadway subway hereinbefore referred to, and thence under Kossuth place to Bushwick avenue.
>
> There are to be two tracks throughout, with necessary switches, connections and sidings as permitted by the general plan of construction.

Fourth Avenue Route

Adopted by the Board of Rapid Transit Railroad Commissioners for The City of New York on the 1st day of June, 1905, approved by said Board of Estimate and Apportionment on the 14th day of July, 1905, by the said Mayor on the 28th day of July, 1905, and by the Appellate Division of the Supreme Court in and for the Second Judicial Department by an order entered in the office of its clerk on the 18th day of June, 1906.

The portion of such route to be constructed under this contract is as follows:

> Beginning at a point under Fourth avenue, near Forty-third street, at the end of the portion of the Fourth Avenue Route now under construction; thence under Fourth avenue to Fort Hamilton.
>
> There are to be two tracks on this line in subway, with necessary switches, connections and sidings as permitted by the general plan of construction, and provision is made so that two tracks may be added in the future.

Bensonhurst, Bath Beach and Coney Island Route

Adopted by the Board of Rapid Transit Railroad Commissioners for The City of New

York on the 7th day of June, 1906, approved by the said Board of Estimate and Apportionment on the 15th day of June, 1906, by the said Mayor on the 18th day of June, 1906, and consented to by the owners of more than one-half in value of property abutting upon the line of such route.

The portion of such route to be constructed under this contract is as follows:

> Beginning at a point under Fourth avenue near Thirty-ninth street in the Borough of Brooklyn at which a connection can conveniently be made with the portion of the Fourth Avenue Route now under construction, extending thence under private property, Fortieth street, private property and New Utrecht avenue to Eighty-first street; thence under private property and various cross-streets to Eighty-sixth street; thence through Eighty-sixth street to a point between Twenty-third and Twenty-fourth avenues where it emerges from the ground and becomes an elevated structure and continues thence over Eighty-sixth street and Stillwell avenue to Coney Island, with a loop at Coney Island.

There are to be three tracks for the subway part, and four tracks for the elevated part of this route, with necessary switches, connections and sidings as permitted by the general plan of construction, and provision is made so that an additional track may be added on the subway part in the future. There are to be two tracks on the loop at Coney Island.

Such routes and the number and location of tracks and the stations are more particularly indicated on the contract drawings hereinafter referred to.

(b) In addition to the construction, as well as the equipment, maintenance and operation, of the portions of the Railroad, hereinbefore in this Article described, the Contractor agrees to equip, maintain and operate the portions of the Railroad already completed or under construction by the City. Such portions comprise parts of the Brooklyn and Manhattan Loop Lines, the Manhattan Bridge Route, Revised and the Fourth Avenue

Route, which were adopted and approved or consented to as aforesaid, and may be described as follows:

Portion to be provided by City

(a) Beginning at a point in the Borough of Manhattan contiguous to the Brooklyn Bridge and extending thence northerly under Centre street to a point at or near Broome street, thence curving easterly into Delancey street and thence easterly under Delancey street to and over the Williamsburg Bridge to the Brooklyn terminal of such bridge.

(b) Beginning at a point in the line just described at or near White street in the Borough of Manhattan and curving thence easterly into Walker street and thence easterly under Walker street and Canal street to and over the Manhattan Bridge to a point in Flatbush avenue extension in the Borough of Brooklyn, thence southerly under Flatbush avenue extension and private property to Fulton street, thence southeasterly under Fulton street and private property to Ashland place and thence under Ashland place and private property to Hanson place and thence under Hanson place, private property, Flatbush avenue and Atlantic avenue to Fourth avenue and thence in a general southerly direction under Fourth avenue to a point therein at or near the intersection of Fourth avenue and Forty-third street.

For convenience a copy of the routes and general plans referred to is hereto appended entitled "**Copy Routes and General Plans**" and the Contractor is required carefully to comply therewith.

Construction of the contract

ARTICLE IV The Contractor shall so construct and equip the Railroad as to meet fully and strictly all the requirements and exigencies of the operation thereof as provided in the Operation Provisions or required by or under the laws of the State of New York.

Marginal notes, etc.

ARTICLE V Titles, headings, running head lines and marginal notes are printed hereon merely for convenience and shall not be deemed to be any part of this contract for any purpose whatever.

Definitions of words

ARTICLE VI The following words and expressions used in this contract shall, except where by the context it is clear that another meaning is intended, be construed as follows:

(1.) The word "City" to mean The City of New York, and any other corporation or division of government to which the ownership, rights, powers and privileges of The City of New York under the Rapid Transit Act shall hereafter come, belong or appertain. "City"

(2.) The word "Commission" to mean the Public Service Commission for the First District, and any other board, body, official or officials, to which or to whom the powers belonging to the Commission shall, by virtue of any act or acts, hereafter pass or be held to appertain. "Commission"

(3.) The word "Contractor" to mean the part* of the second part to this contract, and† "Contractor"

*Here and in like blanks hereafter insert *y* or *ies*, as the case may be.

†Here insert, as the case may be, either *its successors* or *his executors, administrators and assigns*, or *their and each of their executors, administrators and assigns*.

and any and every person or corporation who or which shall at any time be liable in the place or for the part of the second part to perform any obligations under this contract assumed by the said part of the second part. For convenience the Contractor is hereinafter spoken of as if the Contractor were an individual. The word " he " shall, as the sense may require, include " him," " she," " her," " it," " they " and " them," and the word " his " shall include " her," " its " and " their."

"Comptroller"

(4.) The word " Comptroller " to mean the Comptroller of The City of New York, and the officer or board to whom or to which his powers now existing under the Rapid Transit Act shall come to appertain.

"Engineer"

(5.) The word " Engineer " to mean the Chief Engineer of the Commission and any successor or successors duly appointed or any deputy or substitute for him who shall be appointed by the Commission or by its authority.

(6.) The words " Rapid Transit Act " to mean chapter 4 of the laws of 1891 as amended by chapters 102 and 556 of the laws of 1892, chapters 528 and 752 of the laws of 1894, chapter 519 of the laws of 1895, chapter 729 of the laws of 1896, chapter 616 of the laws of 1900, chapter 587 of the laws of 1901, chapters 533, 542, 544 and 584 of the laws of 1902, chapters 562 and 564 of the laws of 1904, chapters 599 and 631 of the laws of 1905, and chapters 472, 606 and 607 of the laws of 1906, chapters 429 and 534 of the laws of 1907, chapter 472 of the laws of 1908, chapter 498 of the laws of 1909, and chapters 205, 504, 505 and 506 of the laws of 1910, or as heretofore or hereafter otherwise amended. "Rapid Transit Act"

"Public Service Commissions Law"

(7.) The words "Public Service Commissions Law" to mean chapter 429 of the laws of 1907 as amended, as the same now exists or as the same may hereafter be amended or supplemented.

"Railroad"

(8) The word "Railroad" to mean the portions of the railroads (described in routes and general plans) referred to in Article III hereof together with all stations and real estate or interests therein belonging to or used in conjunction therewith, and all appurtenances thereto and all other property to be used thereon or in connection therewith, and the extensions, additions and changes provided for in Chapter III hereof; excepting, however, the Equipment. Wherever reference is made to the construction of the Railroad the same shall be deemed to refer to the portion of the Railroad to be constructed by the Contractor. Likewise when reference is made to any

matter involved in the equipment, maintenance or operation of the Railroad, or to additions to or changes in the Railroad provided for in the Operation Provisions, the same shall be deemed to refer to the portion of the Railroad constructed or under construction by the City as well as to the portion to be constructed by the Contractor.

"Construction prov

(9) The words "Construction Provisions" to mean the provisions of Chapter II of this contract as explained or modified by the provisions of this chapter.

"Construction."

(10) The word "Construction" to mean all the work of constructing the Railroad, including the doing of work, the providing of materials, the restoration and reconstruction of street surfaces, sewers and other sub-surface structures and all other work to be done or materials to be furnished of every nature whatsoever under the Construc-

tion Provisions, together with all real estate and interests therein that may be necessary for terminal and storage yards.

"Construction cost" (11) The words "cost of construction" or "construction cost" as used herein shall mean (1) the actual and necessary net cost in money to the Contractor of all labor and materials entering into the construction of the Railroad, including premiums actually and necessarily paid on insurance against damages during construction; (2) the actual and necessary net cost in money to the Contractor of any real estate or interest therein acquired for terminals or storage yards, together with the actual and necessary expense in connection with such acquisition; (3) taxes, assessments and interest actually and necessarily paid upon Items 1, 2, 4 and 5 of this paragraph pending the beginning of operation of the

Railroad; (4) the sum actually and necessarily paid by the Contractor for superintendence, engineering and administration in and about the construction of the Railroad and (5) a sum for the actual and necessary organization and preliminary expenditures of the Contractor to be determined by the Commission. If any profit from whatever source derived shall accrue directly or indirectly to the Contractor, or on his behalf, in any manner out of the construction of the Railroad then the amount of any such profit shall be deducted from the cost of the other items in this paragraph referred to.

(12) The words "cost of equipment or "equipment cost" as used herein shall mean (1) the actual and necessary net cost in money to the Contractor of all labor and materials entering into the Equipment of the Railroad, (2) the actual and

"Equipment cost"

necessary net cost in money to the Contractor of any real estate or interest therein acquired as part of Equipment together with the actual and necessary expense in connection with such acquisition, (3) taxes, assessments and interest actually and necessarily paid on Equipment pending the beginning of operation of the Railroad and (4) the sum actually and necessarily paid by the Contractor for superintendence, engineering and administration in and about the acquisition of the Equipment. If any profit from whatever source derived shall accrue directly or indirectly to the Contractor or on his behalf in any manner out of the provision of Equipment of the Railroad, then the amount of any such profit shall be deducted from the cost of the other items in this paragraph referred to.

(13) The words "New York" to mean the City of New York according to its boundaries as now or hereafter fixed. "New York"

(14) The words "daily newspaper" to mean any paper regularly published in the City of New York on every day or every day except Sundays and holidays. "Daily newspaper"

(15) The word "notice" to mean a written notice and the word "direction" to mean a written direction (save in the specifications, where it may mean either a written or oral direction). Every such notice or direction to be served upon the Contractor, or upon any surety, if not delivered personally, shall either be delivered at such office in New York as shall have been designated by the Contractor or surety, or shall be mailed by deposit in the general or any branch postoffice in New York, postage prepaid, addressed to the office so "Notice" "Direction"

designated, or to such office as the Contractor shall designate by written notice delivered to the Commission, or if no such office shall have been designated, or if such designation shall have for any reason become inoperative, then addressed to the person or corporation intended, at New York. Such delivery or mailing shall be equivalent to direct personal notice.

Operation provisions"

(16) The words "Operation Provisions" to mean the provisions of Chapter III of this contract as modified or explained by the provisions of this chapter.

"Equipment"

(17) The word "Equipment" to mean all equipment used or intended for use on the Railroad, including all motors, cars, whether used for passengers, freight, express or any other purpose, and all other rolling stock, all boilers, engines, wires, ways, conduits (other than any system,

which is built as a part of the permanent railroad structure), mechanisms, machinery, power houses, all real estate upon which any such power houses shall stand or which shall be necessary for the generation or transmission of power, all tools, implements and devices of every nature whatsoever used for such generation or transmission of power, all apparatus and all devices for lighting, heating, signalling and ventilation, all rails, ties, ballast or other supports or appliances constituting the tracks, all pumps, fire supply lines and appurtenances, and all telephone and telegraph wires or appliances—whether such equipment be situate on or near or separate from the railway, provided that the same be used or intended for use in connection therewith or for any of the purposes of the Railroad, and including all such equipment in existence at any time during or at the end of the term of the Operation Provisions. Provided, however, that real estate or rights, franchises, easements or privileges therein or thereon acquired for terminals, storage-yards, roadbed, stations, station approaches or otherwise for the Railroad shall not be included in Equipment, but shall be part of the Railroad and the property of the City.

"Operation" (18) The word "Operation" to mean using, operating and maintaining the Railroad according to the Operation Provisions.

ARTICLE VII All parts of the Railroad shall, when and as constructed, immediately be and become the property of the City.

Statutes incorporated herein

ARTICLE VIII This contract is made pursuant to the Rapid Transit Act which is to be deemed a part hereof as if it were incorporated herein.

Security by Contractor

ARTICLE IX Simultaneously with the execution of this contract the Contractor shall give security for the performance of his obligations as follows:

1

Deposit of cash or securities

(*a*) By depositing with the Comptroller the sum of two million dollars ($2,000,000) in cash or in value of securities as the Contractor may elect. If securities be deposited they shall be securities of which a schedule shall be hereto annexed, entitled **Schedule of Construction Securities,** together with the written approval of the Commission which it shall give when satisfied as to the character and value thereof. In case any of the securities shall, in the opinion of the Commission, at any time cease to be of the character of securities in which the savings banks of the State of New York are then authorized by law to invest moneys, or shall, in the opinion of the Commission, at any time become of less value than the value stated for it or them in the said schedule, then within ten days after notice to the Contractor of the objection of the Commission the Contractor shall either substitute therefor securities which shall be approved by the Commission as of the character aforesaid and as being of at least the value of the former securities to which the Commission shall have objected as such value was originally stated in the said schedule, or shall deposit with the Comptroller in cash the amount of such value of such former securities as so originally stated. In case the Contractor shall not within such ten days substitute such new securities or deposit cash as aforesaid, he shall, if the Commission so elect, be deemed to be in default in the performance of his obligations under this contract.

The securities so objected to shall upon such substitution of securities or deposit of cash in lieu thereof be returned to the Contractor.

When Contractor may substitute cash or securities

(*b*) If and as the Commission shall consent, and the law permits, the Contractor may, from time to time substitute cash for securities or securities of the character aforesaid for cash, but always so that the total amount and value of the deposit shall not be reduced.

Interest on deposit

(*c*) The Contractor shall be entitled to receive, when and as received by the City, a sum which shall be equal to the interest, dividends or other income which the City shall receive from such securities (if securities be deposited), or, not oftener than semi-annually, to a sum which shall be equal to the interest on said deposit (if made in cash) at the average rate of interest received by the City on its bank balances during the period for which such interest has run. If, however, any of the cash or securities so deposited shall have been used or applied for any of the purposes mentioned herein then the Contractor shall not be entitled to interest or other return on the amount of cash or securities so applied from the time of such application.

Security for

(*d*) The said deposit whether in cash or securities, in the form and as the same shall at any time be, shall be security for the faithful performance by the Contractor of all the covenants, conditions and requirements specified and provided for in the Construction Provisions. In case of any default on the part of the Contractor in such performance, and in the further case that the City shall for or by reason of such failure, whether by reason of employment of another contractor or contractors or otherwise, incur or become liable for expense through such default as in the Construction Provisions provided, then the Comptroller shall forthwith pay or apply to the use of the City the amount of such expense out of the said deposit in cash or securities or out of the portion of the deposit remaining at the time.

(*e*) The Comptroller shall, upon the requirement of the Commission, in order to make such payment or application to the use of the City, sell at public auction in New York any of the securities which may then constitute part of such deposit upon notice to be published in three daily newspapers, the first publication to be as much as ten days before the sale and such publication to be made three times within such ten days. Any such sale shall be adjourned from time to time if requested by the Commission. The Comptroller shall, upon the requirement of the Commission, deduct from the proceeds of any such sale, all expenses thereof and of such advertisement, and pay and apply to the use of the City so much of the residue of such proceeds as may be necessary for

Sale of securities

the purpose aforesaid. And the Contractor within ten days after notice from the Commission so to do shall (unless the time be extended by the Commission) by further deposit according to the requirement of the Commission, of money or securities of the character aforesaid approved by the Commission, restore the said deposit with the Comptroller to the full amount originally required. In addition to, or in lieu of, the sale above provided for, the Commission may, in the name of and in behalf of the City, bring any appropriate suit or proceeding in any proper court to enforce the lien and claim of the City in and upon the said deposit, whether such deposit be in money or securities.

Reservations

(*f*) If at any time when the Contractor shall otherwise be entitled to a return of the said deposit, there shall be pending any claim for damages or loss caused to others by the Contractor, for which it shall be claimed that the City shall be liable, then and in that case the said deposit, or such part thereof as the Commission shall prescribe, shall, upon the requirement of the Commission, be reserved by the Comptroller for a reasonable time as security to the City against such claims. And the amount of any such damages or costs paid by the City to others or for which the City shall be liable to others shall be deducted from the said deposit before the same shall be returned to the Contractor as hereinafter provided.

(*g*) When the Contractor shall have completed approximately one-quarter (¼) of the Construction of all the work required to be constructed according to the terms of this contract the Commission shall so certify, and upon such certificate the Comptroller shall pay and deliver to the Contractor one-half (½) of the said deposit, or so **Returnable, when** much thereof as shall not have been reserved or used or applied for any of the purposes above mentioned, and when the Contractor shall have completed approximately one-half (½) of all the work required to be constructed according to the terms of this contract the Commission shall so certify, and upon such certificate the Comptroller shall pay and deliver to the Contractor the balance of the said deposit, or so much thereof as shall not have been reserved or used or applied for any of the purposes above mentioned.

1 A

Construction bond

By filing with the Comptroller a bond in due form executed by the Contractor and by two or more sureties being corporations or persons approved by the Commission, in the sum of two million dollars ($2,000,000), the said bond to be substantially in the form hereto annexed and entitled "**Bond for Construction and Equipment.**"

When the Contractor shall have fully completed the Construction and Equipment of the Railroad according to the terms of this contract, and the Railroad exclusive of extensions shall be completely in operation, the Commission shall so certify and upon such certificate the Comptroller shall deliver such bond duly cancelled to the Contractor.

2

(*a*) By filing with the Comptroller a bond in due form executed by the Contractor and by two or more sureties being corporations or persons approved by the Commission, in the sum of three million dollars ($3,000,000), the said bond to be substantially in the form hereto annexed and entitled "**Bond for Construction, Equipment, Maintenance and Operation.**" In case any of the sureties upon either the Bond for Con-

Continuing bond

struction and Equipment or the Bond for Construction, Equipment, Maintenance and Operation shall become insolvent or unable in the opinion of the Commission to pay promptly the amount of such bond to the extent to which such surety might be liable, then the Contractor, within thirty days after notice by the Commission to the Contractor, shall, by supplemental bond or otherwise, substitute another and sufficient surety to be approved by the Commission in place of the surety so insolvent or unable. If the Contractor shall fail, within such thirty days or such further time as the Commission may grant, to substitute another and sufficient surety, then the Contractor shall, for all the purposes of this contract, be deemed to be in default in the performance of his obligations hereunder and upon the said bond, and the Commission may terminate the contract or may bring any proper suit or proceeding against the Contractor and the sureties, or either or any of them.

(*b*) In lieu of said last mentioned bond the Contractor may, upon the approval of the Commission, deposit with the Comptroller of the City cash equal in amount to the entire amount of the said bond or securities which are lawful for the investment of the funds of savings banks within the State of New York and are worth not less than the entire amount of such bond. If such bond shall have been given then after the deposit of cash and securities in lieu thereof as aforesaid, and the approval thereof by the Commission, the said bond shall be surrendered by the City to the Contractor duly cancelled by the Comptroller. If securities be deposited on the signing of this contract they shall be securities of which a schedule shall be here-

Continuing security

to annexed, entitled "**Schedule of Continuing Securities,**" together with the written approval of the Commission which it shall give when satisfied as to the character and value thereof. If securities be deposited at any time in lieu of such bond the provisions of paragraphs (*a*), (*b*), (*c*), (*e*) and (*f*) of subdivision 1 of this article shall apply. Paragraph (*d*) of such subdivision and article shall also apply except that the deposit here referred to shall be for the purposes specified in and for such bond.

The Contractor shall only be entitled to a return of said deposit upon the termination of the Operation Provisions.

City's lien on Equipment

ARTICLE X The City shall also have a first lien upon the Equipment as further security for the faithful performance by the Contractor of the covenants, conditions and agreements of this contract on its part to be fulfilled and performed. Such lien shall arise immediately upon the acquisition by the Contractor of any part of the Equipment for use on or in connection with the Railroad or any part of it, or intended for such use, whether or not such equipment be set up or delivered upon or at the Railroad. The Contractor shall upon the provision of the Equipment and before such provision shall be deemed complete, execute and deliver or procure to be executed and delivered, such instrument or instruments in form for record in form approved by the Commission as may properly or conveniently recite or prove such first lien of the City upon the Equipment and shall also submit to the Commission reasonable proof of the title of the Equipment and the character and rank of such lien. Such further instruments and proof with respect to such lien shall from time to time be provided by the Contractor as may reasonably be desired or required by the Commission. The Commission may from time to time relieve from such lien any of the property to which the same may attach upon the provision of additional property which, in the opinion of the Commission, is equivalent in value and in the convenience and certainty with which the lien thereon shall be enforceable to the property which it is proposed to release, and upon such terms as to the Commission shall deem just.

Assignment of sub-contractors' bonds

ARTICLE XI The Contractor, upon receiving from any sub-contractor for any part of the work or for the supply of any material as herein provided, any bond, surety, obligation or security of any kind given to the Contractor to secure the performance of such sub-contract shall forthwith assign to the City in form to be approved by the Commission, the beneficial interest of the Contractor in such bond, surety, obligation or security so given by such sub-contractor, such beneficial interest to be held and applied by the Commission for the City as additional security for the performance by the Contractor of the provisions of this contract relating to the construction and equipment of the Railroad.

On Contractor's default in construction

ARTICLE XII In case the Contractor shall fail to complete the Construction of the Railroad, or shall at any time fail to proceed with such Construction with reasonable diligence, or so that it shall not be reasonably probable that the same will be completed within the period herein prescribed therefor, then and in any such case the Commission upon a notice to the Contractor of not less than thirty days may—

City may complete

(1) By resolution declare the Contractor to be in default; and the City by the Commission in addition to every other, or in substitution for any other, remedy which it may have

by law or hereunder, may thereupon forthwith, so far as the City may now have or may hereafter secure statutory power, procure by contract or otherwise, either for the Contractor, for his account and at his risk or otherwise as the Commission shall determine, the completion of such Construction, or, in any case where the Commission shall deem it for the interest of the City, the performance of any part of such Construction; and the Contractor shall be liable to the City and shall, as the Commission may from time to time require, forthwith pay to the City the cost to the City of the completion of such Construction or of such performance or provision of any part thereof, and also the amount, if any, which shall be due to the City by reason of any delay in completion of the Construction, or in such performance or provision of any part thereof. Or

(2) By resolution declare this contract at an end, and make a new contract for construction, upon advertisement of a new invitation to contractors, upon such terms as the Commission may deem proper; in which event the City shall be under no obligation to pay for any work done or for any materials or labor furnished hereunder but shall hold the same free and clear from any claim of the Contractor, or of any one claiming under him. And

or make new contract

(3) The City may also proceed as to the Commission shall seem proper upon the Bond for Construction and Equipment, or with respect to the deposits of cash or securities made as aforesaid, or with respect to the bonds, surety, obligations or securities given by sub-contractors and assigned as aforesaid. And

or proceed upon bond

(4) The City may also bring any suit or proceeding for specific performance or for injunc-

or may bring suit

tion or to recover damages or to obtain any relief or for any purpose proper under this contract.

City's assurances to Contractor of right to construct and operate

ARTICLE XIII The City hereby stipulates and covenants to and with the Contractor that the City will secure and assure to the Contractor, so long as the Contractor shall perform the stipulations of this contract, the right to construct and to operate the Railroad as prescribed in this contract, free of all right, claim or other interference, whether by injunction, suit for damages or otherwise, on the part of any owner, abutting owner, or other person; but not including any interference, legal or otherwise, by patentees or persons claiming to be patentees of tools, methods or appliances. Provided, however, that the Contractor shall enforce his rights against the City under this provision solely by claim for money, and shall have no right to set up any failure or default on the part of the City to perform or satisfy this stipulation or covenant in defense, or by way of exculpation or any excuse whatsoever (otherwise than as a claim or counter-claim for money) of the Contractor for any default or failure of any character whatsoever on its part. Nothing herein contained shall be construed to require the Contractor to do any act in violation of a valid injunction issued by a Court of competent jurisdiction forbidding such act.

Claims for infringement

ARTICLE XIV The Contractor shall hold himself responsible for any claims made against the City for any infringements of patents by the use of patented articles in the performance and completion of the work, or of any process connected with the work agreed to be performed under this contract, or of any materials used upon the said work, and shall save harmless and indemnify the City for all costs, expenses and damages which the City shall be obliged to pay by reason of any infringement of patents used in the performance and completion of the work, and any amount which the Contractor may be required to pay under the provision shall not be deemed a part of the cost of construction.

Beauty of material as well as efficiency

ARTICLE XV The Railroad and its equipment as contemplated by the contract constitute a great public work. All parts of the structure where exposed to public sight shall, therefore, be designed, constructed and maintained with a view to the beauty of their appearance, as well as to their efficiency.

Changes in the Contract

ARTICLE XVI No correction or change in this contract shall be made except by written instrument duly authorized by the Commission, and consented to by the Contractor, and by the sureties upon his bonds; but this provision shall not limit or affect the right to prescribe variations whether of construction or location of route as in this contract elsewhere provided.

Members of Commission not liable

ARTICLE XVII No claim shall be made by the Contractor against any member or members of the Commission personally by reason of this contract or of any of its articles or provisions.

Contract, when assignable

ARTICLE XVIII This contract shall not be assigned without the written consent of the Commission.

Provisions in case Commission ceases

ARTICLE XIX In case the Commission shall cease to exist or in case the powers it now exercises under different laws are separated and devolved upon different officers or boards, the Legislature may provide what public officer or officers shall exercise the powers and duties of the Commission under and by virtue of this contract; and in default of such provision, such powers and duties shall be deemed to be vested in the Mayor of the City. In case any officer or officers other than the Commission shall hereafter have the powers of the Commission or any of them, then the provisions of this contract shall be applicable to such officer or officers to the extent to which the powers of the Commission shall appertain to such officer or officers, and any official act or determination of such officer or officers or of this Commission shall be sufficient hereunder, anything herein to the contrary notwithstanding, if the same be done or had by lawful vote or resolution or in such manner as the Legislature may from time to time prescribe.

ARTICLE XX The Contractor agrees to comply with the provisions of the Labor Law, including Section three thereof as re-enacted by Chapter 36 of the Laws of 1909 so far as applicable. The Contractor further agrees and stipulates that no laborer, workman or mechanic in the employ of the Contractor, sub-contractor or other person doing or contracting to do the whole or a part of the work contemplated by this contract, shall be permitted or required to work more than eight hours in any one calendar day, except in case of extraordinary emergency caused by fire, flood or danger to life or property; and further that the wages to be paid for a legal day's work as hereinbefore defined to all classes of such laborers, workmen or mechanics upon the work contemplated by this contract or upon any material to be used upon or in connection therewith, shall not be less than **Labor Law** the prevailing rate for a day's work in the same trade or occupation in that Borough of the City where the portion of the work hereby contemplated, about or in connection with which such labor is performed, is in its final or completed form to be situated, erected or used; and that each such laborer, workman or mechanic employed by the Contractor or by any sub-contractor or other person on, about or upon the work contemplated by this contract, shall receive such wages herein provided for. This contract shall be void and of no effect unless the Contractor shall comply with the provisions of this paragraph.

In obedience to the requirements of Section fourteen of the Labor Law it is further provided that if the provisions of the said Section, so far as applicable, are not complied with this contract shall be void.

All necessary legal provisions deemed inserted herein

ARTICLE XXI It is the intent and understanding of the parties to this agreement that each and every provision of law required to be inserted in this contract should be and is inserted herein. Furthermore, it is hereby stipulated that every such provision is to be deemed to be inserted herein; and if, through mistake or otherwise, any such provision is omitted or is not inserted in correct form, then the contract shall forthwith, upon the application of either party, be amended by such insertion so as to comply strictly with the law and without prejudice to the rights of either party hereunder.

Provision in case of unlawful provision

ARTICLE XXII If this contract contain any unlawful provision not an essential part of the general structure of the contract and which shall not appear to have been a controlling or very material inducement to the making thereof the same shall be deemed of no effect, and shall upon the application of either party be stricken from the contract without affecting the binding force of the contract as it shall remain after omitting such provision.

CHAPTER II

CONSTRUCTION PROVISIONS

Work to be done

ARTICLE XXIII The Contractor will at his own cost and expense, and in strict conformity with the specifications hereinafter contained and called the **Specifications** and also in strict conformity with the plans which are made a part hereof and with all the provisions of this contract, whether included in the specifications or not, furnish all the materials and labor necessary and proper for the purpose, and, in a good, substantial and workmanlike manner, construct and provide the Railroad, including therein the stations, sidetracks, switches, cross-overs, terminal and storage yards and all other appurtenances complete and ready for operation excepting tracks and ties upon the bridges; provided, however, that said plans may from time to time be altered or modified as hereinafter provided.

On the bridges

The City will provide and lay tracks and ties upon the bridges, but the Contractor will be required to equip and maintain the same as provided with respect to the rest of the Railroad in the Operation Provisions.

Construction includes sewer and other incidentals

ARTICLE XXIV In order to construct the Railroad it will be necessary to take up and relay the pavement or other surface material, to protect and support during construction all buildings and other structures, including their foundations, and all elevated, surface and sub-surface railways, water mains, gas pipes, electrical subways, poles and wires, pneumatic tubes, steam pipes, vaults, including vaults of abutting property, and other surface, sub-surface and overhead structures, together with their necessary connections, as the same may be met with along the route; to build sewers both along the route and other streets; to make or remake the necessary manholes, catch basins and other sewer connections therewith; to move, alter, readjust or rebuild overhead telegraph, telephone and other electric wires, watermains, gas pipes, electrical subways, pneumatic tubes, steam pipes, vaults, including vaults of abutting property, and other surface, subsurface and overhead structures, together with their necessary connections; and to do all such additional and incidental work as may be necessary for the completion of the Railroad and the reconstruction and restoration of the street pavements or other surfaces adjacent to the route of the Railroad and which may have been directly or indirectly disturbed or injured by the Contractor in the progress of the work of construction, to as useful and good a condition as existed before construction shall have been begun. All such work of every description, including under-pinning wherever necessary, of all buildings of whatsoever nature, monuments, elevated, surface and sub-surface railways affected by or interfered with during the construction of the Railroad, is part of the work which is included in this contract and which the Contractor agrees to perform.

Commission may modify plans

ARTICLE XXV The Commission reserves the right during the progress of the work of construction to make such modifications, alterations or revisions of the plans or changes in the specifications (within, however, the purview of a rapid transit railroad as described in the appended copy of the routes and general plans) as may in the judgment of the Commission be found necessary to best subserve the public interests. By way of illustration, but of illustration only, the location of stations as stated in the Schedule of Stations, the location of entrances to and exits from such stations and also the location of ventilating shafts as indicated on the detailed plans, may be changed, or stations, station entrances or exits or ventilating shafts may be added or omitted at any time during the progress of the work.

On the Bensonhurst, Bath Beach and Coney Island Route east of Neptune avenue the Commission will probably consider it advisable, if the necessary steps are taken and the necessary approvals and consents secured, to change the line and terminal station or either of them and construct the same as indicated upon one of the contract drawings hereinafter referred to. The Contractor therefore agrees that upon demand of the Commission he will construct such line and terminal station or either of them as so indicated and will if requested enter into such modifying or

At Coney Island

other agreements for such purpose as may be desired by the Commission.

Acquisition of real estate

ARTICLE XXVI For the purpose of constructing or operating the Railroad, the City will acquire by conveyance or grant to the City to be delivered to the Commission and to contain such terms, conditions, provisos and limitations as the Commission shall deem proper or by condemnation or other legal or other proceedings, any real estate and any rights, terms, interests therein, any and all rights, privileges, franchises and easements, whether of owners or abuttors, or others to interfere with the construction or operation of the Railroad or to recover damages therefor, which, in the opinion of the Commission, it shall be necessary to acquire or extinguish for the purpose of constructing and operating the Railroad free of interference or right of interference; provided, however, that this covenant shall not apply to or include any damages for physical injuries to property referred to in Articles L, LIII and LVI hereof whether or not compensation for such damages be awarded in a condemnation proceeding. If compensation for any such damages shall be included in an award in condemnation proceedings the Contractor shall, upon demand, promptly reimburse the City for any payments made by it for such purposes.

Time for completion to be extended in case of delay in acquiring real estate

ARTICLE XXVII In case the Contractor shall at any time give notice to the Commission that any real estate is necessary under this contract for any of the purposes specified in this contract, which notice shall give a brief description of such real estate, the Commission shall (if it finds that such necessity exists) begin and conduct with diligence proceedings to acquire the real estate described; and in case the Commission shall fail to put the

Contractor in possession of such real estate within three months from the delivery of such notice, then the period for completion of Construction shall be extended for such a time as such completion is necessarily delayed by the failure of the Commission to furnish such real estate; provided, however, that in any suit or proceeding under this article of the contract the burden of proof shall be on the Contractor to show that the real estate which he described was in fact necessary.

Contractor may agree for purchases of real estate, etc.

ARTICLE XXVIII Subject to the approval of the Commission in each case, the Contractor may enter into agreements with the owners of any real estate for the purchase of the same, or of any rights, terms, franchises, easements or privileges therein which may be required as aforesaid, to be conveyed to the City upon such prices and subject to such terms, conditions and provisos and limitations as may be agreed upon and approved by the Commission.

City to acquire real estate for equipment if required

ARTICLE XXIX In case the Contractor shall give notice to the Commission that any real estate is needed for Equipment and that it cannot be purchased from the owner or owners upon reasonable terms, the City shall begin and conduct with diligence proceedings to acquire such real estate so required.

The Contractor agrees to indemnify and promptly reimburse the City for all expenditures made or obligations incurred by it in or about the acquisition of real estate for Equipment. Upon being notified by the Commission that any moneys are necessary to pay for any real estate acquired or to be acquired by purchase or to pay awards in condemnation proceedings with interest thereon, the Contractor shall within the time specified in any such notice pay to the Comptroller such amount as may be specified in any such notice.

Sites for terminals

ARTICLE XXX. The site or sites for terminal and storage yards (except the terminal under Battery Park) shall be proposed by the Contractor but shall be subject to the approval of the Commission.

ARTICLE XXXI The Contractor shall cause to be vested in the City a good and marketable title, free of all liens and incumbrances, to all real estate acquired by him for terminals and storage-yards and shall submit to the Commission such proof as may be required of such title and shall execute and deliver, or cause to be executed and delivered, such instrument or instruments in form approved by the Commission, and so proved as to entitle them to be recorded, as may properly or conveniently recite or prove the City's ownership of, or title to, such real estate. The Contractor shall further provide such further instruments and proof with respect to such ownership or title as may from time to time be required by the Commission.

Contractor bound to complete in best manner

ARTICLE XXXII The Contractor shall complete the entire work in accordance with the specifications and contract-drawings and according to the other provisions of this contract and within the times specified in this contract, at the lowest advantageous cost, in the most workman-like manner and with the highest regard to the safety of life and property and according to the lines, levels and directions given by the Engineer.

Best materials, machinery, tools, etc., to be used

ARTICLE XXXIII The Contractor is to furnish of the best description all materials, machinery, implements, tools and labor necessary to construct and put in complete working order all work covered by the specifications, contract-drawings and other provisions of this contract, including all additional specifications, drawings and details issued or required as herein provided.

No acceptance to obviate the necessity for sound work, etc.

ARTICLE XXXIV No acceptance of any part of the work or materials in construction shall relieve the Contractor of his obligation to furnish sound material and perform sound work, whether with respect to such part or to any other part of the work or materials in Construction.

Inspection

ARTICLE XXXV The Commission contemplates, and the Contractor hereby approves, the most thorough and minute inspection by the Commission and its Engineer, and by their representatives or subordinates, of all work and materials and of the manufacture or preparation of such materials from the beginning of Construction to the final completion of Construction and Equipment. It is the intention of the Commission that its Engineer shall draw the attention of the Contractor to all errors or variations from the requirements of this contract or other defects in workmanship or materials. But it is expressly agreed that no omission on the part of the Commission or its Engineers or any officer, member or subordinate of the Commission to point out such errors, variations or defects shall give the Contractor any right or claim against the City or shall in any way relieve the Contractor from his obligations according to the terms of this contract.

Contractor to afford facilities for inspection

ARTICLE XXXVI. The Contractor shall at all times give to the Commission and its members, to the Engineer and his assistants and subordinates, and to any person designated by the Commission or its Chairman, all facilities, whether necessary or convenient, for inspecting the materials to be furnished and the work to be done under this contract. The members of the Commission, the Engineer and any assistant or other person bearing his authorization or the authorization of the Commission or its Chairman, shall be admitted at any time summarily and without delay to any part of the work or to the inspection of materials at any place or stage of their manufacture, preparation, shipment or delivery.

Work to be subject to approval of Engineer

ARTICLE XXXVII. The work is to be done and the materials are to be furnished subject to the direction and approval of the Engineer. The Contractor shall promptly obey and follow every direction which shall be given by the Engineer, including any direction which he shall give by way of withdrawal, modification or reversal of any previous direction given by him. If any additional specification be prescribed or additional drawing be required to be followed, or additional detail required, or if any question shall arise as to the quality, character or amount of materials or work, or as to the obligation of the Contractor to do any particular work or furnish any particular materials, or if any other dispute, question or doubt as to what is the obligation of the Contractor shall arise prior to the time of the complete Construction of the work and the declaration thereof by the Commission, the determination of the Engineer shall be final and conclusive.

Substitute for Chief Engineer

ARTICLE XXXVIII Any Engineer substituted by the Commission in place of the Chief Engineer during his absence, illness or inability or when the Commission shall so determine, shall during his official connection, have all the power and authority of the Chief Engineer, and in all respects be recognized as such Chief Engineer.

Supervision of operations of Contractor

ARTICLE XXXIX Inasmuch as the City is to share in the profits of the Railroad and as the City may take over the Railroad as provided in the Operation Provisions, the Contractor shall strictly comply with the provisions hereof for assuring to the Commission supervision by it of all operations of the Contractor. The Contractor shall, therefore, in addition to providing facilities for inspection as hereinbefore provided, provide the Commission with all facilities necessary or convenient to afford the Commission full and complete supervision of all operations of the Contractor in or about the enterprise of constructing, equipping, maintaining and operating the Railroad. The Contractor shall keep, and shall require, in any contract, agreement, mortgage or other undertaking, any and all contractors, sub-contractors, bankers and persons furnishing money, material or supplies directly or indirectly to such enterprise to keep books, records and memoranda of such operations to the extent that such books, records and memoranda have to do therewith as, and in the form that, may be required from time to time by the Commission. Such books, records and memoranda whether of the Contractor or of any contractor, sub-contractor, banker or person furnishing money, material or supplies directly or indirectly to such enterprise to the extent that such books, records or memoranda have to do with such operations of the Contractor shall be at all times accessible to and open to the use and examination of the Commission and subject to production at such time or place as may be specified in any notice given by the Commission, and the Contractor shall in any and all contracts, agreements, mortgages or undertakings insert appropriate provisions to assure to the Commission access to and the examination, use and production of any and all such books, records and memoranda to the extent that they have to do with the enterprise of the Contractor.

Contractor's agreements subject to approval of Commission

ARTICLE XL The Contractor shall (unless permission to do otherwise is expressly granted by the Commission) before entering into any contract, agreement, mortgage or undertaking having to do with the enterprise of constructing, equipping, maintaining and operating the Railroad, submit the same to the Commission for its approval and the Commission may as a condition of its approval require the insertion of such terms and conditions therein as it may deem necessary. The Commission may further require the Contractor before making any contract for the performance of any work or the furnishing of any materials in or about the construction or equipment of the Railroad or any section thereof to ask for proposals for constructing or providing specified portions thereof, upon forms of contracts satisfactory to the Commission, in a specific manner and for a specified time and to award the contract to such bidder as may be approved by the Commission.

Determination of cost

ARTICLE XLI The cost of construction and the cost of equipment shall be determined as follows: The Engineer shall, on or about the first days of January, April, July and October, in each year during construction, render a determination in writing, in duplicate, to the Commission and to the Contractor of the cost of construction and of the cost of equipment to the date of the last day of the last preceding quarter, including therein separately a determination of the cost of construction and the cost of equipment during the quarter year immediately preceding the date of such determination. If either the Commission or the Contractor shall be dissatisfied with such separate determination or any item or items thereof it or he shall within twenty (20) days after the receipt of such determination file with the Engineer a statement in writing of the item or items objected to and the reasons for such objection. If within such period of twenty (20) days the Commission or the Contractor shall fail to file such statement with the Engineer, such separate determination shall be final and conclusive upon the party so failing. The Engineer shall thereupon reconsider such determination, or any item or items thereof, so objected to and shall state his conclusions thereon in his determination for the quarter year succeeding the quarter year for which the determination so objected to was made. Such redetermination shall be final and conclusive unless the Commission or the Contractor shall within twenty (20) days after the receipt thereof appeal therefrom to the Board of Arbitration hereinafter provided for. The appeal shall be taken by a written notice addressed, if the Commission be the appellant, to the Contractor, or, if the Contractor be the appellant, then to the Secretary of the Commission. The notice of appeal shall state the determination appealed from, the grounds of appeal and the precise award or redress desired.

Article XLII The Contractor and the Commission shall within three months after the delivery of this contract each appoint a disinterested person to act as arbitrator. Within thirty days after their appointment the Commission and the Contractor shall agree upon a third disinterested person to act with the two arbitrators so ap- **Board of Arbitration** pointed; but if the Commission and the Contractor shall fail to agree upon such third arbitrator within thirty (30) days after the date of the appointment of the second arbitrator appointed, the third arbitrator shall be named by the Executive Committee for the time being of the Chamber of Commerce of the State of New York; or if within thirty days after being requested by either of the parties to make such nomination said Committee shall decline or fail to make a nomination then the third arbitrator shall be named by the Executive Committee for the time being of the Association of the Bar of The City of New York. Such three arbitrators shall be known as and constitute the Board of Arbitration. Any member of the Board of Arbitration appointed by the Commission may at any time be removed by the Commission and likewise any member of the Board of Arbitration appointed by the Contractor may at any time be removed by the Contractor. The Board of Arbitration shall hear the parties and their counsel or any statements or evidence which the parties or either of them, desire to submit and may resort to any other sources of information in reference to the question submitted for determination. Within thirty days after the date of the service of the notice of appeal, unless such time shall be extended for good cause by written order of the Board of Arbitration, the Board of Arbitration shall make its determination in duplicate, one to be delivered to the Commission and the other to the Contractor. In case any vacancy shall at any time occur by reason of the death, resignation, removal or inability to serve of any arbitrator, his successor, (who shall also be a disinterested person), shall be appointed in the same manner and within the same times as above provided for the original appointment of such arbitrator. Any determination by a majority of the Board of Arbitration shall be final and conclusive. Every member of the Board of Arbitration shall be deemed employed by both the City and the Contractor but the fees of the arbitrators and the expenses of the Board of Arbitration shall be borne and paid by the Contractor upon vouchers to be approved by the Commission and such fees and expenses shall be deemed part of the cost of construction or equipment as the case may be. Every arbitrator shall before entering upon his duties be sworn as nearly as may be in the same manner as referees in actions at law are required to be sworn. Within six months after the completion of the Railroad, as indicated by the certificate hereinbefore required as a condition to the return of the Contractor's bond for construction and equipment, the powers and duties of the Board of Arbitration, provided for in this Article, shall cease and the construction and equipment cost of any work or equipment thereafter ordered shall be determined as provided in the Operation Provisions. Provided, however, that if in any case or for any reason an arbitration cannot validly be had as aforesaid then the City or the Contractor, if in no way responsible for the failure of the arbitration, may bring such action or suit as either of them may be advised for the purpose of determining any of the matters for which the arbitration is herein provided.

Commencement and completion of work

ARTICLE XLIII Time is of the essence of this contract. The Contractor shall begin actual work within sixty (60) days after the delivery of this contract. The entire work covered by this contract shall be completely constructed ready for immediate, full and continuous operation within four years from the date of the delivery of this contract.

Damages for delay

ARTICLE XLIV In the event of delay in such complete Construction, beyond the prescribed period, and in case any such delay shall not be excusable, as hereinafter provided, the City shall be paid damages for such delay. Inasmuch as the amount of damages will be extremely difficult to ascertain, it is hereby expressly agreed that the same shall be liquidated by the payment to the City as liquidated damages for such delay (and not as a penalty) of the sum of two thousand dollars ($2,000) for each and every day after the expiration of the said period, and during such time the running of the interest provided for in Item 3 of paragraph 12 of Article VI shall be suspended.

Extension of time

But in case the Contractor shall be delayed by reason of any labor strike not caused or instituted or provoked by the Contractor, or by any sub-contractor, agent or representative of the Contractor (which fact the Contractor shall prove to the satisfaction of the Commission), or in case the Contractor shall be delayed by any injunction or by any interference of public authority, and in case the Contractor cannot, notwithstanding such injunction, strike or interference, with reasonable diligence make up for the delay so occasioned by speedier work when the Contractor shall not be so interfered with, then the said date for completion shall be extended by the Commission to a date later than the expiration of the said period by the amount of the time of such delay.

ARTICLE XLV The time for completion of construction shall not be deemed extended in the By resolution of Commission absence of a resolution duly adopted by the Commission extending such time.

Commission may intervene in case of injunction

ARTICLE XLVI But no injunction, strike, or interference of public authority shall be ground for such extension unless and from the time when the Contractor shall give the Commission notice of the injunction or other cause of delay, with copies of the injunction or other orders and of the papers upon which the same shall have been granted. The Commission and the City or either shall be accorded the right to intervene or become a party to any suit or proceeding in which any such injunction shall be obtained, and to move to dissolve the same or otherwise, as the Commission or City may deem proper. If deemed necessary by the Commission either or both the Corporation Counsel or the Counsel to the Commission shall be authorized by the Contractor to appear, for that purpose, as counsel or attorneys for it.

ARTICLE XLVII The Commission reserves the right of temporarily suspending the execution of the whole or any part of the work herein contracted to be done, if it shall deem it for the interest of the City so to do, without compensation to the Contractor for such suspension, other than extending the time for completing the work as much as it may have been delayed by such suspension.

Suspension of work and additional time for performance

ARTICLE XLVIII The permitting of the Contractor to go on and finish the work, or any part of it, after the time fixed for its completion, or after the date to which the time for completion may have been extended, shall in no wise operate as a waiver on the part of the City of any of its rights under this contract.

Permission to complete contract not a waiver

ARTICLE XLIX If the Contractor shall cause any part of this contract to be performed by a sub-contractor, the provisions of this contract

Contractor responsible for acts of sub-contractor's employees shall apply to such sub-contractor and his officers, agents and employees in all respects as if he and they were employees of the Contractor; and the Contractor shall not be in any manner thereby discharged from his obligations and liabilities hereunder, but shall be liable hereunder for all acts and negligence of the sub-contractor, his officers, agents and employees as if they were employees of the Contractor. The employees of the sub-contractor shall be subject to the same provisions hereof as employees of the Contractor; and the work or materials furnished by the sub-contractor shall be subject to the provisions hereof, as if furnished directly by the Contractor.

Contractor approves plans as involving no damage

ARTICLE L. The Contractor expressly admits and covenants to and with the City that the plans and specifications and other provisions of this contract for construction, if the work be done without fault or negligence on the part of the Contractor, do not involve any danger to the foundations, walls or other parts of adjacent buildings or structures or to navigation; and the Contractor shall at his own expense make good any damage that shall, in the course of construction, be done to any such foundations, walls or other parts of adjacent buildings or structures or to navigation. The liability of the Contractor in respect of these matters is absolute and is not dependent upon any question of negligence on his part, or on the part of his agents, servants or employees, and the neglect of the Engineer to direct the Contractor to take any particular precautions or to refrain from doing any particular thing shall not excuse the Contractor in case of any such damage. When the work is required to be done by tunneling the same admission and covenant shall also apply to the foundations, walls and other parts of buildings and to any railroad track or structure, subway, street, conduit, pipe, sewer or other structure or surface over the tunnel. But this admission and covenant shall not apply to the foundation, walls or other parts of buildings or any part thereof standing upon private property within the outside lines of the Railroad, acquired for purposes of construction, and which necessity requires should be razed.

Engineer may order adjacent property supported

ARTICLE LI The Contractor shall obey any order of the Engineer to support or secure adjacent property or any surface or structure thereon; but the Contractor shall not be relieved of responsibility either by compliance with any such order or by any failure or omission of the Engineer to give any such order or to give notice of any danger.

ARTICLE LII The Contractor shall during the performance of the work safely maintain the traffic on streets, avenues, highways, parks, waters or other public places in connection with the work as provided in the specifications, and shall take all necessary precautions to place proper guards for the prevention of accidents, and put up and keep at night suitable and sufficient lights. Traffic to be maintained

ARTICLE LIII The Contractor shall be held solely responsible for all injuries to persons or property occurring on account of and during Construction, and shall indemnify and save harmless the City from liability upon any and all claims for damages on account of such injuries to persons or property, and from all costs and expenses in suits which may be brought against the City for such injuries to persons or property; it being distinctly understood, stipulated and agreed that the Indemnification for accidents, etc.

Contractor shall be solely responsible and liable for and shall fully protect and indemnify the City against all claims for damages to persons or property occasioned by or resulting from the construction of the Railroad, whether such damages be attributable to the method of doing the work or to the negligence of the Contractor or his agents or employees or otherwise.

Security to secure claims

ARTICLE LIV In case any claim shall be made by any person or corporation against the Contractor or the City for loss or damage to person or property as aforesaid, the City shall be secured by the security required or reserved by this contract.

Damage to Works during construction

ARTICLE LV All risk or loss or damage to the Railroad or stations or anything constructed hereunder or to the materials therefor, prior to final completion of the Railroad, unless caused by the fault of the City, is assumed and shall be borne by the Contractor, and any such loss or damage shall be made good by the Contractor at his own cost, and the Construction shall be carried forward by him in accordance with this contract without cost to the City by reason of such loss or damage.

Article LVI Any amounts paid by the Contractor on account of damages to persons or property, or to indemnify the City for amounts paid by it, or for damage to the works shall not be considered a part of the cost of construction, but the Contractor will be permitted, upon terms and conditions to be approved by the Commission, to carry insurance against accident, which insurance shall run to both the City and the Contractor, and the premiums upon such insurance will be treated as part of the cost of construction.

Accident insurance

Specifications and drawings subject to requirement of railroad of highest grade

ARTICLE LVII The specifications and contract drawings hereinafter mentioned and the other and additional provisions of this contract, are intended by the Commission to be full and comprehensive, and to show all the work required to be done. But in a work of this magnitude it is impossible either to show in advance all details or precisely to forecast all exigencies. The specifications and contract drawings are to be taken, therefore, as indicating the amount of work, its nature and the method of construction so far as the same are now distinctly apprehended. The Railroad is to be constructed for actual use and operation as an intra-urban railroad of the highest class, adapted to the necessities of the people of New York. The Contractor shall construct and complete the Railroad in the best manner, according to the best rules and usages of railroad construction, so that the Railroad shall be thoroughly fitted for safe and efficient operation. If, in the specifications or contract-drawings or in the provisions of this contract, any detail or other matter or thing requisite for such operation in such manner and subject to such requirements be not mentioned, nevertheless the same is deemed to be included, and the Contractor hereby undertakes to do the same as part of his work hereunder.

Where text of contract doubtful, best materials and workmanship required

ARTICLE LVIII In the event of any doubt as to the meaning of any portion or portions of the specifications or contract-drawings, or of the text of the contract, the same shall be interpreted as calling for the best construction, both as to materials and workmanship, capable of being supplied or applied under the then existing local conditions. This provision, by way of illustration (but of illustration only), implies the requirement that the interior surface of every part of the tunnel containing the railway shall be entirely free from percolation of ground or other water from without; the requirement throughout of a structure whose component parts shall be of as permanent and durable a character as practicable; the requirement that the steel and such other parts of the structure as are liable to rust and decay shall be fully protected from such action; the requirement that the road-bed shall be such that trains can be run thereon with safety and comfort at the highest practically attainable speeds; and the requirement that there shall be adequate and comfortable stations. All the clauses of the specifications, and all the parts of the contract-drawings, are, therefore, to be understood, construed and interpreted as intending to produce the results hereinbefore stated.

ARTICLE LIX The plans referred to in the specifications hereinafter contained bear date the 15th day of June, 1910, are each countersigned by the Engineer, are stamped with the seal of the Commission and bear the general titles **Route No. , Contract Drawing No.** The sheets are designated or numbered as follows:

General Notes; Map and Profile;

ROUTE NO. 5:

B101, B102; C1001 to C1005 inclusive, C1008 to C1016 inclusive, C1024, C1026 to C1030 inclusive, and C1032.

Section No. 1

A1, A2; B1, B2; C1 to C23 inclusive, C401, C501 to C506 inclusive.

Section No. 2

A3; B3, B4; C1 to C27 inclusive, C401, C501 to C504 inclusive.

Section No. 2-A

A4; B5; C1 to C11 inclusive, C401, C501 to C504 inclusive.

Section No. 3

A5; B6; C1 to C7 inclusive, C401, C501, and C502.

Section No. 4

A6; B7, B8; C1 to C18 inclusive, C401, C501 and C502.

Section No. 5

A7; B11, B12; C1 to C12 inclusive, C401, C501 to C504 inclusive.

Section No. 6

A8; B13, B14, B15; C1 to C18 inclusive, C401, C501 to C504 inclusive.

Section No. 7

A9; B16, B17; C1 to C39 inclusive, C401, C501 to C506 inclusive.

Section No. 8

A10; B18, B19; C1 to C11 inclusive, C401, C501 and C502.

Section No. 9

A11; B20, B21, B22; C1 to C17 inclusive, C401, C501, C502, C505 and C506.

Section No. 10

A12; B23, B24; C1 to C12 inclusive, C401, C501 to C503 inclusive.

Section No. 11

A13; B25, B26; C1 to C19 inclusive, C401, C501 to C504 inclusive.

Section No. 12

A14; B27, B28, B32, B33; C1 to C18 inclusive, C401, C501 to C504 inclusive.

Section No. 13

A15; B29, B30; C1 to C27 inclusive, C401, C501 to C504 inclusive.

Section No. 14

A16, A16K; B31; C1 to C11 inclusive, and C401.

Section No. 15

A17, A18, A19; B36, B37 and B38; C264 to C315 inclusive, C401, C501 to C508 inclusive.

ROUTE NOS. 19 & 22:

B101, B102; C1005 and C1008.

Section No. 1

A1 to A6 inclusive; B1 to B8 inclusive; C1 to C38 inclusive, C401, C402, C403, C501 to C509 inclusive, and C1001 to C1004 inclusive.

Section No. 2

A7 to A15 inclusive; C1 to C31 inclusive, C501 to C505 inclusive. Route No. 16. Route 19 and 22. Section No. 2. C1001.

ROUTE NO. 16:

A20 to A30 inclusive; C1 to C40 inclusive, C501 to C509 inclusive. Route No. 16. Route 19 and 22. Section No. 2. Contract Drawing C1001.

ROUTE NO. 20:

B101, B102; C1001 to C1004 inclusive, C1006 and C1007.

Section No. 1

A1; B1, B4; C1 to C26 inclusive, C401, C501 to C504 inclusive.

Section No. 2

A2, A3; B2, B3; C1 to C32 inclusive, C401, C501 to C505 inclusive.

ROUTE NOS. 9-A-3 & 9-F:

B101, B102; C1001 to C1005 inclusive and C1007.

Section No. 1

A1, A2; B1, B2, B3, B12; C1 to C51 inclusive, C401, C402, C501 to C506 inclusive.

Section No. 2

A3, A8, A9; B4 to B7 inclusive, B13, B14, B15; C1 to C25 inclusive, C30 to C47 inclusive, C401, C402, C501 to C508 inclusive.

Section No. 3

A4 to A7 inclusive; B8 to B11 inclusive, B16, B17, B18; C1 to C28 inclusive, C401, C501 to C508 inclusive.

ROUTE NOS. 11-B & 11-F-1:

C1001 to C1005 inclusive.

ROUTE NO. 11-B:

A1 to A7 inclusive; B1 to B8 inclusive, B101, B102; C1 to C30 inclusive, C401 to C404 inclusive, C501 to C506 inclusive.

ROUTE NO. 11-F-1:

A1 to A9 inclusive; B1 to B14 inclusive, B101, B102, B103; C1 to C34 inclusive, C401, C402, C403, C501 to C507 inclusive.

ROUTE NO. 11-F-2:

A10 to A14 inclusive; C60 to C71 inclusive, C501 to C503 inclusive, and C1001.

Plans and Contract drawings

ARTICLE LX The sections and dimensions of all parts shown on the contract drawings are typical sections and dimensions which should be applicable to the greater part of the work, and where no extraordinary conditions exist. Where such conditions do exist, or where unforeseen contingencies arise, such as the encountering of quicksand, peat or other bad material, or when there are buildings, monuments or other structures whose foundations are of such a character as to bring an undue thrust upon the tunnel, or other similar circumstances exist, then and in every such case the Commission may issue such special plans, duly countersigned by the Engineer, and accompanied by specifications explanatory thereof, or describing the method of construction, changing the sections or the dimensions of the parts or the materials of the structure; and such special plans and specifications when so issued shall be binding on the Contractor as though originally contained in this contract.

Supplementary drawings

ARTICLE LXI In addition to the contract drawings already mentioned, the Commission has had prepared a set of maps and plans, bearing the same seal and general title as the contract drawings, but designated as **Supplementary Drawings.** These supplementary drawings exhibit certain information which the Commission has received from its Engineer of the nature of the soil underlying portions of the routes, the nature and position of elevated and surface railways, water mains, gas and other pipes, sewers, electrical subways, manholes, hydrants, catch basins, and other surface and subsurface structures. The supplementary drawings can be seen at the office of the Engineer, also samples of material taken in connection with test borings. They are exhibited to the Contractor without any guaranty on the part of the Commission as to their completeness or correctness; and the Contractor may, at his option and at the expense of the Commission, have copies thereof for such aid, if any, as the Contractor may derive from them. If, upon opening the streets by tunneling or otherwise, difficulties of any nature be encountered which are not indicated or suggested by the supplementary drawings, or by the samples of the test borings, or if additional surface or subsurface structures or obstructions be discovered or found of different size or in different positions or of different nature from those shown on the supplementary drawings, or if in any way such supplementary drawings be found erroneous, the Contractor shall have no claim whatever for any such failure, discrepancy, or error, but is to take every necessary or proper precaution to overcome the unforeseen difficulty, and is to take care of, protect, remove, adjust or readjust, as the case may be, the additional or different surface or subsurface structures according to the direction of the Engineer.

ARTICLE LXII It is expressly understood that the specifications do not include all requirements, but are requirements in addition to those heretofore or elsewhere given or provided in this contract. The specifications or other provisions of this contract, and the contract drawings, are intended to be explanatory of each other. Should, however, any discrepancy appear or any misunderstanding arise as to the import of anything contained in either, the explanation of the Engineer shall be final and conclusive. Specifications not exclusive

These specifications are grouped in subdivisions as follows:

1

BRIEF DESCRIPTION OF THE WORK

Generally The rapid transit railroad described in the Routes and General Plans, which is included in the Railroad covered by the contract, is to be in part an underground railroad or subway, and in part an elevated structure or viaduct. It is to be constructed under, along and over certain streets and highways and other City property in the Boroughs of Manhattan, Brooklyn and The Bronx, passing in places under or over private property, with a crossing under the Harlem River and with connections over certain bridges crossing the East River.

Stations are to be constructed at such places as are indicated on the plans, and loops or other methods are to be provided for convenience in operation, including necessary turnouts, cross-overs, sidings, etc. Stations to be constructed, etc.

The Railroad as above generally described comprises several routes or parts thereof, all of which are more fully described in the contract and indicated on the plans.

In addition to the construction of the Railroad itself, it will be necessary to construct or reconstruct certain sewers, together with house and other sewer connections, and to adjust, re-adjust and maintain railways, pipes, subways and other surface and sub-surface structures, and to relay the street pavement, both on streets occupied by, and on streets other than those occupied by, the route of the Railroad. Surface and sub-surface structures

In order to provide for a frequent renewal of air in the railroad, chambers for the installation Ventilating chambers and gratings of the necessary ventilating devices, shall be built at the sides of the railroad and in connection therewith. These chambers shall be generally of the forms and dimensions as shown on the plans, varying somewhat with the requirements of local condtions. They will be so arranged that the air will discharge through gratings placed generally in the sidewalks in the roofs of the chambers. If, owing to local conditions, it becomes necessary to lead the air to gratings or other outlets away from the chambers, suitable air-ways, ducts or flues shall be constructed.

The chambers will be built at the places and as indicated on the plans.

Other openings with gratings will be built at or over the stations, for the purpose of admitting air to the railroad.

The chambers will be provided with suitable doors or openings, and with ladders reaching to the street for use as exits in case of emergency.

The devices for ventilation to be placed in the chambers and in connection therewith, above referred to, will form a part of the "Equipment," and are more particularly described in the subdivision of these specifications relating thereto.

Galvanized iron pipe hand rails

Galvanized iron pipe hand-rails will be placed in the Railroad over the benches containing the ducts. They shall be securely fastened to the walls of the tunnel by means of expansion bolts, and as shown on the contract drawings.

2

GENERAL CLAUSES

It is the very essence of these specifications to secure an underground railroad structure which shall be free from the percolation of ground or outside water. The mixing and placing of the concrete and the placing and protection of the waterproofing shall be with this end in view.

Best quality of work

All materials and workmanship must be of the best class in every respect, and the Engineer is to be the sole judge of their quality and efficiency.

Rapidity and safety

All the work shall be prosecuted in the manner, according to local conditions, best calculated to promote rapidity in construction, to secure safety to life and property and to reduce to the minimum any interference with the public travel. Decking of the streets, paving, or other surface work affecting, or affected by, street traffic shall be prosecuted during such hours as will reduce such interference to a minimum. Night work shall be conducted in accordance with the directions of the Engineer, so that annoyance to occupants of abutting property shall be reduced, and the Engineer may, if in his judgment conditions so require, direct that night work be omitted.

This contract is for an extensive rapid transit railroad system, which the interests of the City imperatively require should be completed and put in operation without delay. If the Contractor shall fail so to prosecute his work that, in the judgment of the Engineer, it shall not be reasonably probable that the work will be completed within the time limited, the Contractor, if directed by the Commission, shall increase the number of shifts and the number of men in each shift, as may be necessary to insure the completion of the work within the time required by this contract, or within the shortest possible time thereafter.

Emergencies

In case of emergencies involving danger to life or property, continuous work with an increased force may be ordered by the Engineer for such time as may be necessary.

Permits

No work shall be begun until the Commission shall issue to the Contractor a permit authorizing him to proceed. No permits for excavation will be given until the Contractor has given satisfactory assurance to the Engineer that the material needed for construction has been acquired and is available. Such permits are to be in such form and cover such sections of the work as the Commission shall prescribe.

When to be filed with Borough President

Before any opening is made in the surface of a street, a copy of the permit issued by the Commission shall have been filed with the Borough President not less than five days, unless the Engineer shall expressly direct work to begin within a less period.

Notice regarding commencement of work

Before commencing work on any part of the route, whether on the Railroad or on the sewers lying off the line of the Railroad, the Contractor shall give notice in writing to the Engineer at least one (1) week in advance of his intention to commence such operations; and before commencing manufacture, or resuming manufacture if the same has been suspended, of any article called for by these specifications, notice shall be given to the Engineer in writing at least one (1) week in advance, with the name and address of the maker and the amount and description of the material to be manufactured.

Shafts and dumping platforms

Plans showing the proposed location, and proposed methods of construction, of shafts, dumping platforms, etc., shall be submitted to the Engineer and receive his approval before permits will be granted for such plant and appliances to be constructed and put in operation.

Ordinances and regulations

In all operations connected with the work, all ordinances of the City, and of the Board of Health, so far as they may be valid and operative with respect thereto, and all laws of this State which are applicable to and control or limit in any way the actions of those engaged in the work or affecting the materials belonging to them, shall be respected and strictly complied with, and the

Contractor shall further strictly comply with all applicable Federal, State and Municipal regulations regarding the transportation in and around the City and Harbor of materials used in, or in connection with, the work.

Requirements of Borough President, etc., to be observed

Whenever the construction of the Works under the provisions of this contract shall interfere with, disturb or endanger any sewer, waterpipe, gas-pipe, or other duly authorized sub-surface structure, the work of construction at such points shall be conducted in accordance with the reasonable requirements of the Borough President or the Commissioner of Water Supply, Gas and Electricity or other officer or local authority having the care of and the jurisdiction or control over such sub-surface structures so interfered with, disturbed or endangered.

Temporary tramways

For the purpose of facilitating construction and to diminish the period of occupancy of any street in The Bronx or along the Fourth Avenue or Bensonhurst, Bath Beach and Coney Island Routes in Brooklyn for the transportation of material, the Contractor may, with the approval of the Commission, lay, upon or over the surface of any street, temporary tramways to be used only for the removal of excavated materials and for the transportation of materials for use in construction; provided, however, that any such tramway shall be forthwith removed upon the direction of the Commission.

Storage on cross-streets

No materials of any nature shall be stored along Broadway, Irving Place or Lexington Avenue in Manhattan, on 138th Street in the Bronx, or on Broadway, Fulton Street or Lafayette Avenue in Brooklyn. On cross-streets adjacent to the work, only such material may be stored as may be necessary, in case of an emergency, to sheet or to support the excavation; or a reasonable amount of such structural material as may be absolutely necessary to avoid delay in construction may be stored; but such material must not be allowed to accumulate, but must be replenished from day to day. The amount to be so allowed shall be determined by the Engineer.

Material stored

Excavated sand, gravel or stone that in the judgment of the Engineer is suitable for use in mortar, concrete, or masonry, also structural and other material to be used in the work, may be stored in such locations and for such periods as are approved by the Engineer.

Approval of Engineer revocable

In any case material may only be so stored with the approval of the Engineer, revocable at any time; and if so ordered, such material shall be removed immediately on receipt of the order, or within a period of time to be therein stated.

Access to fire hydrants

Wherever the work is being carried on, free access must be given to every fire hydrant and fire alarm box, and when required hydrants shall be extended by suitable tube or piping to an accessible point as approved by the Engineer, and to the satisfaction of the Chief of the Fire Department. Materials must not be piled at any time or place within ten (10) feet of any fire hydrant or fire alarm box; and where materials are unavoidably piled or placed in the vicinity of a fire hydrant or fire alarm box, and to such height as to obscure a sight of the same, the position of such hydrant or fire alarm box shall be indicated by suitable signals, both day and night.

Work to be cleared

At his own expense and as directed from time to time by the Engineer, the Contractor is to clear the work, streets and all public places occupied by him of all refuse and rubbish that may accumulate from any source whatever and leave them in a neat condition.

Assistance to be rendered owners of buildings

Where access to any adjacent property is temporarily cut off, owing to the occupancy of the street by the Contractor, he must render every assistance to the owner or occupant in handling such materials of any description, including all material to be removed by the Department of Street Cleaning, that has to be taken to or removed from such property; such material shall be taken to or from the nearest accessible point that in the opinion of the Engineer is convenient for handling.

Waste material of any character will under no conditions be permitted to remain on the streets, but must immediately on its becoming unfit for use in the work be carted away and disposed of by the Contractor as hereinbefore provided; nor shall such materials be allowed to accumulate in the trenches. **Waste material**

Necessary conveniences, properly secluded from public observation, shall be constructed and maintained wherever needed for the use of the Contractor's employees, to the satisfaction of the Engineer and the sanitary authorities. **Conveniences for men**

Wherever necessary the Contractor shall erect and maintain fences for the protection of adjoining property and of the adjoining public places. **Fences**

The using of fences and buildings during construction for advertising purposes, other than the name and address of the Contractor, is forbidden; all temporary buildings and fences erected by the Contractor shall be neat in appearance and shall be painted as directed by the Engineer. **Advertisements forbidden**

All barricades and bridges erected by the Contractor for the protection of the work or use of the public shall be substantial in character and neat in appearance. **Barricades**

The Engineer will prepare and furnish to the Contractor, from time to time as required, draw- **Detailed drawings**

ings and plans amplifying such details of the contract drawings as may be necessary, and drawings and plans necessary to show the adjustment and reconstruction of all surface and sub-surface structures wherever the reconstruction of the same is necessitated by the construction of the railroad. These plans must be strictly followed, unless local conditions should develop, during construction, suggesting changes, when, with the approval of the Engineer, such changes may be permitted.

Working and shop drawings

The Contractor shall make all working or shop drawings which may be required in addition to the contract drawings, or in addition to such other drawings as the Commission may issue in amplification of such contract drawings, as explained above. All working or shop drawings shall be submitted in duplicate to the Engineer for his approval, which approval shall be indicated by his countersigning one set of such working or shop drawings and returning the same to the Contractor. Should the working or shop drawings be not approved by the Engineer, then the Engineer shall return one set of such working or shop drawings, with the necessary corrections and changes indicated thereon; and the Contractor must make such corrections and changes, and again submit plans in duplicate for the approval of the Engineer; and no work shall be done under said working or shop drawings until the approval of the Engineer be obtained, which must be given or refused within ten (10) working days after delivery to him at his office of such plans in duplicate.

Lines and grades

During the progress of the work the Commission will give, through the Engineer, to the Contractor, suitable points, marks or benches, indicating the line and grade of the Railroad and of the sewers; such points or bench marks to be established at such intervals as the Engineer deems necessary for the Contractor to be able to perform his work. The principal lines and grades are to be given by the Engineer, who may change them from time to time as may be authorized and directed by the Commission. The stakes and marks given by the Engineer shall be carefully preserved by the Contractor, who shall give to the Engineer all necessary assistance and facilities for establishing benches and plugs for making measurements.

Notice, how given

When the Contractor is absent from any part of the work where it may be necessary to give instructions, orders will be given by the Engineer to, and shall be received and promptly obeyed by, the superintendent or overseer of the Contractor, who may have charge of the particular work in relation to which the orders are given, and a confirmation in writing of such orders will be given to the Contractor by the Engineer if so requested.

Imperfect work

Any imperfect construction which may be discovered before the final acceptance of the work, shall be corrected immediately on the requirement of the Engineer, notwithstanding that it may have been overlooked by the proper inspector.

In all work of whatever kind which during its progress and before its final acceptance shall become damaged from any cause, so much of it as may be objectionable shall be broken up or removed and be replaced by good and sound work.

Condemned materials to be removed

If the work or any part thereof, or any material found or brought on the ground for use in the work or selected for the same, shall be condemned by the Engineer as unsuitable or not in conformity with the specifications, the Contractor shall forthwith rebuild or remedy such work and remove such materials as may be directed by the Engineer.

Competent men

The Contractor shall employ only competent, skillful and faithful men to do the work. Whenever the Engineer shall notify the Contractor in writing that in his opinion any man on the work is incompetent, unfaithful or disorderly, such man shall be discharged from the work and shall not again be employed on it.

3

MANNER OF PROSECUTION AND MAINTENANCE OF TRAFFIC

Access to buildings, etc.

No building shall, without the consent of the occupant, and after notice to the Engineer be deprived of means of access thereto; and, where streets are open suitable bridges shall be built and maintained to permit owners and occupants to reach their premises. Where necessary, proper and easy means for passengers to reach or leave street cars shall be maintained.

Tube tunnel under Astor House and St. Paul's Churchyard

Provision is made for cast-iron tube tunnels, which will begin at a point about sixty (60) feet north of the north building line of Fulton Street, passing thence under property at St. Paul's Church to Vesey Street, thence crossing under Vesey Street and under the Astor House to Broadway, and thence northerly under Broadway to a point about forty-five (45) feet south of the south building line of Park Place produced. The Contractor will be required to prosecute his work so as to avoid damage to the above-mentioned properties.

The Contractor's attention is called to the necessity for extreme care in tunneling under St. Paul's Churchyard in order to avoid disturbance of the graves and vaults therein.

Harlem River

For the prosecution of the work from 131st Street in Manhattan to 138th in The Bronx, including those portions of the Railroad lying beneath the Harlem River and the approaches thereto, the work may be conducted by means of compressed air, dredging, open caissons founded on piles, or such other means as the Contractor may prefer and as may be approved by the Engineer.

Whatever method, however, is pursued, must give the tunnel a firm foundation without danger of settlement, and must during construction give a free and unobstructed waterway, at least two hundred (200) feet in width, for the passage of vessels. If necessary, the Contractor must keep a channel dredged to a depth at least equal to the minimum channel depth existing in the Harlem River at the time of commencing construction. The Contractor must also maintain suitable signals during both day and night, and during foggy weather to indicate the position of its temporary work and must, if required by the Engineer, protect the same by guard piles. When construction is finished, all temporary piles must be drawn and all parts of caissons or other work removed, so that there will be an unobstructed depth of water over the top of the tunnel for the full width of the river measured between the established bulkhead lines as shown by the plans.

Depth of channel and navigation signals

For that portion of the route adjoining wharves and docks the work must be so prosecuted as to permit free access to neighboring wharves and docks.

Wharves and docks

All regulations of the United States Government in respect of navigation shall carefully be complied with.

Generally the Contractor will be permitted to conduct its work in the most expeditious manner possible, having due regard for the safety of persons and property and facilities for traffic and

Other portions of the route

under such instructions as the Engineer may give from time to time.

All necessary facilities are to be furnished by the Contractor for the benefit of street travel, both on longitudinal and cross streets. Facilities for travel

In order to provide the minimum interference with traffic and the minimum inconvenience to abutting property owners, during the construction of the Railroad, on all parts of the work, except as is hereinafter especially provided, the streets and sidewalks shall be substantially decked or covered over, and every precaution must be taken to keep surface railways free from interruption of service. Decking of streets and sidewalks

The Contractor will be permitted to prosecute his work within the limits of Battery Park in open trench excavation without cover. Care must be taken to prevent damage to the park outside of the lines of excavation, and wherever practicable the cross-walks must be maintained across the excavation. Battery Park

From Church Street near Dey Street to a point on Broadway between Vesey and Barclay Streets, the Railroad will pass under private property as indicated on the contract drawings. The surface of the property between these points is not to be disturbed, except that, if needed by the Contractor, the building on the northeast corner of Fulton Street to Broadway

Fulton Street and Church Street may be razed, and the property itself be used during construction by the Contractor for his plant and for other purposes in the prosecution of the work.

On Broadway, between White and Grand Streets

On the west side of Broadway from a point north of White Street to a point near Grand Street as indicated on the contract drawings the Railroad will pass under private property to be acquired by the City. Where necessary the buildings on this property will be razed, and the Contractor will be permitted to prosecute his work in open trench excavation without cover within the limits of the property so acquired.

Broadway and Ninth Street to Irving Place and Fourteenth Street

From the point where the Railroad leaves Broadway between East Ninth Street and East Tenth Street to the point where the Railroad enters private property on the east side of Fourth Avenue the same will pass under private property and the Contractor will be required to prosecute his work by tunneling or other method so as not to disturb or injure overhead surfaces and structures. From the east side of Fourth Avenue to Irving Place at Fourteenth Street the Railroad will pass under private property which will be acquired by the City. The buildings thereon will probably be razed, in which event the Contractor will be permitted to prosecute his work in open trench excavation without cover within the limits of the property so acquired. In the event that it is deemed necessary to so conduct the work as to avoid such demolition of buildings the plans may be so changed as to permit of tunneling.

North of East 131st Street the Contractor will generally be permitted to prosecute his work in open trench excavation without cover in streets and, where necessary, private property under which the Railroad will extend, except that traffic and access to abutting property must be maintained and the tracks of the New York Central and Hudson River Railroad Company protected and supported.

On Lafayette Avenue east of Bedford Avenue, and on Bushwick Avenue in the Borough of Brooklyn, the Contractor will generally be permitted to prosecute his work in open trench excavation without cover except that traffic and access to abutting property must be maintained.

Street intersections

The street intersections, except in cases where open trench excavation without cover is permitted, shall be kept at all times open for traffic for their full width. The street intersections in cases where open trench excavation without cover is permitted must be kept at all times open to traffic for at least one-half the width of the cross-roadway, except that cross-roadways in which surface railroads are located shall be kept at all times open to traffic for their full width.

Where portions of a street intersection are opened the same shall be substantially and neatly bridged for foot traffic. In all cases the Contractor shall at all times keep all the street crossings on the lines of the sidewalks in a clean and neat condition, bridging gutters and low places where water might collect.

Close observance of above requirements

The Commission will insist upon the close observance of the above requirements, and no departure therefrom will be allowed, excepting upon the written permission of the Commission.

Openings for ventilation

Wherever the excavations are decked, where gas pipes are maintained in service or where gases are liable to accumulate, suitable openings shall be provided for proper ventilation.

Temporary pipes, etc.

Temporary pipes, if laid above the street or sidewalk surfaces, shall be neatly and substantially placed, and in a manner to cause the minimum of inconvenience to the abutting property owners and to the public.

In general

In general, work will as provided herein be carried on under covered roadways. In exceptional cases however where rock is within a few feet of the street or sidewalk surface, it may be impracticable to operate drills while the street is covered, until a sufficient depth of excavation has been obtained.

In such cases such latitude will be allowed the Contractor as may prove absolutely necessary for the execution of its contract, and as the Engineer with the approval of the Commission may deem advisable, after a thorough understanding of the exact conditions and the necessities has been determined.

4

MAINTENANCE OF STREET RAILROAD TRACKS, MAINS AND OTHER SURFACE OR SUB-SURFACE STRUCTURES

Surface and sub-surface structures to be maintained

The Contractor shall at all times, by suitable bridging or other supports, maintain and support in an entirely safe condition for their usual service and to the reasonable satisfaction of the owners, all elevated and sub-surface railroad structures, street railroads of whatever character, telegraph, telephone or electric light poles or wires, water and gas mains, steam pipes, pneumatic tubes, electric subways, sewers, drains, and all other surface or sub-surface structures encountered during the progress of the work. The sidewalks, curbs, areas, vaults and stoops along the line of the work must also be protected from any injury; but should any injury occur to any surface or sub-surface structure as mentioned above, or sidewalk, curb, area, vault or stoop, the Contractor shall fully restore the same to as good a condition as existed before the injury was done.

Notice to be given

Notice is to be given by the Contractor to all companies and the proper city officials, owning or having charge of surface or sub-surface structures along any part of the work, of his intention to commence operations along such part of the route, at least one (1) week in advance, and the Contractor shall file with the Engineer at the same time a copy of said notice; and he shall co-operate with the proper officers or officials in charge of such structures and shall furnish them with all reasonable facilities to inspect the methods of caring for their property.

Plans furnished

In the re-arrangement of sub-surface structures a tentative plan will be made by the Engineer, which will be submitted to the parties interested; if any reasonable changes are then requested by any of the said parties within ten days after the submission of the tentative plan, such changes will then be made, if in the judgment of the Engineer they will best conserve the interest of all parties concerned; a further plan will then be made which, on the approval of the Engineer, will be final.

Owners of structures may do work

Whenever it becomes necessary to cut, move, change, or reconstruct any such structures as named above, or connections therewith, such work shall be done according to the reasonable satisfaction of the owners of such pipes or other structures, and should they so desire, and the Engineer approve, by the owners themselves, at the expense of the Contractor; such expense not to exceed the actual and proper cost of labor and materials used, together with a reasonable allowance for the use of plant and tools not exceeding seven and a half ($7\frac{1}{2}$) per cent.

Reasonable dispatch

All work of reconstruction or alteration if performed by the City or owners shall be done with reasonable dispatch, and facilities are to be provided so that said work will interfere as little as possible with the practical working and use of such structures. Failure to make such alterations within a reasonable time, as shall be adjudged by the Commission, may be considered by the Contractor as a waiver on the part of said City or owners of the right to do said work.

Facilities to be given to make extensions

In the event of the owners or the City being required to make any alteration to their structures as above provided, or in case they shall consider it necessary or desirable to make any further alterations in, or do any work to or in connection with surface or sub-surface structures owned by them or it, at the time the work under this contract is in progress, the Contractor shall give said owners or the City all reasonable opportunity to perform such work; provided such work or alteration for the benefit solely of the owners of sub-surface structures does not cause the Contractor any serious loss or delay, as shall be determined by the Commission.

Parks and parkways, trees, etc.

In any park or parkway or where any grass plots or trees exist along any street occupied by the Contractor, proper precautions must be taken to protect from injury all such trees or grass plots. For every tree removed, injured or destroyed, the Contractor shall set out a new thrifty tree of the same kind removed, injured or destroyed and not less than fifteen (15) feet in height and not less than three and one-half ($3\frac{1}{2}$) inches in diameter, measured at a height of two feet above the surface of the ground, and in such position as the Commissioner of Parks shall indicate. All roads, cross-paths, grass plots, shrubbery and other plants removed or affected by the construction of the Works, shall be restored as soon as possible to as good a condition as existed before the commencement of the work.

Replanting under direction of Park Commissioner

In replanting trees and the replanting of grass plots the Contractor must be governed by the reasonable requirements of the Commissioner of Parks or by other authorities specially charged with the care of these trees or grass plots, and the nature and depth of the soil to be placed therein must be as approved by such authorities and the Commission.

5

EXCAVATION

Width of excavation

Special care must be taken to avoid damage wherever open excavation is permitted. The width of such excavation shall not exceed the width actually necessary, in the opinion of the Engineer, for the proper prosecution of the work. All excavations shall be of such width, in addition to that of the Railroad, as shall be necessary, for the proper and expeditious progress of the work, and to permit the laying and readjusting of all sewers, mains, subways and other sub-surface structures encountered along the route and contiguous to the Railroad.

Depth of trenches

Trenches shall be excavated to such depth, both in soft ground and in rock, as may be necessary to permit the laying of such concrete bed or special foundation as may be deemed necessary by the Engineer.

Filling back of sheeting

Sheeting shall be driven wherever possible, but when it is placed against the sides of the excavation, the spaces or voids back of the sheeting wherever possible and if so ordered by the Engineer, must be immediately and carefully filled with suitable material to prevent as far as possible the natural ground back of the sheeting from moving.

Buildings underpinned, and sides to be secured

To secure adjacent ground or the buildings thereon, or to prevent bringing an unusual pressure on the structure when completed, the Contractor shall secure the sides of the excavation by suitable timbering, and by underpinning of adjacent buildings. As a part of this obligation the Contractor shall use such methods of construction or underpinning, pneumatic or otherwise, as special conditions may require and the Engineer shall approve. Unless specially directed by the Engineer, the Contractor will not be required to remove rangers or draw sheeting.

Sides to be secured

The sides of the excavations shall be secured against slips by suitable sheet-piling or sheeting, held in place by braces, shores, or waling timbers, special precautions being taken where there is additional pressure due to the presence of buildings or other structures. Where a movement of the ground might cause the settlement of an adjacent building, the sheeting must be started, if near the building, before the elevation of the bottom of the foundation of the building is reached; if away from the building, at such depth of the excavation as the Engineer may permit; and the excavation must not be made in advance of or below the bottom of the sheeting.

Timber for temporary purposes

All timber used for sheeting, shoring, bracing, decking or other temporary purposes, shall be sound and free from any defects that may impair its strength. The top or wearing surface of all decking used for carriageways shall be of hard yellow pine, sound, straight, and free from all shakes, and large loose knots. All sheeting and timber used temporarily shall be put in place by skilled mechanics, keyed tight by wedges where necessary, and so arranged as to be withdrawn readily without endangering the adjoining soil.

Wherever vaults are broken through or otherwise disturbed, the Contractor shall erect a temporary partition on or about the building line, or as directed, that will afford proper protection to the owner or occupant of the adjoining premises. Vaults disturbed

Ledge rock in place and boulders within the ordered line for excavation requiring blasting will be measured as rock excavation. Rock

Whenever rock is encountered in the trench, it shall be stripped of earth in sections of not less than twenty feet; and the Engineer in charge shall be duly notified, in order that he may measure or cross-section the same. Rock measurement

Whenever rock or material requiring blasting is encountered in any trench or tunnel, all necessary precautions must be exercised by the Contractor, as required by the ordinances of the City relative to blasting. Explosives shall be used only of such character and strength as may be permitted by the Commission, and the right is reserved for the Engineer to direct that in special cases ordinary blasting powder only, in small charges, shall be used. Blasting shall not be done between the hours of 11 P. M. and 7 A. M. with- Blasting out the express permission of the Engineer, and under such restrictions as he may impose.

Storage of explosives

No larger quantity of explosives shall be kept on the line of the work than will be actually required for the twelve (12) hours of work next ensuing, and kept under lock, the key to which is to be only in the hands of the foreman or other equally trustworthy person. The amount of explosives kept in any one place shall not exceed the limit permitted by any ordinance of the City, or as may be determined by the Commission. Caps and exploders shall not be kept in the same place with dynamite and other explosives. During freezing weather, special precautions shall be taken as to the care and manipulation of dynamite.

Near pipes and mains

Whenever any pipe or main is encountered in or alongside of the trench, the right is reserved to direct that all rock within five (5) feet of the same shall be removed by means other than blasting.

General precautions in blasting

In rock excavation in the trenches for the Railroad the work must be so regulated as to avoid, as far as possible, shattering the rock beyond the established line for excavation.

Blasting

Generally the central portion of the excavation must, when directed by the Engineer, be kept some distance in advance of the excavation near the sides, and if the rock, owing to its general character and structure, has a tendency to break large, or the strike and dip of the stratification indicate a liability to slip or slide into the excavation, the Contractor must place the drill holes at close intervals on the established lines for excavation, in order to avoid excessive excavation and to preserve the established lines thereof.

Pumping

Whenever water is encountered in trenches, the same shall be removed by bailing or pumping, great care being taken when pumping that the surrounding particles of soil be not disturbed or removed. If necessary to prevent such disturbance, the pumping must be done by a series of driven wells whose points are protected by fine wire cloths, the rate of flow at each well being made so slow as not to remove the particles of soil; or the pumping must be done by other means approved by the Engineer. The delivery from all pumps shall be conducted into the adjacent sewers, and the delivery pipes shall be so arranged as to be readily inspected at all times to ascertain if the water is free from particles of soil.

Carts to be tight

All carts, buckets or other vehicles used by the Contractor for the removal of material, shall be tight and so arranged and so loaded as not to spill over. Whenever a cart, bucket or other vehicle so used is leaky or unsuitable, it shall be immediately withdrawn from the work on notification by the Engineer, or his duly qualified assistant, in charge of that portion of the work.

Removed expeditiously

Excavated material shall be removed expeditiously and disposed of, in any place selected by the Contractor, subject to the ordinances and regulations of the City authorities governing the disposal of such material, and the regulations of the United States Government as to the disposal or dumping of material in and about or near the Harbor of New York.

If at any time during the course of construction the City shall desire any part of the material excavated for City purposes and the cost of such disposal shall not exceed the cost to the Contractor of the method in which he is then disposing of it, the Commission may order such material dumped or turned over to the City at a point designated, without cost to the City.

6

TUNNELING

How lined

All tunnels shall be lined with steel or cast-iron and concrete, or with concrete or brick masonry.

Where tunnels are lined with concrete or brick work without metal tubes proper provisions shall be made for keeping the tunnels dry by the use of drains, and by other methods as elsewhere provided.

The space between the extrados of the arch or back of the sidewalls and the rock or other materials of excavation, shall be filled with concrete to a height of two feet above the spring line of the arch—above this concrete the space shall be filled with dry masonry packing. Packing

After the tunnel lining and packing is in place if required by the Engineer a grout, consisting of one (1) part fine, clean and sharp sand, and one (1) part Portland cement, shall be pumped in under pressure from time to time behind the masonry, so as to completely fill all the voids. Where tunnels are made by the use of a shield, similar grout shall be pumped in to completely fill the space left by the tail piece of the shield as soon as the shield is moved forward. Grout

The tunnels shall be excavated to the lines as shown on the plans. Drilling and blasting must be conducted with all possible care and in such a manner as not to shatter the roof and sides outside of the prescribed lines, nor endanger adjoining property. Blasts shall not be fired between the hours of 11 P. M. and 7 A. M. where tunnels are in front of private residences, without the express permission of the Commission and under such restrictions as it may impose. Blasting

Whenever any loose rock occurs outside of the lines of the excavation, whose fall or settlement might, in the judgment of the Engineer, produce Loose rock to be removed an unequal or concentrated pressure on the masonry, the same shall be removed, and the space refilled with such class of concrete or dry masonry as ordered by the Engineer.

Drains

All seams carrying water shall be carefully drained, as specified under the clauses relating to drainage.

Soft ground

In soft ground the Contractor must take every precaution, and such precautions as the Engineer may direct, by suitable shields, timbering, lagging or other supports, to prevent any settlement or movement of surrounding ground. Such timber as cannot be drawn without endangering the work or the ground above, shall be left in place and thoroughly surrounded by masonry and grouted.

Compressed air

If for the work under the Harlem River and for the approaches thereto a method is adopted requiring the use of compressed air, a plant must be provided of sufficient capacity, in the judgment of the Engineer, to insure at all times and under all conditions an ample supply of air to prosecute the work with safety and dispatch.

Where compressed air is used proper air locks shall be built with safety locks in addition, to provide for the escape of workmen at times of accident.

Methods to be approved

All methods of tunneling shall be subject to the approval of the Engineer, and be changed from time to time if, in his judgment, the local conditions so require, and during construction approved methods of ventilation and lighting shall be used.

In arched cut and cover work the arching and sidewalls shall be of concrete or brick masonry, with proper precaution taken in each case to prevent leaks, as prescribed in the clauses relating to waterproofing. If so ordered concrete must be placed back of the sidewalls where the excavation is in rock. Arched cut and cover

7

BACKFILLING

The trenches at the sides of and over the top of the subway and wherever backfilling is necessary, shall be backfilled with sand, gravel or other good clean earth, free from perishable material and from stones exceeding six (6) inches in diameter, and not containing in any place a proportion of stone of or below that size exceeding one (1) part of stone to five (5) parts of earth. The filling shall be compacted by flooding with water or in cases where flooding with water is not practicable, it shall be compacted by ramming in layers not exceeding six (6) inches in depth. Quality of material How placed

Whenever pipes, sewers, or other sub-surface structures are met with, the filling must be carefully packed, rammed and tamped under such Sub-surface structures sub-surface structures, using special tools for the purpose. No filling of trenches with frozen earth will in any case be permitted, nor will any filling be permitted over frozen material.

Frozen material not permitted

Sheeting removed

As fast as the work of filling permits, sheeting and other timber supporting the sides of the excavations shall be carefully withdrawn, or shall be left in place, as may be directed by the Engineer, and when removed the spaces left by the removal of such material shall be carefully backfilled.

8

PILING AND TIMBERING

Piles

If in the judgment of the Engineer the ground is of such a character as to require piling, the Contractor shall drive such piles as the Engineer directs. The piles shall be of good, sound pine or spruce, straight and free from shakes; they shall be not less than twelve (12) inches in diameter at the butt end, or less than six (6) inches in diameter at the point, and shall be driven to the satisfaction of the Engineer and by means of a steam hammer driver if so required by him. If necessary the points of the piles shall be protected by proper shoes, and the butts by rings or caps. Piles shall not be spliced unless permitted by the Engineer, and then in such manner as he directs. Piles shall be carefully cut off to the grade given by the Engineer.

If in the judgment of the Engineer special conditions so require, piles of re-inforced concrete of an approved form of construction shall be used. Concrete piles

Timber grillage foundations shall be built if so directed by the Engineer. Grillage

All foundation timber shall be of pine or spruce, or other timber permitted by the Engineer, sound and free from shakes. It shall be of such dimensions, and laid in such manner, as the special plans to be issued shall require, and held in place by spikes or good seasoned oak or locust treenails. Foundation timber

9

CEMENT

All cement used in the work shall be true Portland cement, by which is meant the finely pulverized product, resulting from the calcination to incipient fusion of a properly proportioned intimate mixture of argillaceous and calcareous earths or rocks, to which no addition greater than three (3) per cent. has been made subsequent to calcination. Portland cement

Before any cement is furnished, the brand shall receive the approval of the Engineer. Cement, to be acceptable, shall be of a well-known brand which has been in successful use for large engineering works in America for at least five (5) years, and which has an established reputation for Brand to be approved uniform character. Preference will be given to cements which, by their records, show a tendency to maintain high strength of mortar with increased age.

Inspection

Cement shall be subject to inspection at the place of manufacture or on the work, and to such tests as may be ordered by the Engineer. The Engineer or his representatives shall have access at all times and places to inspect the methods of manufacture, storage and protection, and shall have liberty to inspect the daily laboratory records of tests and analyses at the cement works.

Tests

In general, tests will conform to the methods recommended by the Committee on Uniform Tests of Cement of the American Society of Civil Engineers. Unless otherwise directed, samples will be taken at the place of manufacture by a representative of the Engineer, and sent to the Commission's laboratory, where the tests will be made. If required, tests will be made on the individual samples, without intermixing.

Specific gravity and color

The cement shall have a specific gravity of not less than 3.10 nor more than 3.25 after being thoroughly dried at a temperature of .212 Fahr.

The color shall be uniform, bluish gray, free from yellow or brown particles.

Chemical analysis

Chemical analyses of cement made from time to time shall show a reasonably uniform composition.

Cement shall not contain more than 1.75 per cent. of sulphuric anhydride (SO_3) nor more than 4 per cent. of magnesia (MgO).

The fineness of the cement shall be such that it shall leave by weight a residue of not more than eight (8) per cent. on a No. 100, and not more than twenty-five (25) per cent. on a No. 200 sieve; the wires of the sieves being respectively 0.0045 and 0.0024 inch in diameter. Fineness

It shall not develop initial set in less than thirty (30) minutes unless a more quickly-setting cement is specifically required, and shall develop hard set in not less than one (1) hour nor more than ten (10) hours. Time of setting

Pats of neat cement, after remaining one (1) day in moist air, shall be kept in air or water of normal temperature for at least twenty-eight (28) days, or shall be exposed to an atmosphere of steam, above boiling water, in a loosely closed vessel for at least five (5) hours; and under any of these conditions, shall remain hard without any indications of checking, cracking, distortion, disintegration or blotching. Soundness

Neat cement briquettes shall have at the end of one (1) day in moist air a breaking strength, per square inch of sectional area, of not less than one hundred and fifty (150) lbs.; at the end of seven (7) days—one (1) day in air, six (6) days in Tensile strength water—of not less than five hundred (500) lbs.; and at the end of twenty-eight (28) days—one (1) day in air, twenty-seven (27) days in water—of not less than six hundred (600) lbs. The strength at twenty-eight (28) days shall not be less than that at seven (7) days.

Mortar briquettes

Mortar briquettes, composed of one (1) part of cement and three (3) parts of standard Ottawa sand, by weight, shall have at the end of seven (7) days—one (1) day in air, six (6) days in water—a breaking strength, per square inch of sectional area, of not less than two hundred (200) lbs.; and at the end of twenty-eight (28) days—one (1) day in air, twenty-seven (27) days in water—of not less than three hundred (300) lbs. The strength at twenty-eight (28) days shall show an increase of not less than fifty (50) lbs. over the strength at seven (7) days.

Long-time tests

Tests will be made from time to time extending over longer periods than twenty-eight (28) days. If such tests show a tendency to unsoundness or unusual reduction in strength with increased age, the Engineer shall have the right to prohibit the further use of that brand and to require that another brand be substituted.

Storage during tests

A sufficient quantity of cement shall be held in storage to allow ample time for tests to be made before the cement is required for use in the work.

How contained

Cement shall be packed and delivered in canvas sacks or other strong, well-made packages, plainly marked with the manufacturer's brand, and sealed in an approved manner. The weights of such packages shall be uniform.

Methods of storing

The Contractor shall at all times keep in store on the work, or at some point convenient thereto, an abundant supply of acceptable cement, so as to guard against possible shortage. It shall be stored in a weather-tight building, with a tight floor a proper distance above the ground, and with sufficient floor space to admit of storing each lot of cement, of not more than two hundred (200) barrels, or its equivalent, separately, so as to facilitate identification of each individual lot in case of necessity for further tests or rejection. Cement that has become partially set or otherwise damaged shall not be used.

10

MORTAR

Cement and sand

All mortar shall be prepared from accepted cement and clean, sharp sand, approved by the Engineer. These ingredients shall be thoroughly mixed dry in the proportions as specified below; water shall then be added, so as to produce a stiff paste. Water used in mortar, grout or concrete must be clean, fresh water, no salt water being permitted. The mortar shall be freshly mixed for

Mixing

the work on hand, in proper boxes made for that purpose, and no mortar shall be used that has stood beyond such limit of time as may be determined by the Engineer.

How measured

For purposes of mixture, three hundred and seventy-five (375) pounds of Portland cement shall be estimated at three and one-half ($3\frac{1}{2}$) cubic feet of volume. The proportional parts of sand and stone or gravel shall be by volume as cast into the measuring box. The proportions for brick and stone masonry shall be one (1) part cement to two (2) parts sand; for pointing, one (1) part cement and one (1) part sand; for concrete masonry, as specified under the head of concrete; for station finish work, as specified under stations; and for other classes of work, as directed by the Engineer; for grout, one (1) part of cement to one (1) part of fine sand.

11

MASONRY

Laid in Portland cement

All masonry, except as otherwise specified, shall be laid in Portland cement mortar, and shall be built of the forms and dimensions shown on the plans, or as directed by the Engineer from time to time; and the system of joining or bonding ordered by the Engineer shall be strictly followed.

Water not to interfere with

Care must be taken that no water shall interfere with the proper laying of masonry in any of its parts.

Freezing weather

During freezing weather such masonry only shall be built whose construction, in the judgment of the Engineer, can not be postponed, except at the cost of delaying the work. The Contractor shall provide such appliances as are necessary for heating the water and the materials used in the masonry according to the specific instructions of the Engineer.

During freezing weather all masonry shall be protected by a suitable covering of salt hay, canvas, tarpaulin or by such material or in such ways as may be necessary to insure it against freezing.

Hot weather

During hot weather all masonry, especially concrete, shall be kept wet by sprinkling and properly covered until it has become thoroughly set and hardened.

Pointing

Unless otherwise permitted, every joint that is to be pointed shall be raked out, within two days after being laid, to a depth of at least two inches.

Pointing of the face joints of masonry shall be thoroughly made with cement mortar mixed in the proportion of one (1) part of cement to one (1) part of sand, except where otherwise specially provided.

No pointing shall be done in freezing weather, and masonry laid between December 1st and April 1st shall not be pointed until permitted by the Engineer.

Defective masonry Any masonry which is found to be defective from any cause whatsoever, before the final completion and acceptance of the work, must be removed and properly rebuilt, or if damaged during such time must be properly repaired.

Stone cleaned All stone before being laid shall be thoroughly cleaned, and washed if so directed by the Engineer.

12

CONCRETE

How composed The concrete shall be composed of gravel or broken stone, or a mixture of both, free from all dirt and dust, and mixed together with the proportion of mortar specified below.

Sand Sand for concrete shall be of the kind herein specified for mortar.

Stone Stone for concrete shall be sound, clean gravel, or sound, hard, broken limestone, or trap rock or a mixture of such gravel and broken stone may be used.

Size of stone and gravel Broken stone or gravel for concrete shall be graded from fine to coarse, and that which is all of one size, or practically so, shall not be used. It shall be screened or washed so as to remove all dust, and it shall contain no pieces that will pass through a hole three-eighths (3/8) inch in diameter and no pieces that will not pass through a hole one and one-half ($1\frac{1}{2}$) inches in diameter. Broken stone or gravel for concrete graded as above but between three-eighths ($\frac{3}{8}$) and three-fourths ($\frac{3}{4}$) inch in diameter may be required and used in special parts of the work.

In concrete where the thickness is thirty (30) inches or more, if permitted by the Engineer, the Contractor may imbed in the same pieces of sound stone whose greatest diameter does not exceed twelve (12) inches and whose least diameter or thickness is not less than three-quarters ($\frac{3}{4}$) of the greatest diameter. These stones shall be set by hand in the concrete as the layers are being rammed, and so placed that each stone is completely and perfectly imbedded. No two (2) stones shall be within six (6) inches of each other and no stones within four (4) inches of an exposed face, nor shall any such stone be placed nearer than six (6) inches to any metal built in the concrete for reinforcing the same. Rubble Concrete

The proportions of cement, sand and stone (or gravel) used in making concrete shall be as follows: Proportions

Concrete in floor, sidewalls and roof, one (1) part of cement, two (2) parts of sand and four (4) parts of stone. Concrete for tube tunnels under the Harlem River will be as indicated on the plans.

Protective concrete outside of waterproofing lines on sides and roof, one (1) part of cement, four (4) parts of sand and eight (8) parts of stone.

Mixing by machine

Whenever practicable, concrete shall be machine-mixed. A rotary machine of a pattern approved by the Engineer, and mixing only one batch at a time shall be used.

Mixing by hand

When concrete is mixed by hand the stone or gravel shall be spread on a platform in a bed about six (6) inches thick, and shall be thoroughly wet. Sand shall be spread on a platform and the requisite portion of cement spread on the sand. After thoroughly mixing the latter, the dry mixture thus formed shall be spread evenly over the bed of stone wet as above, and the whole turned over until thoroughly mixed, but not less than two (2) turnings on the mixing board shall be allowed in any case, water being added as necessary. Care shall be taken to keep the bed of concrete wet and avoid piling.

How laid

Concrete shall be placed immediately after mixing in layers of such thickness as may be directed by the Engineer, and shall be thoroughly compacted throughout the mass by ramming or spading, special tamping bars or tools being used as approved by the Engineer. The amount of water used in making the concrete shall be as approved by the Engineer. If a small amount of water has been used in mixing, ramming shall be continued until the water flushes to the surface; as a rule, however, concrete shall be placed wet.

Made smooth to receive water-proofing

Concrete to which waterproofing is to be applied shall be made smooth at the time of laying and shall be carefully protected from injury by barricades or otherwise, if necessary, until thoroughly set.

Time for hardening

Concrete shall be allowed to set for twelve (12) hours, or more, if so directed, before any work shall be laid upon it; and no walking over or working upon it shall be allowed while it is setting. Concrete shall not be flooded with water before being thoroughly set.

Rock surface to be cleaned

Before laying concrete on rock surfaces the latter shall be swept clean of all debris and dirt, and when laid on earth the earth shall be rammed as directed before placing the concrete.

Surface rough for bonding

Wherever a section of concrete is necessarily left unfinished, leaving a surface which will be hard set before additional concrete is laid, the surface shall be left rough to form a bond with the new work; and if deemed necessary by the Engineer, the joints shall be reinforced with steel bars or dowels, to be furnished by the Contractor.

Joints cleaned

In all cases of joints of old with new work the old surfaces shall be thoroughly cleaned and wet, and a coating of mortar or cement shall be applied, if required, before placing the concrete.

Forms

Suitable forms shall be provided by the Contractor to support the concrete while being placed in the walls or roofs. These forms shall be immediately replaced by new ones as soon as they commence to lose their proper shape. Before being used they shall be carefully cleaned of cement and dirt in order to provide a perfectly smooth face to the exposed surface of the concrete. The forms shall be made of wood, kept carefully planed; or made of metal sufficiently thick to retain their shape without the use of wood.

No forms made of wood and covered with iron will be permitted.

The forms if made of wood, shall be made of boards with tight joints, tongued and grooved if required by the Engineer.

Precautions in placing

Every precaution shall be taken in placing or assembling the forms to do so in such a manner that when removed, after the concrete has been placed, the faces of the concrete that are to remain exposed shall present a smooth and even surface.

Forms, how set

Forms removed

The forms shall be set true to line, firmly secured, and be so tight as not to allow water in the mortar to escape; they shall be thoroughly wet before placing the concrete and shall be removed as soon after the concrete has been placed as in the judgment of the Engineer may be done with safety to the work. Immediately on the removal thereof the faces that will remain exposed shall be carefully examined and any irregularities of the surface corrected; projections shall be removed and voids filled with mortar. If, however, the voids are such as to indicate an excessive loss of mortar, portions of the concrete shall be cut out to the fullness of such defects and the space refilled with a rich concrete or mortar in such proportions and in such manner as the Engineer may direct.

Surface irregularities corrected

Defective work replaced

Where reinforcement steel is used, efficient means shall be provided to maintain it in the exact position it is to occupy in the completed work, and to prevent it from becoming dislodged, or moved in any manner, when concrete is placed.

Reinforcement steel

The exposed faces of the concrete, excepting within station limits, shall be left with the natural cement finish; therefore, immediately following the removal of the forms, followed by the removal of the projections and the filling of voids as provided above, these entire surfaces shall be rubbed down in such a manner, approved by the Engineer, as will leave a smooth and even surface, the object in view being to obtain a generally smooth finished surface with uniformity in color.

Surfaces not to be painted

It is intended to obtain concrete impervious to water; the concrete shall be mixed and deposited

Impervious to water

with this end in view, and on the roof of the railroad, if waterproofing is not used, the top surface of the concrete shall be carefully troweled as may be directed in order to add to its imperviousness.

(For Concrete in Sewers, see **SEWERS.**)

13

BRICK MASONRY

Quality

Bricks for masonry shall be of the best quality common bricks, burned hard entirely through, regular and uniform in shape and size and of compact texture.

Hollow terra cotta blocks

Hollow terra cotta blocks or bricks may be required in station work, on the outside of walls of the structure or at such other places as indicated on the plans or as the Engineer may direct. They shall be of the best porous terra cotta as approved by the Engineer, and shall be laid in such manner as hereinafter specified or as the Engineer may direct.

How laid

All brick masonry shall be laid in mortar of the quality above described, except that in exposed locations coloring matter may be added, if required by the Engineer. The bricks shall be laid to line with joints in the face work (except in stations) not exceeding one-quarter (1/4) of an inch in the beds, and three-eighths (3/8) of an inch on ends; the bricks to be thoroughly wet before laying and to be completely embedded in mortar under the bottom and on the sides and ends at one operation, care being taken to have every joint full of mortar.

All exterior surfaces shall be smooth and regular.

The inside faces of all arches and other exposed parts shall have all the mortar scraped off and washed clean immediately after the centres have been struck, and shall be pointed and left in neat condition. Cleaned

All bricks of whatever nature shall be carefully culled and if necessary gauged before laying, at the expense of the Contractor. No " bats " shall be used except in large masses of brick-work, where a moderate proportion, to be determined by the Engineer, may be used, but nothing smaller than half bricks. No "bats" or culls

All unfinished work shall be racked back or toothed, as directed by the Engineer, and before new work is joined to it the faces of the brick in the old work must be scraped entirely clean, scrubbed with a stiff brush and be well moistened. Racked or toothed

Where necessary to make a neat joint in connection with steel framework, or at corners, curves, or other similar places, special bricks of proper shape shall be furnished and used. All centers and forms shall be made to fit the curves of the work; they shall be put up and removed in a manner satisfactory to the Engineer. Special bricks

14

STONE MASONRY

Footings for columns

In general columns will be set on a concrete base; in special cases, however, footing stones may be required.

Footing stones

If footing stones for columns are required they shall be of the dimensions and shapes shown on detailed plans, which will be provided; they shall be strong and free from defects, and shall be set in cement mortar. Before being set the tops shall be rough-pointed without chisel draft, the vertical sides shall be left quarry faced, the portion of the top where the column base plate is to rest shall be dressed true with pean hammers, and the top brought to a plane, so that at no point will it be more than one-eighth (1/8) of an inch from a straight edge laid across in any direction. In case the Contractor fails to set the footing stones true to line and surface, then they shall be set with their tops about one-eighth (1/8) of an inch above the grade called for by the plans, and not less than two (2) days after being set they shall have their tops dressed with pean hammers, so as to form accurate seats for the base plates of the columns.

To be set high

Anchor bolt holes

Holes shall be accurately drilled for anchor bolts, and filled with neat cement mortar after the bolts are set in place.

Columns during erection shall be set on iron shims, if shims are necessary; wooden shims are prohibited.

Where shims are used the voids under column bases shall be filled with cement grout consisting of one part of cement and one part of sand.

15

WATERPROOFING

In general, waterproofing of the structure will be limited to the roof and sidewalls at the stations, and to those surfaces near ground water or mean high water if ground water is found for any reason to be below mean high water. At other places free drainage shall be provided by pipe drains, hollow tile or broken stone. **General limits of waterproofing**

The protecting masonry shall be hollow terra cotta blocks, common bricks or concrete, laid as herein elsewhere provided, and shall not be less than four inches in thickness. **Protecting masonry**

In places where permanent sheeting is placed at the waterproofing line, the waterproofing, if permitted by the Engineer, may be applied against the sheeting. **Laid against sheeting**

Surfaces to be made smooth

All surfaces to which waterproofing is to be applied shall be made as smooth as possible; on these surfaces there shall be spread either hot melted pitch or asphaltum in a thick layer of uniform thickness; on this layer of pitch or asphaltum shall be laid a woven fabric of such material as may be approved by the Engineer; this process shall be repeated until such number of layers as may be required by the Engineer have been placed and a final coat of pitch or asphaltum shall then be applied.

Definition of term "ply"

The term "ply" as used in these specifications shall mean a layer of treated woven fabric both sides of which shall be coated with pitch or asphaltum at the time of laying.

Number of ply

The number of plies of waterproofing on the sides at the stations shall in no case be less than three (3), except as hereinafter provided where brick laid in asphalt mastic is used.

Brick in asphalt mastic

Over the roof of the structure within station limits and over the tracks passing through the stations within said limits, also on the sides and bottom of the structure below a line of two (2) feet above ground water, or if ground water is below mean high water level, then two (2) feet above mean high water, one (1) ply of waterproofing, as described above, shall be used with one or more layers of brick laid in asphalt mastic; the number of layers of bricks, not exceeding two (2), to be determined by the Engineer.

In any case where brick laid in asphalt mastic is not used, the number of plies, should local conditions require it, may be increased as directed by the Engineer; not to exceed, however, six (6) plies.

Quality of brick

The quality of brick shall be the same as elsewhere provided in the specifications under brick masonry. The brick shall be properly dried and shall be heated before laying.

Six (6) plies of waterproofing may be substituted for brick in asphalt mastic, if approved by the Engineer.

Asphalt mastic

Asphalt mastic shall contain one-third (1-3) pure bitumen, the other ingredients to be sand and lime dust or cement, in proportions governed by local requirements and weather conditions.

Leaks stopped

Any masonry that is found to leak at any time prior to the completion of the work and final acceptance thereof by the Commission shall be cut out and the leak stopped.

Quality of pitch

Pitch shall consist of either coal-tar or natural asphalt as the Engineer shall elect, it must be delivered on the work in packages that are plainly marked with the manufacturer's brand, and indicating the grade and quality of the material.

Coal-tar pitch

The coal-tar pitch shall be straight-run pitch, containing not less than 25 and not more than 32 per cent. of pure carbon, which will soften at approximately 70° F., and melt at 100° F., being a grade in which distillate oils distilled therefrom shall have a specific gravity of 1.05.

Quality of asphalt

The asphalt used shall be the best grade of Bermudez, or lake, or other natural asphalts, subject to the approval of the Engineer, and shall comply with the following requirements:

The asphalt shall contain in its refined state not less than ninety-five (95) per cent. of natural bitumen soluble in rectified carbon bisulphide or in chloroform. The remaining ingredients shall be such as not to exert an injurious effect on the work. Not less than two-thirds (2-3) of the total bitumen shall be soluble in petroleum naphtha of seventy (70) degrees Baume or in acetone. The asphalt shall not lose more than four (4) per cent. of its weight when maintained for ten (10) hours at a temperature of three hundred (300) degrees Fahrenheit.

Woven fabric for waterproofing

The fabric to be used shall be a woven fabric which shall have been treated with pitch or asphaltum before being brought on the work. The fabric and the material used in its treatment shall be approved by the Engineer.

All concrete shall be dry before waterproofing is attached. If, in the judgment of the Engineer it is impracticable to have the concrete dry, then there shall be first laid a layer of the treated fabric, on the upper surface of which is to be spread the first layer of pitch or asphaltum; the said layer of fabric shall not be counted as one of the required plies.

Concrete to be dry

Each layer of pitch or asphaltum fluxed as directed by the Engineer must completely and entirely cover the surface on which it is spread without cracks or blowholes.

Fabric for waterproofing to be carefully laid

The fabric must be rolled out into the pitch or asphaltum while the latter is still hot, and pressed against it so as to insure its being completely stuck over its entire surface, great care being taken that all joints are well broken by overlapping, and that the ends of the rolls of the bottom layers are carried up on the inside of the layers on the sides, and those of the roof down on the outside of the layers on the sides so as to secure a full lap of at least one (1) foot. Especial care must be taken with this detail.

None but competent men, especially skilled in work of this kind, shall be employed to lay the waterproofing.

Skilled labor to be employed

When the finishing layer of concrete is laid over or next to the waterproofing material, care must be taken not to break, tear or injure in any way the outer surface of the pitch or asphaltum.

16

STEEL AND IRON

Open hearth process

Steel shall be made in an open hearth furnace.

Chemical and physical properties

The chemical and physical properties of finished material shall conform to the following limits:

Properties.	Structural Steel.	Carbon Rivet Steel.	Steel Castings.
Phos. (Max.) ...	.04%	.04%	.05%
Sulph. "	.05%	.04%	.05%
Mn. "	.60%	.60%	.80%
Si. "	.10%	.10%	.35%
Ult. Str........	60000±4000	50000±4000	65000±(Min.)
Yield Point....	55% Ult.	55% Ult.	35000±(Min.)
Elongation.....	$\frac{1500000}{\text{Ult. Str.}}$	$\frac{1500000}{\text{Ult. Str.}}$	20% in 2″
Fracture.......	Silky.	Silky.	Fine granular.
Cold Bend	180° flat.	180° flat.	120° (d.=3+.)

Yield point

The yield point shall be that strain, beyond which the elongation ceases to be proportional to the weight imposed, and may be indicated by drop of beam. The speed of testing shall be governed by the inspector.

Sufficient discard shall be made to insure sound material free from piping or excessive segregation. The material shall be finished straight and smooth, and shall be free from all seams or other defects. Any imperfection which may develop during the progress of the work will be sufficient cause for rejection. Finish

Steel castings shall be true to pattern and free from injurious imperfections. Steel castings

The tensile strength, yield point and ductility of the material shall be determined from a standard test piece of not more than two (2) inches in width, and about one-half ($\frac{1}{2}$) square inch in sectional area, cut from a full sized bar, with sides turned or planed parallel so as to give a uniform minimum section for at least nine (9) inches. Whenever practicable the two sides of the test piece shall be left as they come from the rolls, but the finish on opposite sides shall be alike in this respect. Standard test pieces

Specimens for bending shall be cut from the material as rolled. Specimens for bending

Rivet rods shall be tested as rolled. Rivet rods

For steel castings the test piece shall be turned to a uniform minimum section of one-half ($\frac{1}{2}$) inch diameter, for a length of at least two and one-half ($2\frac{1}{2}$) inches. Specimens for bending shall be one (1) inch by one-half ($\frac{1}{2}$) inch in section. Steel castings

Ductility and elongation

In determining the ductility, the elongation shall be measured after breaking on an original length as specified, in which length shall occur the curve of reduction each side of the point of fracture.

Where taken from

For rollers the specimens shall be cut from the finished bar so that the center of the specimen shall be one inch from the outside of the bar.

For steel castings the specimens shall be cut from coupons cast on some portion of a casting from each melt, and shall be annealed with the casting before it is cut off.

Treatment of test specimens

The material from which test specimens are cut shall receive the same treatment as the material which it represents in the finished structure.

Number of tests

At least one tensile and one bending test shall be made from each melt of steel as rolled. In case steel differing three-eighths (3/8) inch or more in thickness is rolled from one melt, a test shall be made from the thickest and from the thinnest material rolled.

Variation in weight

A variation in weight of any piece of steel of two and one-half per centum (2½ per cent.) from that specified, shall be sufficient cause for rejection, except in case of sheared plates exceeding one hundred (100) inches in width, where the variation may be five (5) per centum.

Each finished piece of steel shall be marked with the melt number, excepting that for bars for reinforcing concrete, the bars shall be bundled and the melt number stamped on a metal tag attached to each bundle. Material marked

Wrought Iron

All wrought iron shall be double rolled, and no scrap used in its manufacture. It shall be thoroughly welded in rolling, shall be tough, ductile, and fibrous, and shall be finished straight and smooth. It shall be uniform in quality and free from surface defects. Double rolled

The methods specified for testing rolled steel shall apply generally to wrought iron. It shall show by the standard test piece an ultimate strength of fifty thousand (50,000) lbs. per square inch, and a yield point of twenty-six thousand (26,000) lbs. per square inch. It shall bend one hundred and thirty-five degrees (135°) with inner radius not to exceed twice the thickness of the piece tested. When nicked and bent the fracture shall show at least ninety (90) per centum fibrous. Method of testing

Cast Iron

All castings shall be true to pattern, out of wind and free from injurious imperfections. They shall be of a good quality of tough gray iron made by the cupola process. Sample test True to pattern Tests pieces, cylindrical in shape, one and one-quarter (1¼) inches in diameter, and fifteen (15) inches long, cast under the same circumstances as those which attended the casting of the full-sized piece, shall sustain at the centre, when resting upon two dull knife edges twelve (12) inches apart, a load of three thousand (3,000) lbs. with a deflection of at least one-tenth (1/10) of an inch before rupture.

Wire Mesh

Wire mesh

Wire mesh, of a character and weight to be approved by the Engineer, is to be furnished and placed around the lower flanges of the roof girders, and at other places as may be required, in order to hold the concrete in place.

Workmanship

Qua ity

All workmanship shall be first class. All parts exposed to view shall be neatly finished. All nuts on the finished structure shall be hexagonal.

Rods deformed sections

Rods to be used for reinforcing concrete shall be deformed as approved by the Engineer; plain bars will not be used.

Bent rods and bars

Bent rods and bars and other bent material shall be bent hot and annealed, except that obtuse bends in material of less than 1 square inch section may be made cold when permitted by the Engineer. The bending shall be done before the material is delivered on the work. Except in special cases all bends shall be made uniformly to template.

Material straightened in shops

All material shall be straightened in the shop before being worked in any way.

Holes accurately spaced

All holes shall be accurately spaced and punched. Unfair holes shall be reamed to exact match; drifting to enlarge the holes will not be allowed. Poor matching of holes will be cause for rejection.

Size of punch

In punching, the diameter of the punch shall not exceed by more than one-sixteenth (1/16) of an inch, the diameter of the rivet to be used, and the diameter of the die shall be as small as may be required to punch a clean hole. When the material is to be sub-punched and reamed, a punch of diameter three-sixteenths (3/16) of an inch smaller than specified above shall be used, and all reaming shall be done after the material is assembled, with twist drills of one-sixteenth (1/16) of an inch greater diameter than the rivet to be used.

Sub-punching and drilling

All material over seven-eighths (7/8) of an inch thick shall be drilled from the solid. Material over five-eighths (5/8) of an inch and not exceeding seven-eighths (7/8) of an inch in thickness shall be sub-punched and reamed. All other material may be direct punched.

Sheared edges

Sheared edges of material exceeding five-eighths (5/8) of an inch in thickness, to be used in main members shall be planed at least one-eighth (1/8) of an inch.

Burrs removed

All burrs shall be removed, and the members shall have all parts firmly drawn together with bolts before reaming or riveting is commenced.

Riveting

Rivets when driven shall completely fill the holes, and shall be machine driven wherever possible. They shall have full concentric heads or they shall be countersunk when so required. Rivet heads shall not be flattened to less than half the diameter of the rivet on the line of the shank unless countersunk.

Use of bolts

Generally the use of bolts instead of rivets will not be permitted, but when used in special cases the holes shall be reamed parallel, and the bolts turned to a driving fit.

Templates

All holes for field rivets, excepting those in connections of lateral and sway bracing, shall be sub-punched and accurately drilled to an iron template, or reamed and match marked while the connecting parts are temporarily assembled in the shop. In case of splices of upper chords or other compression members, the abutting members shall be brought to a forcible contact.

Finished members

Finished members shall be true and free from kinks, twists or open joints. Ends of floor beams and stringers shall be finished square and true.

Rods and bars which are to receive a thread shall be properly upset. Where threads are cut on steel, they shall be properly filleted. Rods upset

Steel, except in minor details, which has been partially heated, shall be properly annealed. All steel castings shall be annealed. Annealing

All abutting surfaces, except flanges of plate girders, shall be neatly planed or faced perpendicular to the direction of strain, so as to insure even bearings. Abutting surfaces faced

Stiffeners of plate girders shall fit neatly against the flange angles. Web splice plates and fillers under stiffeners shall be cut to fit within one-eighth (1/8) of an inch of flange angles. Stiffeners

The Contractor shall submit plans, subject to the approval of the Engineer, of all the machinery or other apparatus, including all necessary housing and a suitable locking device, required for the operation of the drawbridge over the Bronx River, and shall provide and install the same in complete working order. Drawbridge machinery

Pins and rollers shall be turned accurately to a gauge, and shall be of full size throughout. All pin-holes shall be bored truly and at right angles to the axes of the members to be connected, and shall fit the pins with a play not exceeding 1/32 inch. Pins and rollers

Bed-plates planed

Bed-plates shall be planed. The bottom of the shoes shall be planed exactly parallel to the centre line unless otherwise shown. The cutting of the planing tool shall be in the direction of expansion.

Details boxed

Nuts, bolts, rivets and other details shall be boxed.

Weight marked

The weight of every piece and box shall be plainly marked upon it.

Inspection

Free access and information shall be given by the Contractor for a thorough inspection of material and workmanship, with proper office facilities.

Mill orders in triplicate

The Engineer shall be furnished copies in triplicate of all mill orders, and no material shall be rolled nor work done before the Engineer has been notified so that he may arrange for the Inspector.

Contractor responsible

The Inspector shall make detailed reports of his inspection to the Engineer and may notify the Contractor of any defects in the material or workmanship, but all acceptances made by him shall be considered temporary, and his inspection shall in no way relieve the Contractor of full responsibility for the character and accuracy of the work until its completion and final acceptance by the Engineer.

Errors in plans

The Contractor shall be responsible for all errors which can be discovered by checking or examining the plans.

Chemical determination of the percentage of carbon, phosphorous, sulphur and manganese shall be made by the manufacturer from a test ingot, so taken, during the casting of each melt of steel, as to fairly represent the melt. Two copies of such analysis shall be furnished to the Engineer or his Inspector. Chemical analysis

Check analyses shall be made, at the discretion of the Engineer, of the finished material, on drillings from pieces selected by the Inspector from parts suspected of being most highly segregated. These analyses shall not show a variation above the ladle analysis of more than twenty-five (25) per centum for phosphorus, nor more than fifty (50) per centum for sulphur. The analyses shall be made by a chemist designated by the Engineer. Check analyses

The Contractor shall furnish, without extra charge, such standard test pieces as may be necessary to determine the uniform quality of the material and also the use of a reliable testing machine, with necessary labor for testing. Contractor to make tests

The Contractor shall furnish for the use of the Inspector a suitably equipped office at the mills and at the shops. Inspector's office

All parts shall be carefully loaded and protected from injuries during transportation by such means as will be satisfactory to the Inspector. After delivery of materials at the work the Con- Loading and shipping tractor will be required to store it on skids at least twelve (12) inches above the ground and to keep it in good condition. Any piece showing injurious effects of rough handling at any stage until the final acceptance of the work may be rejected.

17

PAINTING

All metal work, excepting as otherwise herein provided, shall be painted with three coats of paint, including the shop coat, of kind and quality approved by the Engineer. Lead or carbon paint will generally be required.

Shop coat

All iron shall be scraped free from scale, and receive one coat of red lead paint as herein specified before leaving the shops. All surfaces which come in contact or are enclosed shall be painted before being assembled. All turned or faced surfaces shall receive a coat of white lead and tallow before leaving the shops.

Quality of red lead

The red lead shall be strictly pure, and shall contain at least 80 per cent. of "true lead" (Pb_3 O_4). The color shall be a clean pure tint. The red lead shall be of the fineness that when washed with water through a No. 19 silk bolting cloth, not more than 1 per cent. shall be left on the screen.

The linseed oil must be absolutely pure, fully aged and ripened, well settled oil. It shall be perfectly clear on receipt, and after heating to 212° Fahr. on a current of hydrogen, shall not show a deposit of foots nor a loss of over 0.4 per cent. for raw oil, nor over 0.2 per cent. for boiled oil. The specific gravity at 60° Fahr. for raw oil shall be between 0.932 and 0.937, and for boiled oil between 0.936 and 0.940. Quality of linseed oil

All material shall be delivered, inspected and sampled in original packages. Original packages

Red lead paint shall be mixed in the proportion of 500 lbs. of red lead to 5½ gallons of boiled linseed oil, and 11 gallons of raw linseed oil. Proportions in mixture

Where the shop coat has become damaged before or after erection, through any cause whatever, it shall be renewed with the same kind of paint as originally used, such renewal to be considered only as a part of the original shop coat. On members or parts of members buried in concrete the shop coat will be omitted. Damaged shop coat renewed

Structural steel and rods to be imbedded in concrete shall be protected from the weather before being put in place, and shall be cleaned and scales removed but not painted before being incased in the concrete. Structural steel and rods

The second coat of paint shall be a carbon paint, approved by the Engineer. It shall be applied Second coat carbon paint after erection, but not until the metal has been cleaned from dirt or other objectionable matter that may be found thereon.

Metal to be cleaned after erection

After erection the metal shall be thoroughly cleaned of all dirt, rust or scales by stiff wire brushes or sand blasts, as directed, and afterward dusted and thoroughly and evenly painted as described above. No paint shall be applied until the cleaning has been passed upon by an Inspector.

Third coat

Between stations the exposed members shall be given a third coat, which shall be a carbon paint of a color and quality approved by the Engineer.

Third coat, when applied

The third or finishing coat shall be applied to all exposed surfaces of the metal after its erection, and after a completion of the masonry or other work; it shall be applied at such time after such completion and before the final acceptance of the work as in the judgment of the Engineer may be advisable. The several field coats shall be sufficiently tinted to be distinctive.

Surfaces in contact

Surfaces of exposed members inaccessible after erecting, shall be cleaned and painted before erecting.

Recesses, etc.

All recesses that might contain water, or through which water could enter, must be filled with thick paint or a waterproof cement of ground skins before receiving final painting.

All surfaces so close together as to prevent the insertion of a brush, must be painted thoroughly by using a piece of cloth, if necessary.

Rainy or freezing weather

No painting in rainy or freezing weather or on wet surfaces shall be permitted.

18

DUCTS AND CONDUITS

[For ducts and conduits to be built as part of Construction]

Vitrified Ducts

All the duct construction, including the necessary manholes, shown on the drawings or otherwise required for the proper installation of the cables required for the operation of the Railroad, which is built along the line of the Railroad, shall be considered a part of construction. Duct lines so constructed shall include all tile ducts built into and forming a part of any section of subway structure, or built over, under or along side of said structure, and all lines built in the street under the elevated sections of the railroad and parallel thereto, whether immediately under or in the street at either side of said elevated structures.

Quality

The ducts to contain cables for transmitting electricity shall be manufactured of the best clay, thoroughly mixed, burnt and vitrified, sound in all respects, straight and free from soft spots, stones, cracks or blisters liable to impair their strength or durability; in lengths generally of from eighteen (18) to thirty-six (36) inches, shorter lengths shall only be used as directed; generally in four-way form with circular holes, the least diameter to be three and one-half ($3\frac{1}{2}$) inches; one, two or three-way ducts shall be used in special cases as determined by the Engineer. The interior surface of the holes to be smooth and clear of warts, tits, pits or blisters, which may tend to injure the electric cable in pulling the same through the duct. The ends to be cut smooth and at right angles to the axis of the duct and beveled on inside for three-quarters ($\frac{3}{4}$) of an inch.

Size

Thickness of ducts

The outside walls and webs of four-way ducts to be three-quarters ($\frac{3}{4}$) of an inch thick; the outside dimensions of ducts to be not less than nine and one-quarter ($9\frac{1}{4}$) nor more than ten (10) inches, and constructed square on outer lines; the dimensions of single, two-way or three-way ducts shall be consistent with the above.

Ends combed

The ends of ducts to be combed with two (2) sets of three (3) combings each, each combing to have a width of one-quarter ($\frac{1}{4}$) of an inch and a depth of one-sixteenth (1/16) of an inch.

Glaze

The inside and outside of ducts to be thoroughly glazed in the most approved manner with good salt glaze.

Inspection

All ducts to be subject to inspection, both at the place of manufacture and on the work. All rejected ducts to be promptly removed by the Contractor at his expense.

The ducts shall be laid in beds of cement mortar about one-quarter ($1/4$) of an inch in thickness, with broken joints and with full bearing. Two (2) strips of thick unbleached muslin six (6) inches wide, and coated with neat cement mortar, shall be used to wrap each joint, the ends of the wrap to lap six (6) inches. The muslin shall be not less than 56x60 count, weight not less than four (4) ounces to the yard and width thirty-six (36) inches. In laying the ducts care must be taken to close abutting joints so that practically the end of ducts shall be in contact on all sides. Where ducts are laid on curves, the wraps must be doubled if required, to protect the openings between the ends of the ducts on the outer line of the duct and to exclude all mortar from duct openings. **How laid**

The ducts shall be laid with a linked mandrel of the length and diameter to be prescribed, the same accurately fitting the duct openings, the mandrel to be left in each duct until the next succeeding duct is laid. **Mandrels**

The ducts shall be laid with dowel pins, at least two pins on the opposite sides horizontally. **Dowel pins**

The ducts shall be so laid that the centre of the holes shall be true to line and grade.

To be rodded

After the ducts are laid, and sufficient time is given to allow the mortar in beds to partially set, they shall be rodded; all mortar or other foreign matter must be cleaned from the duct openings, leaving a clear and smooth opening. If obstructions are found in rodding the ducts which cannot be removed by cleaners, so as to give a clear and smooth opening of three and one-half ($3\frac{1}{2}$) inches in all duct openings, the ducts shall be removed and relaid; all ducts, during construction and after being rodded, shall be plugged with suitable plugs, to be furnished by the Contractor. If wooden plugs are used they shall be immersed in water for at least eight hours before being put in place.

Other forms of ducts

Other forms of ducts may be permitted, such as iron pipe tubing or ducts formed directly in the concrete benches, by special methods during construction, but only under plans and methods approved by the Engineer.

Duct manholes

Duct manholes will be built at the sides of the railroad in connection therewith and as indicated on the plans. These manholes shall be generally at intervals of about three hundred feet, and shall be on either or both sides of the Railroad as necessary, in accordance with the location of the duct lines. They may vary in form as may be necessary to accommodate the work to local conditions.

Duct manholes will be built at the ends of the stations to provide for the passage of the ducts under the station platforms, and if found necessary on account of the lengths of stations, additional manholes will be constructed under the platforms. At stations

At manholes the ducts will be laid to conform to the special conditions.

Iron pipe or fibre conduits built into and forming a part of any subway structure or other building or other structure called for under the construction specifications shall be installed as a part of construction. Iron pipe or fibre conduits

All other pipe conduit shall be installed as a part of the equipment, as hereinafter specified.

In all work where iron pipe or fibre conduits are installed for a part of their length in the structure and for another part as open construction, the ends of such runs shall be carried outside of said structure as open construction and shall terminate in outlet or junction boxes located by the Engineer. All of this portion of the work shall be done as a part of construction, the remainder of the work being installed as a part of equipment, as specified hereinafter.

All iron conduit used for any purpose in connection with the work herein shall be of the best Quality grade (Galvaduct or equal) standard weight wrought iron or steel piping, protected inside and out by a coat of zinc or enamel. It shall be delivered to the work in bundles of full length pipes, each length marked with the trade-mark of the manufacturer. It shall bend cold 90 degrees about a radius equal to ten diameters without signs of flaw or fracture in either pipe or enamel.

Installation

All conduit shall be carefully cleaned before and after erection, and all ends shall be reamed free from burrs, and inside surfaces shall be free from all imperfections liable to injure the cable.

Joints water-tight

All joints shall be made with standard couplings, well treated with red lead, and screwed up to make a water-tight job.

Fibre conduits, quality, laying, etc.

All fibre conduits shall be made of impregnated fibre equal to that manufactured by the Fibre Conduit Company of Orangeburg, N. Y.

It shall be of uniform thickness, having walls of not less than one-quarter ($\frac{1}{4}$) inch and true cylindrical holes not less than two (2) inches in diameter. Lengths shall be not less than five (5) feet, and all ends shall be finished.

All joints shall be made by suitable finished sleeves fitting closely over the ends of the conduit and made water tight by making up with an approved bituminous compound.

After laying, all ducts shall provide a clear true opening, free from obstructions and imperfections in any way injurious to the wires to be installed. All ducts shall be rodded and cleaned with an approved mandrel not less than one and three-quarter (1¾) inches in diameter and eighteen (18) inches long.

Conduits built into concrete or other parts of the structure shall be properly protected and supported, so that the same shall not be injured by the building operations. Built in concrete, etc.

Conduit not built into the structure shall be supported by approved pipe straps located not more than eight feet apart, or in any other manner designated by the Engineer, and they shall be kept boxed or otherwise suitably protected from injury. Not built in concrete

Bends and offsets may be made in the field if proper tools are used, but in no case shall deformed, split or crushed conduit be erected. Not more than two right angle bends shall be made between any two outlet boxes without special approval of the Engineer. Bends and offsets

All outlet and pull boxes shall be made of cast iron, with openings threaded for the conduit ends, Outlet and pull boxes and conduits shall be screwed into these openings and made up with red lead to effect a water-tight joint. Covers shall be of cast iron and water-tight, and no other boxes or covers shall be used except under special permission of the Engineer.

19

DRAINS AND PUMPS

Railroad to be drained

Every part of the Railroad, the stations and appurtenances connected therewith, must be arranged so far as possible that any water finding access thereto will be led away automatically to the City sewers.

Where the Railroad is on an inclined gradient, and is constructed in dry, porous soil, the floor of the Railroad may be depended on to act as a conduit. At the bottom of the inclined gradient connections must be made with a sewer or with sub-drains lying beneath the Railroad and draining into the sewers.

Sub-drains

Along such parts of the work where the soil is not porous, or where the floor of the Railroad cannot, in the judgment of the Engineer, be used as a conduit, there shall be laid, beneath the rail level and on a continuous descending gradient, drain pipes of vitrified salt-glazed stoneware, of the quality described in these specifications for sewer pipe. These drain pipes shall be of such diameter not exceeding fifteen (15) inches, as the Engineer may direct, and there shall be one (1) such drain for each two (2) tracks. Each drain shall be laid in the concrete or directly in the soil with tight or open joints, as directed, and in such manner and in such position as, in the opinion of the Engineer, local circumstances require.

Connections and cross drains

Where drain pipes connect with the City sewers, the junction shall be protected by suitable traps, and back-pressure valves or gate valves where necessary, to prevent back rush of water or gas from the sewers. Connections with the Railroad shall be as necessity demands and all as directed by the Engineer. Where the Railroad is in rock, or partly in rock, cross drains to connect with the main drains will be placed at such places and in such manner as the Engineer shall direct.

Broken stone for drainage

On the roof of the Railroad and at other points as may be directed or indicated on the plans, broken stone shall be placed for the purposes of drainage.

Sumps

At the low points of the grade of the Railroad where the same passes below the bottom of adjacent sewers there shall be constructed sumps connected with the subdrains or the floor of the Railroad. Such sumps must be watertight, with a capacity of not less than eight hundred (800) gallons each.

Pumps for tunnel drainage

Adjacent to each sump a suitable enclosure shall be provided in which two pumps shall be installed, each of which shall have ample capacity to remove all the water entering the sump at that point under ordinary conditions. These pumps shall each have a separate source of power, and shall be arranged to operate automatically.

Capacity

If in the opinion of the Engineer the service requires it, each of these pumps shall be able to remove from the sump eight hundred gallons per minute.

Delivery to sewers

The delivery of such pumps shall be into the City sewers, and all piping, valves, etc., in connection therewith, shall be installed as a part of this contract.

The pumps called for herein shall be a part of the equipment.

20

SEWERS

In accordance with plans and specifications

All sewers and appurtenances shall be built of the materials, of the sizes and dimensions, on the lines and grades, at the depths, with the connections, and in the manner called for by these specifications and shown on the drawings.

Change of location

If, in the opinion of the Engineer, it is impracticable during the progress of the work to construct any sewers, manholes, or other appurtenances, according to the contract drawings, owing to the presence of unknown sub-surface structures or other contingencies, the Contractor shall construct such sewers, manholes or appurtenances in the location given by and according to the directions of the Engineer.

General clauses apply

The general clauses in this contract relating to excavation, both in open trench and tunnel, backfilling, cement, mortar, masonry, waterproofing, piling, timber work of all kinds, care of streets and public places, maintenance of surface and sub-surface structures, protection of persons and property, repaving or restoring of the surface of the street or other public places, responsibility of the Contractor, authority of the Engineer to examine and condemn materials, and the power of the Commission and the Engineer in all or any other respects to enforce this contract, apply to the construction and reconstruction of sewers, water mains, or pavements, unless specifically amended or exempted, both along the route occupied by the Railroad and elsewhere.

No claims for damages

Should postponement or delay be occasioned by the precedence of paving or other contracts, which may be either let or executed by the Borough President, Commissioner of Water Supply, Gas and Electricity, or other heads of departments, either before or after the execution of this contract, on the line of the work, no claims for damages therefor shall be made or allowed; nor shall any claim for damages be made or allowed in consequence of the street or the adjoining sewers not being in the condition contemplated by the parties at the time of making the contract, except that if the Contractor shall be delayed in the performance of his work by reason of the street or the adjoining sewers not being in such condition, an allowance of time may be given for the completion of the work, as elsewhere provided in this contract.

Size of trenches

The trenches for sewers and basin culverts both in earth and in rock, in streets along the route of the Railroad, shall have vertical sides and shall be not less than six inches wider than the greatest external width of the sewer or its foundation on the side farthest away from the subway; and in other streets the trenches shall have vertical sides, and shall be not less than six inches wider on each side than the greatest external diameter of the sewer, but shall be not less than four feet in width. They shall be excavated to the depth and to the form of the sewer or its foundation.

Limit of trench opening

Not more than one hundred (100) feet of trench in sewers off the line of the Railroad shall be opened at any one time in advance of the sewer already completed, unless by permission of the Engineer, and for a distance specified.

The excavation of trenches shall be fully completed a sufficient distance in advance of the laying of the sewer, and the exposed end of the sewer shall in all cases be fully protected.

Where the foundation for a manhole or a receiving basin extends beyond the line of such manhole or receiving basin, the minimum excavation required in earth shall be to the lines of the smallest rectangle enclosing the full dimensions of the exterior of the foundation, and shall have vertical sides to the surface, but it shall, in all cases, be not less than six inches larger than the greatest external dimension of the manhole or receiving basin. **Trenches for manholes and receiving basins**

In rock excavation, the trench shall be six inches larger than the greatest external dimension of the manhole or receiving basin, or its foundation, and shall have vertical sides to the surface.

Where the ground does not afford a sufficiently solid foundation, the trench shall be excavated to such increased depth as the Engineer may deem necessary, and this extra depth, and all other irregularities in the bottom of the trench, shall be filled up to the required level and form, with such material, and in such manner, as the Engineer shall direct. If so directed, piles shall be driven and a timber or reinforced concrete foundation shall be constructed, as elsewhere provided in these specifications, to support the sewer. **Foundations**

When the trench is properly prepared, and before laying any sewer, the Contractor shall notify the Engineer, who will, thereupon, cause the grades for the sewer to be tested, and if correct **Inspection of grades** the sewer shall then be laid in the presence of a duly authorized inspector, and no construction work shall be done in his absence.

Trenches to be kept free from water

The trenches shall be kept entirely free from water while the foundation and the masonry are being constructed or the sewer laid. In no case shall water be allowed to flow over the invert or foundation or through the sewer until the mortar is thoroughly set.

Tunneling

When tunneling for sewers shall be deemed advisable, it shall be done in a manner approved by the Engineer.

Gutter and passageway to be kept open

At all times, gutters shall be kept open for surface drainage, and the streets and sidewalks shall be kept clear and free for the passage of carts, wagons, carriages and street or steam railroad cars or pedestrians, and as otherwise provided in these specifications.

Cross-walk, side-walk and roadway to be kept clear

Where any cross-walk or roadway is cut by the trench, it shall be temporarily replaced by a timber bridge with side railings, according to the direction and approval of the Engineer. The work shall at all times be conducted so as to cause as little inconvenience as practicable to the public.

Disposition of paving material

All curb, gutter, flagging, paving and macadam stones, necessary to be removed, which in the judgment of the Engineer are suitable to be used again, shall be stored in such places as the Engineer shall direct, or shall be removed as provided in these specifications; in all cases a passageway on the sidewalks and in the roadway shall be preserved free from needless obstructions.

Flow of sewers to be maintained

The Contractor shall provide for the flow of all sewers, drains and water-courses interrupted during the progress of the work, and shall restore and make good all connections, and shall immediately cart away all offensive matter, in such manner and with such precautions as the Engineer may direct. All temporary house connections shall be made by closed iron pipes, with suitable provision for preventing leakage at joints. Wooden troughs for such connections will not be permitted.

Brick

In the construction of brick masonry none but the best quality of common brick burned hard entirely through, regular and uniform in shape and size and of compact texture, shall be used. They shall be culled as they are brought on the ground, and bats and bricks of improper quality are to be removed from the work. A limited number of bats may be used in manholes and closures, and in the outer ring of the sewers where more than two rings of brick are required.

How laid

The bricks shall be properly wet immediately before laying. Every brick is required to be laid in a full joint of mortar, made as described in these specifications, on its bed, end and side, at one operation. In no case is mortar to be slushed or grouted in afterward. The bricks shall be neatly and truly laid, every second course to line, and the joints to be carefully struck on the inside.

Racked back or toothed

All brick work, as it progresses, shall be racked back in courses, and in no case will it be allowed to be toothed, unless by special permission from the Engineer.

Brick or stone inverts

All inverts, or bottom curves, shall be formed from profiles accurately made according to the dimensions of the sewer, and correctly set according to the grades furnished. The masonry shall be allowed to set for twenty-four (24) hours before the arch is turned. Vitrified brick or granite paving blocks shall be used for the inner ring of the invert when required by the Engineer, and whenever so used they must be thoroughly jointed, so as to be water-tight along the inner surface of the sewer. The last course of the invert masonry below the springing line shall be laid as headers.

Brick arches

The arches or upper curves shall be formed on strong centres of correct form, according to the sizes and shapes required, and keyed with stretchers in full joints of mortar. The extrados of the arch shall be plastered with mortar one inch thick, mixed in the proportion of one part of cement to two parts of sand. The centres shall not be removed nor withdrawn in less than thirty-six hours, or until the work is thoroughly set, and until the filling on the arch is properly put into place to a depth which is at least one foot above the crown of the arch. The centres in all cases shall be struck and not drawn, so as not to crack or injure the work. Should any crack or settlement appear in the arch after the centres are removed, so much of the work as the Engineer may require shall be taken down immediately and replaced.

Spurs

Vitrified or iron sewer pipes or spurs, equal in every respect to those described elsewhere in these specifications, and of a size required by the Engineer, but not less than six inches interior diameter with hubs moulded for house connections, and of sufficient length to project at least four inches beyond the exterior of the sewer, shall be built into the walls of brick sewers and at such an angle as indicated on the plans or as the Engineer may direct.

How built in

Spurs shall be built in wherever similar house connections exist in the present sewer which is to be reconstructed under this contract, but in no case shall the distance be more than twenty feet between spurs. In the case of the construction of new sewers where no sewers existed previously, except sewers under public parks or those crossing intersecting streets, they shall be built opposite each house, and where there are no houses, they shall be not more than fifteen feet apart on each side of the sewer or at such frequent intervals as local conditions may require. They shall be set so that their inner ends shall be flush with the inner face of the sewer, at such height in the walls as the Engineer may direct, and each pipe shall be sealed on the outside with an approved earthen-ware cover set in mortar.

Iron chair spurs

Where the sewers to be built under this contract will be at a depth greater than thirteen feet below the established grade of the street (or below the surface of the street where final grades have not been established), cast iron chair spurs, of the design shown on the drawings, not less than six inches in diameter and of the weight of extra heavy soil pipe, shall be used unless otherwise ordered by the Engineer. Where house drains are to be connected to these spurs, extra heavy soil pipe and fittings shall be used for the riser between the spur and the house drain. Where the spurs are provided for future connections, risers of extra heavy soil pipe shall be placed in each spur and shall be brought to a point thirteen feet below the established grade of the street, the end of which shall be sealed with an approved cover laid in cement mortar. The joints of this pipe shall be packed, leaded and caulked in accordance with these specifications for laying watermains.

Under station platforms

Wherever the sewer passes under a station platform or other structure, extra heavy soil pipe shall be laid from the spur to the outside of such station or other structure, brought up to a point thirteen feet below the established grade of the street, caulked and sealed as provided above. All pipes passing under such structures shall be laid in concrete.

Sewers, interchange of concrete and brick

If, during the construction of the sewers, it is deemed advisable to interchange concrete and brick, the Contractor may, with the approval of the Engineer, build such sewers of either kind and quality herein specified.

Steel bars used if ordered

Concrete sewers shall be reinforced with steel bars, if so indicated on the plans or directed by the Engineer.

Profiles and inverted centres for inverts

Proper profiles for the concrete inverts shall be set up at the required distances, and the concrete for the bottom and invert of the sewer shall be deposited in place and rammed and worked down to the required shape. The concrete for the bottom and invert, if so directed, shall be placed in alternate lengths extending between every other pair of profiles, so that opportunity may be given to properly work the concrete in place.

Invert to be protected

The concrete of the invert shall be protected during the progress of the work with planking, or by such other suitable methods as the Engineer shall direct and for so long a time as he may require.

Forms, moulds, etc.

Suitable forms or moulds, of the size and design to be approved by the Engineer, shall be provided by the Contractor to support the concrete of the side walls and roof while the same is being rammed into the permanent work.

Defective work

If any voids, or irregular or defective work is discovered upon removing the forms or moulds, such voids or work shall be cut out and filled with a rich concrete or mortar mixed in such proportions and of such materials as provided elsewhere in these specifications.

Joints

No joints between different sections of the walls of a sewer shall, in any case, be a straight line, but shall always be stepped or toothed, so as to give a broken joint in the manner to be approved by the Engineer.

Spur pipes, branches, etc.

In so far as they will be applicable to sewers constructed of concrete, the provisions and requirements for spurs, branches, etc., in brick sewers shall be understood to govern in such construction.

Vitrified pipe sewers

Pipe sewers shall be built of vitrified, salt glazed stone-ware pipe, with or without hub, as the Engineer may direct. The pipe shall be of the best

Quality of pipe

quality, thoroughly and perfectly burnt, without warps, cracks or imperfections, well and smoothly glazed over the entire inner and outer surfaces and perfect in shape. The pipe shall be subject to all tests ordered in conformity with any requirements of the Bureau of Sewers, at any time previous to its being used.

Thickness

The size of the pipes shall be designated by their interior diameters. Each pipe shall be a true cylinder, and of even thickness throughout, according to the following schedule:

6″ pipes shall be not less than 5/8 of an inch thick;

8″ pipes shall be not less than 3/4 of an inch thick;

10″ pipes shall be not less than 7/8 of an inch thick;

12″ pipes shall be not less than one inch thick;

15″ pipes shall be not less than 1 1/4 inches thick;

18″ pipes shall be not less than 1 1/2 inches thick;

24″ pipes shall be not less than two inches thick;

30″ pipes shall be not less than 2 1/2 inches thick.

Lengths

No pipe shall be less than two feet in length, and pipes of 12 inches, 15 inches and 18 inches in diameter shall be not less than three feet in length.

Curved and split pipes

When required, curved pipes shall be furnished and laid, curved to such a radius as may be required or as indicated on the plan of the work. No curved pipe shall exceed three feet in length. Split pipes shall be used when found necessary.

Hub and spigot pipe

In case the Engineer shall order hub and spigot pipe to be used, the hub shall have a depth of at least three (3) inches from its face to the shoulder of the pipe on which it is moulded, and shall have an interior diameter not less than one (1) nor more than two (2) inches greater than the exterior diameter of the pipe which is to be fitted into it.

Straight pipe with collars.

In case the Engineer shall order pipe without hubs to be used, it shall be fitted with a collar of the same thickness as the pipe and not less than five inches wide. Each collar must have an internal diameter of not less than one-half inch nor more than one and one-half inches greater than the external diameter of the pipe to which it is to be fitted.

Spur pipes

Pipes having spurs not less than six inches in diameter with hubs moulded thereon for house connections shall be furnished and laid at such points as indicated on the plan or as directed by the Engineer, and when not immediately used, they shall be sealed on the outside with approved vitrified earthen-ware covers set in mortar.

Risers

The provisions for risers on brick sewers shall also apply to pipe sewers.

Bends

Bends, siphons and special pipe shall be furnished and laid of the size and forms shown on the plans of the work, or as required.

Pipe sewers, how laid

All pipes shall be laid in concrete cradles of the required form and dimensions. The first layer of concrete shall be four inches thick, for the full width of the cradle, and after being thoroughly tamped shall be allowed to set for a period of not less than twenty-four hours. Upon the bed thus prepared, the pipe shall be laid true according to the lines and grades furnished. The ends of the pipes shall abut against each other and in such manner that there shall be no shoulder or unevenness of any kind along the bottom half of the sewer on the inside. Unless otherwise ordered, not less than fifteen feet of pipe shall be laid at any one time, in any one length of trench. The remainder of the concrete shall then be put in place and shall be exposed for at least twenty-four hours for inspection, as required for the bottom course.

Jointing hub and spigot pipes

When hub and spigot pipes are used, the lower half of each hub shall be plastered on the inside with a layer of cement mortar mixed in the proportion of one part of cement to one part of sand and of a sufficient thickness to bring the inner surface of the abutting pipes flush and even with the established flow line. After the pipes are fitted, the space between the inside of the upper half of each hub and the outside of the entering pipe shall be filled with cement mortar mixed as above specified, and the outside of the joint shall be thoroughly sealed with the same kind of mortar and the joints carefully wiped inside and outside.

Jointing pipes without hubs

When pipe without hubs is used, a collar or ring shall be used at joints and shall lap equally the ends of each abutting pipe. Such collar or ring shall consist of not more than three pieces, the largest of which shall be placed at the bottom.

The space between the ring and the pipes shall be as uniform as possible and shall be thoroughly filled with cement mortar mixed in the proportions specified for hub and spigot pipe. The joints shall be carefully wiped and pointed inside and outside and all mortar that may be left on the inside shall be removed and the inside of the pipe left clean and smooth throughout.

Iron pipe sewers

Sewers of iron pipe, of quality and laid in the manner described elsewhere in these specifications for the laying of water mains, shall be laid wherever indicated on the plans or at such places as the Engineer shall direct.

Special castings

Wherever such pipes are laid under station platforms, or through vaults, they shall, when required by the Engineer, be provided with special castings for manholes, which shall be fitted with a cover bolted on so as to make an air-tight joint, according to the plans to be furnished by the Engineer.

Ventilators

Whenever, in the opinion of the Engineer, it becomes necessary to provide ventilation for sewers under station platforms, or other structures, iron pipe shall be laid from the sewer to the surface of the street and fitted with proper gratings according to the plans to be furnished by the Engineer.

Connections

All existing sewers, culverts, drains and house connections intercepted by the proposed sewers, culverts or receiving basins shall be connected with the new work by proper curves and grades and in such manner as the Engineer shall direct; and all drains, basins or culverts rendered unnecessary or becoming disused by the work herein contemplated shall be filled in and made solid with good wholesome earth in the manner directed. Provision shall also be made for the connection of future sewers or basins by constructing brick spurs or inserting vitrified pipe at the points indicated on the contract drawings and at other points as the Engineer may direct. These connections shall be closed with bulkheads not less than eight inches in thickness and of the quality specified for brick masonry.

Fresh work to be protected

All fresh work shall be carefully protected from injury in every way. No wheeling or walking will be allowed on it and any portion injured must be relaid by the Contractor; no walking or working over the pipes after they are laid, except as may be necessary in tamping the earth and refilling, will be allowed until there is at least two and one-half feet of earth over them.

Pipes to be kept clean

The interior of pipe sewers shall be carefully freed from all dirt, cement and superfluous material of every description as the work progresses, for which purpose a disc, mould or plate, attached to a rod sufficiently long to pass two joints from the end of the pipe last laid, shall be continuously worked through.

Exposed ends of pipes to be protected

The exposed ends of pipe sewers shall, in all cases, be protected with a board or other stopper carefully fitted to the pipe, to prevent earth or other substances from washing in, and in no case shall brick or stone be used for that purpose.

Manholes

The masonry of manholes shall be carried up so that the top of the iron head when set shall be at the level of the established grade of the street at that point or to such height as the Engineer may direct, and from templates correctly made and set at top and bottom, between which not less than eight lines shall be drawn. Where manholes are not built to the established grade of the street, they shall be covered, when necessary, by selected bluestone slabs eight inches in thickness, to support the manhole heads. All joints shall be neatly struck and pointed on the inside. Each manhole shall be plastered thoroughly on the outside with cement mortar one inch in thickness, mixed in the proportion of one part of cement to two parts of sand.

Foundations

The foundations for manholes shall be of concrete or masonry of the kind indicated on the plans and shall be not less than twelve inches below the invert elevation of the sewer, except as otherwise indicated on the plans. When foundation additional to that indicated on the plans is required, it shall be built as directed by the Engineer.

Sewer pipes shall be built in and trimmed, when necessary, so as to be flush with the inner face of the manhole, and an arch, laid in cement mortar, shall be turned over the pipe.

The invert shall be built of vitrified brick, granite blocks or concrete masonry, as indicated on the contract drawings. Vitrified bricks or granite blocks

A reasonable number of bats not smaller than half bricks may be used in the construction of manholes or receiving basins, provided all interstices are thoroughly filled with mortar. Use of bats

Standard steps of good quality of galvanized wrought iron, of the size, length and shape required for steps, shall be built into the interior sides of all manholes at a distance apart of not more than fifteen (15) inches vertically and they shall be so arranged that the lowest step shall be not more than two feet above the bench at the bottom of the manholes nor more than two feet above the invert of the sewer where there is no bench. Each manhole head shall be cast with a wrought iron step on the inside, when directed by the Engineer. Steps

Hammer-dressed bluestone shall be furnished and laid of the form and thickness required as indicated on the plans or as otherwise directed. Bluestone

Manhole head and cover

A cast-iron manhole head and cover of the quality specified for cast-iron, and except in special cases, of the pattern adopted by the President of the Borough in which the work is located, and in dimensions, weight and all other respects satisfactory to the Engineer shall be fitted on a bed of mortar to each of the above described manholes. Manhole heads and covers which do not conform to these specifications shall be at once removed from the work.

Perforations

Covers to be used on manholes in the street shall be perforated. Those used on sidewalk manholes shall be tight-fitting, without perforations.

Weights

Each manhole head and cover shall have its weight distinctly marked upon it with oil paint. The following shall be allowed as the minimum and maximum weights:

Street manhole head, 475 to 500 pounds;
Street manhole cover, 135 to 150 pounds;
Sidewalk manhole head, 300 to 310 pounds;
Sidewalk manhole cover, 100 to 110 pounds.

Noiseless heads and covers

When the pavement of the street is asphalt or wooden block, the manhole shall be fitted with a noiseless head and cover, to be approved by the Engineer, where new heads and covers are necessary.

Sealed manhole heads and covers

All manholes in station platforms, vaults or other structures shall be provided with sealed manhole heads and covers according to the design indicated on the plans.

Emergency manholes

Where a sewer crosses under the subway, emergency manholes shall be provided when directed by the Engineer and according to plans to be furnished by him.

Manholes to be completed

Manholes shall in all cases be fully and completely built and fitted with their covers as the work progresses, and the sewers shall not be laid beyond or in advance of any uncompleted manhole.

Receiving basins

Receiving basins shall be built as located on the plans or as the Engineer shall direct and in accordance with the plans to be furnished. Each portion of the basin shall be built of the size and materials designated on said drawings and shall be thoroughly plastered, both inside and outside, with cement mortar in the proportion of one part of cement to two parts of sand.

Foundations

The foundations for receiving basins shall be of concrete or masonry of the kind indicated on the plans and shall extend not less than twelve inches below the finished floor of the basin, except as otherwise indicated on the plans. When additional foundation is required, it shall be built as directed by the Engineer.

Stone flooring

The flooring shall be of hammer-dressed North River bluestone flagging, not less than three inches thick, in not more than two pieces, and shall be well set in a full bed of mortar and rammed into place. The floor may be finished with cement mortar mixed in the proportion of one part of cement to one part of sand if so directed by the Engineer. The mortar shall be spread, while fresh, upon the concrete base and before the latter shall have reached its first set; it shall be in such quantity that after thorough manipulation it shall be one inch in thickness.

Head stone and gutter stone

Where head stone and gutter stone are required they shall be of sound, durable granite of the dimensions indicated on the plan, hammer dressed to an even surface and cut to the satisfaction of the Engineer. Cast-iron basin heads and gutter pieces of the design indicated on the plans shall be set instead of the above when required.

Cast-iron cover

A cast-iron cover of approved pattern weighing not less than eighty nor more than ninety-five pounds shall be fitted to the opening in the head stone.

Grate bar

A grate bar made according to the plan shall be fastened solidly into the said head stone in the manner indicated.

Cast-iron trap

A cast-iron trap of the form and dimensions indicated on the plan and free from imperfections, and properly coated with coal pitch varnish shall be furnished and built into place as directed by the Engineer.

Joints

The joints shall be tightly fitted with an oakum gasket or with cement mortar if so directed.

Iron steps

Galvanized iron steps of the same design required for manholes shall be built into the walls.

Culvert pipes

The culvert pipe for connections with sewers shall be 12″ vitrified pipe unless otherwise indicated on the plan, and of the kind and quality previously described, and shall be laid, in all cases, in a concrete cradle of the form and dimensions required for pipe sewers and in accordance with the directions of the Engineer. In case it becomes necessary to connect any basin already built, with the work to be constructed, so much of such culverts as in the opinion of the Engineer, may be necessary shall be taken up and rebuilt or relaid with vitrified pipe, or brick as the case may be, in the manner described above and reconnected in a straight line from the basin to the sewer.

Flush tanks

Automatic flush tanks of a type approved by the Engineer shall be built where indicated on the plans or where directed by the Engineer.

Water service

The Contractor shall furnish all materials, perform all work and make all arrangements for the installation of water service in flush tanks, in strict compliance with the regulations of the Department of Water Supply, Gas and Electricity.

Water-proofing

Whenever, in the opinion of the Engineer, it is necessary to waterproof a sewer, chamber or receiving basin, or their appurtenances, it shall be done as indicated on the plans or as directed by the Engineer and in the manner described elsewhere in these specifications.

Mortar

All masonry shall be laid in Portland cement mortar of the quality described in these specifications. It shall be mixed in the proportion of one (1) part of cement to two (2) parts of sand, excepting as otherwise specially provided.

Concrete

All concrete for sewers shall be made in the proportions of one (1) part of cement to two and one-half ($2\frac{1}{2}$) parts of sand and four and one-half ($4\frac{1}{2}$) parts of stone of the quality described in these specifications.

Paving

On the completion of each section of one hundred feet of sewer, the regrading and temporary paving over the same shall be done and all surplus earth, sand and rubbish shall be immediately removed. After the completion of the work a permanent pavement shall be placed over the entire length of the trench as provided elsewhere in these specifications.

Permits for connections

The Commissioner of Public Works shall have the right to connect any sewer or sewers with the sewers herein described or to grant permits to any person or persons to make connections therewith at any time before it is finally completed, and the Contractor shall not interfere with or place obstructions in the way of such person or persons as may be employed in building such new sewer or sewers or in making such connections. This is not to be construed, however, as permitting the introduction of storm water or sewage into any sewer being constructed under this contract before its final completion.

Sewers, etc. to be kept clean

During the progress of the work, and until the entire completion and final acceptance thereof, the sewers, drains, basins, culverts and connections shall be kept thoroughly cleaned throughout, and left clean, and the drainage of any old sewer that may be taken up or intercepted shall be provided for and taken care of by the Contractor.

Siphons at 106th and 110th Streets

The Contractor shall pay to the City annually for the maintenance and operation of the siphons for sewers at 106th and 110th Streets in the Borough of Manhattan an amount to be determined by the Commission as the necessary and reasonable cost of inspection, maintenance and repair of the said siphons and the furnishing of current for the pumps, but not to exceed seven thousand five hundred dollars ($7,500), and the City shall assume all responsibility for such siphons and the maintenance and operation thereof.

21
WATER MAINS

Whenever it is necessary to relay any water main, all new material required for the same shall be of the quality and laid in the manner specified below, and subject to the various clauses of these specifications applicable thereto.

Pipes to be cylinders The pipes shall be circular cylinders, with the inner and outer surfaces concentric, and of the full interior diameter required.

Hubs and spigots The hub or socket and the spigot end shall be shaped in exact conformity with the standards of the Department of Water Supply, to be furnished by the Commission, and will be tested by circular gauges.

The seat or shoulder of the socket and the end of the spigot shall be straight and even, and at right angles to the axis of the pipe, so as to make a smooth, tight joint. Special care will be required in making the sockets and spigots to conform to the drawings, and all pipes will be rigorously inspected at these points. No pipe will be received whose eccentricity at either the spigot and socket ends, exceeds one-eighth (1/8) of an inch, or whose dimensions differ by more than one-eighth (1/8) of an inch from those required.

The pipes shall be designated by dimensions of the interior diameter.

Bands, lugs, buttons, or ribs shall, if required, be cast on the pipes, of such forms and dimensions as the Engineer may direct.

The straight pipe shall be twelve (12) feet long, exclusive of hub; other pipe as may be directed. Length of pipe

All straight pipes shall be straight in the direction of the axis of the cylinder.

The thickness of the pipes, branches and special castings shall correspond with the standards of the Department of Water Supply. The weight for straight pipe shall be approximately as follows: Thickness and weights

60-inch pipes, 12,835 pounds each.
48-inch pipes, 8,270 pounds each.
42-inch pipes, 6,860 pounds each.
36-inch pipes, 5,305 pounds each.
30-inch pipes, 3,940 pounds each.
24-inch pipes, 2,660 pounds each.
20-inch pipes, 2,005 pounds each.
16-inch pipes, 1,475 pounds each.
12-inch pipes, 1,015 pounds each.
8-inch pipes, 580 pounds each.
6-inch pipes, 415 pounds each.

For high-pressure fire system, standard spigot and grooves, the weights for straight pipes, with lugs, shall be approximately as follows, in pounds per length: High-pressure fire system

	Of 3 ft.	Of 4 ft.	Of 6 ft.	Of 12 ft.
8-inch...........	355	420	550	935
12-inch...........	615	745	1,000	1,765
16-inch...........	1,005	1,215	1,635	2,905
20-inch...........	1,475	1,795	2,425	4,320
24-inch...........	2,105	2,585	3,535	6,385

All requirements as to weights, laying, tests, etc., shall be in strict accordance with the standard requirements of the Department of Water Supply, Gas and Electricity.

The thickness of the metal of the pipes and special castings will be tested by calipers after the castings have been freed from sand and cleaned.

Variations in thickness No pipe will be received when the thickness of metal is less by more than one-twelfth (1/12) of an inch than the thickness required by the standards.

No straight pipe or casting will be received which weighs less than the weights above mentioned by more than five (5) per cent., for pipes 16 inches or less in diameter, or more than four (4) per cent. for pipes more than 16 inches in diameter. No special casting will be received which weighs less than the standard weight by more than ten (10) per cent. for pipes 12 inches or less in diameter, and eight (8) per cent. for larger pipes.

All straight pipes shall be cast vertically, and all pipes 12 inches or more in diameter shall be cast with the hub end down.

Castings, how marked All the castings shall be made in such moulding-sand or loam as will leave the surface clean and smooth.

All the castings shall have the year in which they are cast, the running number of the castings of the same size and form, the letters D. W. S., and the initials or name of the Contractor, and of the foundry where cast, cast on the outer side in raised letters of not less than two (2) inches in length and one-eighth (1/8) of an inch in relief, in such manner as the Engineer may designate; and, in case any pipe shall be condemned, the letters D. W. S. shall be erased by the Contractor.

Quality of cast iron

The metal of which the castings are to be cast (which shall be remelted in a cupola or air-furnace) shall be pig-iron, made without any admixture of cinder-iron, or other inferior metal, and shall be of such character as to make a pipe strong, tough and of an even grain, entirely free from uncombined carbon when seen under the microscope, and such as will bear, satisfactorily, drilling and cutting, and shall have a tensile strength of at least sixteen thousand (16,000) pounds to the square inch.

The castings shall be free from scoria, sand holes, air bubbles, and other defects and imperfections.

Castings to be clean

The castings shall be perfectly cleaned and no lumps shall be left on the inner surface of the barrels or sockets, or on the outer surface of the spigot end. The castings shall be subject to hammer inspection. Iron-wire brushes shall be used, as well as softer brushes, to remove the loose dust. No acid or other liquid shall be used in cleaning the castings.

Pipes to be coated

Every pipe, branch and special casting shall be carefully coated inside and out with coal pitch and oil. Every casting shall likewise be entirely free from rust when the coating is applied. If the casting cannot be dipped immediately after being cleaned, the surface shall be oiled with linseed oil, to preserve it until it is ready to be dipped. No casting shall be dipped after rust has set in.

Pitch

The coal-tar pitch shall be made from coal tar distilled until the naphtha is entirely removed and the material mixed with linseed oil so as to make a smooth, tough and tenacious coating. Pitch which becomes hard and brittle when cold will not answer for this use.

Pitch of the proper quality having been obtained, it shall be carefully heated in a suitable vessel to a temperature of three hundred (300°) degrees Fahrenheit, and shall be maintained at not less than this temperature during the time of dipping. The material will thicken and deteriorate after a number of pipes have been dipped; fresh pitch shall, therefore, be frequently added, and occasionally the vessel shall be entirely emptied of its old contents and refilled with fresh pitch.

Every casting shall attain a temperature of three hundred (300°) degrees Fahrenheit, before being removed from the vessel of hot pitch. It shall then be slowly removed and laid on skids to drip.

No casting shall be dipped until the authorized inspector has examined it as to cleaning and rust, and subjected it thoroughly to the hammer test. It may then be dipped, after which it will be passed to the hydraulic press to meet the required water test. The proper coating shall be tough and tenacious when cold on the pipes, and not brittle or with any tendency to scale off. **To be inspected before dipping**

The castings must be capable of sustaining a pressure, in the hydraulic press, of three hundred (300) pounds to a square inch, and any casting which shows any defect by leaking, sweating or otherwise, will be rejected. This test shall be made at the foundry, and at the expense of the Contractor. **Tests**

The castings shall be weighed, and the weight distinctly marked on the castings in white paint. The Contractor shall provide at the foundry where the pipes and castings are to be manufactured proper sealed scales and weights for weighing the castings, which shall be done at the expense of the Contractor, under the supervision of the inspector. **Weighed and marked**

Each pipe over eight (8) inches inside diameter, unless otherwise ordered, shall be placed on two (2) blocks and four (4) wedges of hemlock timber, the wedges to rest on the blocks and the pipe on the wedges. **Blocking and wedges**

The blocks and wedges shall be of sound hemlock timber; 48 and 36-inch pipe shall be laid on blocks 4 feet long, 12 inches wide and 6 inches thick, with wedges 18 inches long, 6 inches wide, 4 inches thick on one end and 1/2 inch thick on the other; 30 and 24 inch pipe on blocks 3 feet long, 10 inches wide and 5 inches thick, with wedges 15 inches long, 5 inches wide and 3 1/2 inches thick on one end and 1/2 inch thick on the other end; 12 and 20 inch pipe on blocks 2 feet long, 8 inches wide and 4 inches thick with wedges 12 inches long, 4 inches wide, 3 inches thick on one end and 1/2 inch thick on the other.

Joints

The spigot end of the pipe shall be inserted into the hub to within from one-fourth (1/4) to one-eighth (1/8) of an inch of the full depth of the hub, and the space around the pipe shall be equalized so as to give as nearly as possible an equal space for the packing. The space between the pipe and hub shall be packed with clean, sound jute packing yarn, free from tar, far enough to leave the proper space for lead. The remaining space shall then be filled by running it full of lead to a depth of four (4) inches, with a bead outside of the face of the hub large enough to allow for caulking, so that when the joint is properly caulked the lead will be flush with the hub of the pipe. After the joint shall have been run with lead, it shall be caulked by means of proper tools, so as to make a water-tight joint.

The lead to be used shall be of the best quality of pure, soft lead, and in every respect suitable for the purpose. Lead

In case it becomes necessary to cut any connection with any other main, house or hydrant, or in any way to interfere with the continuous and normal flow of water, due notice shall be sent at least forty-eight (48) hours in advance to the Engineer and to the Commissioner of Water Supply, and the Contractor shall, if so ordered, make a temporary by-pass or other arrangement to preserve the flow of water while breaking connections. Notice of interruption to be given

All connections cut, interfered with or injured shall be restored under the directions of the Engineer, without delay and in accordance with the rules and regulations of the Department of Water Supply governing such matters, to a suitable condition as good as existed before commencing work.

Stop cocks, boxes, branches, curved pipe, and other specials according to the standards of the Department of Water Supply shall be set where necessary.

22

PAVING

Pavement to be restored

As soon as the work in any open excavation or trench made under this contract within a street shall have been completed, and the trench properly backfilled, as provided under the clauses relating to backfilling, a temporary paving shall be laid and maintained in a condition satisfactory to the Engineer; and after the earth shall have become, in his opinion, sufficiently settled, the Contractor shall proceed to restore the surface to a condition similar to, and equally as good as that existing previous to the commencement of construction.

Other pavements may be laid

Nothing contained in these specifications shall be understood or construed as prohibiting the Contractor, with the approval of the Commission, from making any arrangement with the President of the Borough, or such other officer of The City of New York as may be in charge of street paving, to lay a better or other form of street pavement; or to make an arrangement with any property owner to lay another style of sidewalk in front of such premises in place of the pavement or sidewalk taken up.

In case the municipal officer in charge of street paving, or any property owner, desires to lay a pavement in any street, or a sidewalk along any street, affected by this contract, different from the one removed, and shall notify the Commission in writing that he has failed to make satisfactory arrangements for such work with the Contractor, then the Commission in its discretion may direct the Contractor to finish and dress off the filling over its work to such grade as the Engineer may select, and further direct it to remove from the street all stones of whatever nature not required to be relaid, and to permit another contractor to lay such pavement or sidewalk; in which case the liability of the Contractor under this contract shall cease as far as that part of its work is concerned, whenever the Engineer shall report to the Commission that the instructions of the Commission have been complied with, exactly the same as if the Contractor had fully completed the repaving as hereinbefore provided. The Engineer shall then report to the Commission the number of square yards of pavement thus disturbed but not relaid, and the Contractor shall forthwith, upon demand, pay to the City such sum as the Engineer shall certify as the reasonable value of the expense of restoring the previous pavement.

23

STATIONS

The contract drawings indicate the general plan and outline and the chief structural and decorative features of the stations.

Station plans furnished

As soon as possible after the letting of the contract, the Engineer will furnish to the Contractor full detail plans and such additional specifications as may be necessary. Said plans may vary in detail, from the plans as shown on the contract drawings, in accordance with the local requirements.

The decorative features and details of the stations, however, will be in general harmony with and substantially similar, as far as possible, to the general details of the stations, as indicated on the above-mentioned contract drawings.

Materials of construction for underground station finish

Marble, enameled bricks, face bricks, glass and glazed tiles, mosaic work, metal laths, plaster, cement floors, concrete, metal covered wood, woodwork, brass and iron grilles, railings, gates, toilet fixtures, lighting conduits, and all other materials used in the decoration and interior finish of the stations shall be of the best merchantable grade of the respective articles, as approved by the Engineer, and shall be fabricated and laid or erected in the most approved manner by workmen especially skilled in their respective trades.

Marble

All marble used for wainscoting or panels on the sidewalls of the stations, closets and passageways, shall be "Pink Georgia," or its equal, as selected for each station.

All marble lintels shall be "Green Veined Vermont," or its equal. All marble work shall be thoroughly anchored with brass wire anchors in a manner satisfactory to the Engineer. The space between the back of the wainscot and panel work and the masonry walls shall be filled in solid with Portland cement grout. All corners shall be curved to standard radii.

Enameled or face bricks shall be of an approved brick of the best quality. For common bricks see specifications for brick masonry. **Face bricks**

Mortar for brick masonry station finish shall consist of: For common brick or hollow blocks, one (1) part cement, three (3) parts sand; for face brick station finish, one (1) part of extra No. one (1) freshly burned and thoroughly slaked lime of an approved brand and sand in proportion to properly work under the trowel, and one (1) part of cement, colored to match the face brick. The lime and sand are to be mixed together, and the cement added as it is being used. **Mortar**

The tile and mosaic work shall consist of scratch coat, straight tile, bull nose and bent tile conforming to standard radii, " art ceramic " or glass tile mosaic bands, friezes, pilasters, panels and name tablets. **Tile and mosaic work**

The tile work shall consist of opal glass or white glazed tile or other approved material, white or colored. All tile shall be brought to the work in large quantities and care taken to avoid strong contrasts in color. No broken or imperfect tile shall be used and the tile work shall be perfectly true, plumb and straight. Tiles shall be furnished in such dimensions as designated. All corners shall be finished with tile curved to standard radii.

The mosaic work shall consist of " art ceramic " or glass tile mosaic or other approved material. It shall be furnished in such colors as may be selected, rendered into ornamental designs.

The tile and mosaic work shall be set in Portland or " plastic " cement as approved. Before the tile and mosaic work is set the walls shall be thoroughly cleaned and well wet and plastered with a scratch coat of cement mortar consisting of one (1) part of approved Portland cement and three (3) parts of clean, sharp sand.

Concrete finish

The concrete in the station shall be finished as specified for finish under concrete.

Vault lights

The roofs of the stations, where under the sidewalks, parks or parkways, shall, to as great an extent as possible, consist of vault light construction. These lights shall be made with lenses not exceeding three (3) inches in diameter, of strong glass set in cement; they shall be provided with non-slipping treads, buttons or other devices all of design approved by the Engineer; and shall be of sufficient strength to carry, when supported in a manner similar to that in which they are to be permanently set, an equally distributed load of at least five hundred (500) lbs. per square foot without signs of failure, deformation or permanent set, when such test load is removed. The right is reserved to test at least one (1) frame or panel in every ten (10), as selected by the Engineer. Should the one selected fail, another will be selected by the Engineer; and, if that fail, then the whole lot may be rejected. The vault lights must be set in place with cement, lead or other means to be absolutely waterproof.

Hollow space in walls

In order to prevent any leaks, and as far as possible, condensation, the Contractor must exercise great care in the construction of station walls and roofs. The walls shall be constructed so as to contain a hollow space. The hollow space shall be obtained by lining the walls on the inside with hollow terra cotta blocks four (4) inches thick, or common brick facing wall four (4) inches thick set away from the sidewalls two (2) inches distance. These hollow block or brick facing walls shall be laid as hereinbefore or after specified in order to provide clearway spaces for drainage from the top to the bottom of the walls. The hollow spaces in the wall shall be connected at the bottom by a pipe leading to the drains. Where directed, openings protected by bronze gratings, shall be provided through the facing walls in order to permit the circulation of air in the hollow spaces behind them. On an average there shall be three (3) openings 2⅜ inches by 4 inches in every fifteen (15) feet.

Where it shall become necessary to cut into or through the hollow blocks or bricks for the purpose of laying electric conduits or any other pipes or tubes, the spaces thus cut out shall be covered with galvanized metal lath, fastened to the hollow blocks with suitable fastenings, before any scratch coat or plastering is applied to the wall surface, thereby securing a clear opening behind the wire mesh for drainage.

Where enamel or face bricks are used in the facing walls, they shall be laid as specified for the common brick, except where otherwise specified.

Laying brick-facing walls

The hollow block, common brick, enamel brick and face brick facing walls shall be laid in running bond, with headers set hard against the station sidewalls, at least once in each square yard. All facing walls shall be anchored to the sidewalls in an approved manner.

Furring for elevated stations

Metal lath and furring shall be provided for tile on toilet walls. Hollow tile shall be laid between studs in toilet room walls to form backing for marble or glass wainscot. All of the interior of building shall be cross-furred to form nailing for finishing sheathing.

Interior finish

The interior walls of the subway stations, including all sidewalls of the stations, closets, toilet rooms, passageways, and the walls of the railroad to the extreme ends of the platforms, shall be finished in marble, enameled brick, face brick, glass or glazed tile, " art ceramic," or glass tile mosaic, concrete, or such other material as indicated on the plans or as may be approved by the Engineer. All materials shall be furnished in such dimensions and of such colors, and laid or set, as the Engineer may direct. In the designs of the stations all angles formed by the intersection of the sidewalls, floors and ceilings shall be avoided by joining these surfaces by curves. In order that such curved surfaces shall present a smooth and workmanlike finish the Contractor shall supply special bricks, tiles or pieces of other materials curved to the radius used.

Interior walls and ceilings, where not otherwise specified, shall be sheathed with first quality oak sheathing. Ceilings of mezzanine platforms under tracks shall be of stamped steel, nailed to furring. Sleepers in under side of concrete track floor and joists between bottom flanges of platform girders shall be provided for nailing furring for metal ceiling. Ceilings of toilet rooms shall be plastered on metal lath. Ceilings in all passageways, when not of metal, shall be as specified for canopy ceilings. Ventilators in ceilings and wind guards on platforms shall be constructed where shown on plans.

All details of the stations must be so arranged as to provide as few lodgment places as possible **Ceilings** for dust and dirt, to facilitate cleaning, and to permit, if desired, a thorough washing of all parts of the station and its approaches by means of a hose.

The ceilings over the platforms, mezzanines, passageways, closets and toilet rooms of subway stations shall be constructed with an air space. Wherever possible this air space is to be obtained by lining the roof with hollow terra cotta blocks two (2) inches thick. The hollow blocks are to be laid, when the roof is constructed, so that a secure bond shall be obtained between the hollow block linings and the concrete roof. This shall be done by laying the blocks against the inside of the concrete forms, as directed by the Engineer, before the concrete is placed. Care shall be taken that the hollow spaces in blocks are not obstructed with cement mortar or concrete.

Where hollow block is not used galvanized metal laths shall be attached to the roof beams or furred out from the roof in an approved manner, so as to leave an air space beneath the same.

Interior ceiling finish

The interior ceilings on terra cotta blocks or metal lath, over the platforms, mezzanines, passageways, closets and toilet rooms, and on concrete over tracks at the stations to the extreme ends of the station platforms, except under vault lights, shall be finished in cement plaster, or other approved material, applied in the following manner, or as directed by the Engineer:

On metal lath, one (1) scratch coat, one (1) brown coat and two (2) finish coats.

On terra cotta blocks, one (1) brown coat and two (2) finish coats.

On concrete, two (2) finish coats.

The brown coat and first finish coat shall be scored to insure a proper bond for the following coats. The scratch and brown coats shall consist of cement mortar of such proportions as directed by the Engineer. The two finish coats shall consist of a mixture of the best grade of white Portland cement and white silica sand, or other material approved by the Engineer. The final coat is to have a smooth, hard finish, and shall be in such colors as directed. All angles shall be coved.

The floors of the stations shall be constructed as hereinafter specified, and generally shall be so arranged as to drain to the edge of the platform and thence into the tracks. Under special conditions, however, they shall be arranged to drain to one or more points as directed, where suitable and proper provisions shall be made for the removal of water used in flushing the same. In subway stations in order to provide a space in which all floor drains, pipes, tubes and electric conduits may be laid, concrete construction under the finish shall be stopped at least six (6) inches below the finish floor grades at all points. Floors

Floor finish

The floors of the station platforms, closets, toilet rooms, mezzanines, and passageways shall be finished in concrete and cement of a minimum thickness of three (3) inches, composed of two (2) inches of concrete and one (1) inch of cement finish. The three (3) inch floor finish shall be laid upon a concrete foundation three (3) inches thick.

The materials and proportions shall be as follows:

Three (3) inch foundation concrete, one (1) part of cement, two and a half (2½) parts of sand, and six (6) parts of broken stone not exceeding three-quarter (¾) inch.

Two (2) inches of concrete, same as specified for foundation concrete.

Cement finish, one (1) part of cement, and two (2) parts of coarse white sand.

The cement for the two (2) inch concrete layer and cement finish and the white sand may be special materials, approved by the Engineer; all other materials shall be as hereinbefore or hereinafter specified.

Method of laying

The top of the foundation concrete shall be left three (3) inches below and parallel to the finish floor elevations. After the foundation concrete has set, the two (2) inch concrete layer shall be spread to an even thickness and rammed so that its top surface shall be one (1) inch below and parallel to the finish floor lines. Before this concrete is set, lay the one (1) inch cement finish and trowel to a smooth uniform hard finished surface.

The floor shall be laid out in blocks about three (3) feet square. These blocks shall be formed by cutting through the two (2) inch concrete, before it has begun to set, with a tool which will make a quarter (¼) inch joint. The cement finish shall be marked with a suitable tool directly over the joint above described.

Reinforced concrete floors for mezzanines, ticket houses, passageways, platforms, toilet and waiting rooms on elevated stations shall be constructed. The floor, except as hereinafter specified, shall be finished and brought to the level of the finished floor with a layer about one (1) inch thick, the same as specified for subway platforms. The floors of toilets and waiting rooms shall be finished with an approved asbestos composition about one-half (½) an inch thick laid directly on the concrete and colored as directed.

At the intersection of the floor and sidewalls a sanitary cove of two (2) inch radius shall be formed. The floor shall be kept moist and protected until perfectly set.

Stairways

The stairways for subway stations shall be supported or self-supporting stairways.

Supported stairways

Supported stairways shall consist of concrete steps built directly on concrete foundations, and the minimum thickness of the concrete between the bottom of the riser and the foundation shall be four (4) inches. The landings shall consist of a concrete slab four (4) inches thick laid on the concrete foundation.

Self-supporting stairways

Self-supporting stairways and landings shall be constructed of concrete reinforced with steel rods.

The concrete shall, when machine mixed, consist of one (1) part of approved Portland cement, two and a half ($2\frac{1}{2}$) parts of first quality Cow Bay sand, or its equal, and four and a half ($4\frac{1}{2}$) parts of three-quarter ($\frac{3}{4}$) inch trap rock or clean gravel of a mixture of paving and roofing sizes. When mixed by hand (1) part of cement, two (2) parts of sand and four (4) parts of stone.

All treads and landings shall have a granolithic finish one (1) inch thick, into which shall be worked the most approved form of treads to prevent slipping. The risers shall be paneled and washed with a cement grout and rubbed down to a hard, even finish. The cement grout shall be applied before the concrete thoroughly sets. The granolithic finish shall consist of one (1) part of Portland cement, one (1) part of finely crushed granite and one (1) part of sand colored with lampblack as directed.

For elevated stations

Stairways for elevated stations shall consist of steel stringers, with angles riveted on for connection of wood risers and treads. All intermediate supports shall consist of steel pipe columns with cast iron bases set on concrete foundations. All treads, risers and platforms shall be of yellow pine set in white lead and secured to the angles. All treads shall be provided with the most approved form of non-slipping treads. Concrete street landings shall be provided at the foot of the stairways.

Number of stairways

At least as many stairways as are shown on the plans shall be provided for each side of the stations. The stairways shall be of as great width as the local conditions will satisfactorily permit.

Elevators, escalators or moving stairways

The Contractor shall establish an approved plant of elevators, escalators or moving stairways, as indicated on the plans, or required by the Engineer, including necessary supports, panel work, etc., as well as all motors and devices for operating the elevators or escalators or moving stairways, complete and ready for operation.

All machinery required for these plants shall be a part of the Equipment.

Safety treads

Along the edge of train platforms adjacent to the tracks, an approved type of non-slipping treads securely anchored to platforms shall be provided.

Ticket booths, doors and news-stands

The ticket booths, doors and frames, and news-stands for subway stations shall be constructed of copper covered wood with mouldings independently applied, or such non-combustible material as may be approved by the Engineer. The ticket booths for elevated stations shall be of quartered oak, with cornices, pilasters, composition bead mouldings, carved brackets and ticket shelves.

The ticket windows of all booths shall be glazed in plate glass, plain or frosted, as indicated, and shall be enclosed with bronze grille. Plate glass coin shelves shall be provided.

Doors for elevated stations shall be veneered on both sides with No. 1 oak. Door frames for elevated stations shall be of two-inch oak and well screwed to studs. Panel boards for elevated stations shall have doors and trim of oak.

Woodwork for elevated stations

Timber shall be New York State spruce unless otherwise specified, and shall be free from winds and other imperfections impairing durability and strength. House roof boarding and outside sheathing shall be best quality of sound, seasoned hemlock or spruce not exceeding six (6) inches in width, planed, tongued and grooved and laid with close joints in courses.

Canopy roof and stair roof boarding shall be first quality North Carolina pine, planed on one side, tongued, grooved and beaded.

All boarding under roofing tin and copper sheathing shall be covered with approved roofing fabric.

Roofs of ticket houses shall be provided with wood cleats to form standing seams in tin work.

The outside walls of ticket houses, excepting sash and doors, shall be covered with copper in design shown and properly backed.

Studs shall be two by four, cross-bridged at half their height.

Sills and plates shall be bolted to the steel upon which they bear, or anchored to the concrete with one-half (½) inch bolts.

Frame for all dormers, gables, ventilators, scuttles, skylights, stove recesses, panel boards, etc., where shown on plans.

All sash (except sash in toilets and sometimes in wind screens) shall be glazed with first quality double-thick American sheet glass. Sash in toilets always, and in wind screens where the same come in front of and close to windows in adjacent buildings, shall be glazed with Florentine glass set in an approved manner. **Glass for elevated stations**

Outside doors to be glazed with first quality American plate glass, ¼ inch thick, secured in an approved manner, without the use of putty.

Panel boards shall be glazed with 3/16-inch American plate glass.

Hardware

All hardware shall be of solid bronze metal without lacquer, and of weight, quality and design as approved by the Engineer.

Railings and grilles—subway

On subway stations the platform and stairway railings and grilles, and the stairway railings and hoods at the street surface, shall be constructed of iron and bronze.

Railings and grilles—elevated

On elevated stations the stair railings and canopies over landings and platforms shall be of cast and wrought iron, and steel as indicated. Railings for train platforms and ticket houses shall be made of cast iron or cast and wrought iron, as indicated.

Newel posts and light standards

Newel posts shall be of cast iron, and those in platform railings shall be furnished with electric light standards. Island platforms beyond canopies shall have free standing electric light standards.

Hand rails

Oak hand-rails supported on iron brackets shall be provided for all stairways.

Gates

All gates shall be as shown on plans and hung on ball-bearing sheaves, and shall be operated by an approved method, invisible where possible.

Name tablets

Cast-iron name tablets shall be provided for elevated stations; same shall have enamel signs secured to face of cast iron.

Saddles for outside doors of elevated stations shall be of cast iron, roughened on top and securely anchored in place. **Saddles**

Each side of every station, unless otherwise ordered by the Engineer, shall be equipped with two (2) toilet rooms, as indicated on the plans, plainly marked, for the use of women and men, respectively, and one (1) porter's closet. The women's rooms shall be furnished with the necessary fixtures, not to exceed two (2) bowls, one (1) basin, and one (1) floor drain; the men's with not to exceed two (2) bowls, two (2) urinals, one (1) basin and one (1) slop sink and one (1) floor drain, unless otherwise noted on the plans. All the toilet fixtures shall be of the most approved design, and provided with most approved flushing devices. The doors leading to these rooms shall be equipped with self-closing springs. Each room in subway stations shall have a ventilating pipe leading direct to the outer air, and covered either by a suitable cast-iron ventilating post set on the sidewalk, or in some other approved manner. A suitable chamber shall be furnished in the wall of the toilet room and connected with the ventilating pipe for the installation of a small electric exhaust fan. **Sanitary arrangements**

All fixtures shall be connected by means of cast-iron drain pipes to the main sewer. These drains shall be furnished with sufficient traps of approved design, set close to the fixtures, which traps shall be back-aired in an efficient and workmanlike manner, such back-air pipes terminating in the sidewalk or other approved situation, and covered by suitable galvanized iron gratings or ventilating post.

On elevated stations the main drain of four (4) inch cast-iron pipe shall be carried down the structural column to the surface of the ground, where it enters a concrete manhole. From the manhole a six (6) inch cast-iron pipe shall be carried to the sewer. Water supply pipe of adequate capacity, to supply all fixtures shall be provided to run from manhole to water main, and to be carried up the column and across on same lines as main drain pipe. Necessary traps, valves, insulated joints, etc., shall be provided. All pipes shall be suitably wrapped and protected.

Soil and other pipes

All soil, waste, vent and water supply pipes, wherever possible, shall be run in specially arranged and accessible wall spaces between an outer marble or glass finish and the sidewalls of the toilets. Where considered necessary by the Engineer, back pressure valves shall be provided on the soil line. When it is impossible to connect the soil pipes directly to the sewer, sewage shall be discharged into a sewage sump of approved form and dimensions, in which an approved automatic sewage ejector may be installed. Between the wall spaces and the sewer all soil and supply pipes shall be run where possible in pipe troughs constructed under the station platforms. All water supply pipes shall be encased in asbestos or other approved non-conducting material, and all pipes exposed in the troughs or wall spaces shall be suitably painted. Wherever practicable, all pipes shall be concealed from view. The toilet room stalls shall be finished in marble or glass as approved by the Engineer. All work must conform with the City Building and Health regulations, which are to be considered as part of these specifications.

Water connections

Both platforms of the stations shall have connection with the water main so as to permit the attaching of hose for the flushing and washing of all parts of the stations and platforms, waiting rooms and stairways, and to furnish an adequate supply for fire purposes.

Sewers under platforms

Where it may be necessary to pass sewers or pipes, or both, beneath the station platforms, in order to reach the same for the purpose of inspection and repair, cast-iron frames capable of being lifted shall be inserted in the floor.

Sheet metal work for elevated stations

The sheet metal work shall be carefully applied, and of the very best quality and workmanship. All mouldings shall be carefully run and true to full size details. Seams shall be carefully locked and, where possible, double locked and soldered. Nailing in all cases shall be with copper or tinned nails. All roofs throughout shall be covered with an approved " I C " tinned plate.

Copper

The outside walls of ticket houses shall be covered with 18-oz. copper. Copper cresting shall be provided.

All panels shall be of fine crimped copper, and moulded as required.

Canopy gutters shall be of No. 24 galvanized iron; gutters on ticket houses shall be of 16-oz. copper and moulded as required.

Copper used on buildings in any form shall not have over two (2) per cent. impurities.

All leaders, except on side of ticket house and next to copper sheathing shall be of No. 24 galvanized iron, corrugated, and where leaders pass through platform floors, they shall be carried in iron pipes. All leaders shall carry down the structural columns, and shall be protected at the discharge by wrought iron pipe with elbow at end. Suitable sheet metal protection for wrapping on soil pipe at foot of structural columns shall be provided. Leaders next to copper sheathing shall be of 18-ounce copper.

Suitable smoke flues, with double lining, shall be provided in connection with stove recesses.

Lighting conduits

Provision shall be made for the illumination of the station platforms, passageways, stairways, toilet rooms, ticket booths, electric signs, closets and mezzanines by supplying and erecting all the necessary conduits, outlet boxes, fittings and all other materials which are built into the structure, for the installation of an approved lighting system.

The lighting system shall be at least equivalent to that furnished by one 16-candle power incandescent lamp for each fifty (50) square feet of floor area. At all points on the station platforms and stairways the light shall, however, be not less than one-foot candle at a point three (3) feet above the floor, and the construction and location of lights shall be such as to give this degree of illumination.

Transformer platforms

Platforms for transformers on elevated stations shall be constructed where required.

Ventilation

Ventilating openings shall be constructed in the roofs of the subway stations. These openings shall be of such dimensions as indicated on the detailed plans, and shall be covered at the sidewalk surface with approved gratings. The openings shall be so arranged as to exclude storm water from the station platforms; and where necessary and as indicated on the plans, vault light slabs or pans shall be placed and provided with proper drains.

Heating

Provision for electric heating shall be made in all toilet rooms and news stands of subway stations and in all ticket booths. On elevated stations, concrete stove recesses shall be built where required.

Pipes, conduits, etc., concealed

At the stations all signal wires, air pipes, electric conduits and wires, pipes or conduits for any purpose whatever shall be concealed from view behind the finished walls or ceilings, or under the platforms or platform overhangs in such manner as approved by the Engineer.

Station painting

All exposed metal work at the stations and between the tracks opposite the stations in the subway, and for at least thirty (30) feet from the ends of the subway station platforms, shall be thoroughly and evenly painted, after all other station finish work has been completed, with three (3) additional coats of paint besides the renewed shop coat. The first coat shall be the same as the first coat applied to all other metal work in the subway or on the elevated after erection, and the other two coats shall be of approved paint and in such colors as may be designated by the Engineer. All woodwork shall be satisfactorily cleaned and smoothed by scraping or sand-papering before any paint, varnish or oil is applied. Pine and cypress stock shall be painted two coats on top of priming. Platform and stair canopies, ceiling in passageways and ceiling of overhang on houses shall receive one coat of pure raw linseed oil, one coat of dark shellac and one coat of spar varnish. All inside oak shall have one coat of hard wood filler, one coat of shellac and two coats of interior varnish, the last coat rubbed to an eggshell gloss.

All window and door frames, sash and wind guards on elevated stations shall be primed on all sides with a coat of lead and oil paint before being taken to the station.

Track houses

Track houses for signal men and train despatchers shall be constructed adjacent to the platforms of all terminal stations and at intermediate points where indicated on plans. Also, provide toilets and locker rooms for train crews in track houses adjacent to all terminal stations. Houses in the subway shall be constructed of masonry, and those on the elevated shall be constructed of asbestos lumber, supported on steel, with wood bolted to steel to afford nailing. Doors and windows to be metal covered wood, glazed with double thick American sheet glass, except in signal towers where American plate glass shall be used, and provided with hardware similar to that specified for stations. Electric heaters and lights shall be provided for all track houses.

Miscellaneous buildings

All spaces within the Railroad, permanently enclosed for offices, signal towers, pump rooms, store houses, or for any other purpose shall be built as a part of the Construction and in accordance with the plans approved by the Engineer. All such rooms or enclosures within the limits of any of the stations shall conform, as to construction and finish, with the station in which it is located.

Floors shall be of concrete, reinforced where necessary, and shall have a granolithic finish, except in signal towers and despatchers' rooms where sleepers shall be bedded in the concrete to provide nailing for wood floors. Ladders or stairways shall be provided where necessary.

Necessary plumbing, etc., for toilets, similar to that specified for station toilets, shall be provided. Automatic sewage ejectors shall be provided where necessary, as hereinafter specified under Equipment. Each toilet shall be provided with necessary fixtures not to exceed eight (8) urinals, five (5) bowls and four (4) basins.

24

TERMINALS, YARDS AND SHOPS

Terminals

Proper terminals shall be provided at the ends of all lines and at any other points where running direction of the trains is reversed in regular service, which will permit such turning of trains quickly and without interference with the regular operation of other trains. At all terminals, the necessary rooms for train crews, dispatchers, signal towers, toilets, and all other rooms or offices, of a permanent character, required for the proper operation of the railroad, shall be built as a part of Construction.

Yards and Shops

Suitable yards shall be located by the Contractor, subject to the approval of the Commission, and sufficient in area to permit the construction of repair shops and inspection sheds complete with all appurtenances required for the proper maintenance of all of the rolling stock equipment furnished under this contract. The area of these yards shall also be sufficient to provide for the storage of such part of said equipment as may be laid up in the hours of light traffic at any time during the period of the Operation Provisions.

Grading

The surface of all yards shall be improved by excavating, filling or other grading as ordered by the Commission, in order to put the same in proper condition for use.

Buildings

All structures, buildings, foundations, pits for transfer-tables or turntables and all similar appurtenances of a permanent character required for shops, inspection sheds, tracks or similar purposes shall be constructed according to the plans and specifications furnished by the Commission or according to the plans and specifications furnished by the Contractor and approved by the Commission.

Buildings fireproof

All buildings shall be constructed of steel, brick or other fireproof materials, and shall present an attractive appearance.

All of the above mentioned permanent structures and the necessary real estate shall be supplied by the Contractor as a part of Construction. All machinery of whatever nature, all track construction, including the necessary ties, ballast, fittings, etc., and all similar material or devices of a movable character shall be furnished by the Contractor and owned by him as a part of the Equipment contemplated and called for in this contract.

25

EQUIPMENT

Equipment to be approved

The general plans for all equipment shall be submitted to the Commission and approved by it both as to design and quantity, and all equipment supplied shall be approved as to workmanship and material and shall be in all respects suitable for the service herein contemplated.

Equipment to be owned by Contractor

The full and complete equipment of the Railroad, including all material, apparatus or devices for the complete installation of the track work, contact rails, signals, emergency systems, telephones, ventilation, drainage, heating and lighting, and all other equipment required to place the line of the Railroad in full and complete operating condition, and all rolling stock of whatever nature, including the complete electrical and mechanical equipment thereof and the tools, implements and other devices necessary for the maintenance and repairs of same, and all power houses, substations or other buildings, including all real estate required therefor and including all necessary machinery, mechanisms, tools and other devices required for the generation or transformation of power, and all wires, conduits, ducts, subways, manholes, or other equipment required for the transmission and distribution of the power required for the operation of the Railroad, and whatever other things may be included in the definition "Equipment" in Chapter I of this contract, excepting only those parts which, as specifically stated in Chapter II, shall be a part of Construction or indicated on the plans, shall be provided by and at the expense of the Contractor and shall be owned by him.

The full and complete equipment of the Railroad shall be ample in all respects to permit the regular operation of all tracks to the limit of their capacity. This equipment shall not be less than that required for the operation of the following schedules for a period of at least two hours. Amount of equipment

Fully loaded express trains of ten (10) cars shall be operated over all main line express tracks at a headway not exceeding one and one-half (1½) minutes, and when so operating shall average not less than twenty-five (25) miles per hour in the run from terminal to terminal of said main line express tracks, including the stops at intermediate stations. This service shall continue to the respective terminals of the branch lines at such headway and at such speed as the local conditions of the branch lines will permit.

Fully loaded local trains of ten (10) cars shall be operated over all main line local tracks at a headway not exceeding one and one-half ($1\frac{1}{2}$) minutes and when so operating shall average not less than fifteen (15) miles per hour in the run from terminal to terminal of said main line local tracks including stops at stations. This service shall be divided between the respective branch lines as the traffic requires and shall be continued to the ends of these branch lines if this course is considered necessary by the Commission.

With the approval of the Commission a partial equipment may be installed for the initial operation, this equipment to be increased from time to time as the traffic conditions demand or as required by the Commission and as set forth in the Operation Provisions.

Such reduction of equipment shall be made only in the rolling stock, the generating or transforming apparatus for power supply and in the number of frogs and switches required for track work. All buildings, ducts, cables, and other equipment called for shall be initially installed for the full and complete equipment as described above and as set forth hereinafter.

Track equipment

The track structure complete, including all ballast, ties, concrete (other than that called for under

Construction), rails, special work, spikes, joints, bolts, tie-plates and all other material or apparatus necessary to complete the track work in the best possible manner and to the satisfaction of the Engineer, shall be provided and installed as a part of the Equipment.

Track, how constructed

It shall be constructed of the best materials and to the standard, and in the manner best calculated to make a track structure upon which the trains herein contemplated can be operated at the highest attainable speed with the minimum of jar and noise. The track shall be laid, as directed by the Engineer, on blocks or ties supported by and surrounded by concrete, or laid on cross ties imbedded in ballast, or in any other manner which may be approved by the Engineer.

All lining, gauging, leveling, spiking, bolting and all other work in connection with the laying and surfacing of the track, shall be done by specially skilled workmen in a manner to give the best construction.

Upon curves the outer track rail shall be elevated and the inner rail depressed, and said curves shall be laid to a true circular arc or shall have the ends thereof laid as transition curves as required by the Engineer.

On tangents the distance between gauge lines of running rails shall be four (4′) feet eight and one-half ($8\frac{1}{2}''$) inches and on curves this distance shall be increased as required by the degree of curvature.

Track rails

The chemical composition, the weight and section of all track rails shall be as approved by the Engineer. Manganese steel or other high grade material shall be used for such portions of the work as, in the opinion of the Engineer, may be improved by this course. First quality rails only shall be laid for running rails of main line tracks.

Guard rails

Guard rails of approved dimensions and material shall be laid on the inside of the inner rail on all curves, and at other special points where directed by the Engineer. The method of attaching these guard rails to the track structure shall be as approved by the Engineer.

Such additional catch rails as may be required in special locations, shall be installed as a part of the track construction.

Track details

All details of track construction, including the design and construction of all joints, bonds, tie plates, bolts, nuts, spikes and all other fittings shall be as approved by the Engineer.

Tie plates of approved form and dimensions, shall be applied to every tie or block at the point of support of the rail.

Joint plates shall be designed to permit proper bonding and joints shall be bonded to provide the greatest possible conductivity in the return circuit. All bolts shall be held by approved lock washers or grip nuts.

All timber used in connection with the track shall be thoroughly sound and free from sap, shakes, decay or any other defects which, in the judgment of the Engineer, might impair its strength, durability or serviceability for the special uses intended. **Timber**

Bearing blocks or cross ties for the support of the rail shall be of white oak, or long leafed yellow pine, made to exact dimensions, as prescribed in plans to be furnished and, if required by the Engineer, shall be treated to prevent decay at such special locations as he may indicate.

Frogs, switches and other special work shall be provided and installed in such locations and of such design as to permit the operation of trains, as hereinafter specified, with the greatest safety and upon such headway as the Commission requires. All of the special work shown on the plans may not be required for the initial operation of the line and such parts as are not so required may be omitted from the initial equipment upon the approval of the Engineer. At any time during the life of the contract such additional special work or tracks shall be added and such changes made in the operation as may be required by the Commission. **Track, special work**

Frogs, switches, etc.

All frogs, switches and other appurtenances of a similar nature, must be of such a design as to give an unbroken or continuous bearing on the main track rails, and all such devices must receive the approval of the Engineer before being laid. Manganese or other hard steel shall be used for such part of this work as the Engineer may require. All switches, as far as practicable, shall be laid trailing.

Ballast

In case ballast is used, said ballast shall be of hard broken stone not subject to granulation, nominally three-quarters (3/4) of an inch in size, all pieces of which shall pass through a ring one and one-half (1 1/2) inches in diameter, and containing no particles smaller than one-quarter (1/4) inch.

Concrete in tracks

In case concrete is used in the track equipment, said concrete shall be made up from the best materials, in all respects equal to those specified for Construction, and shall be mixed in such proportions as may be required by the Engineer. All forms and all methods used in mixing or installing this concrete and all work in connection with the lining and leveling of the track shall be done under the direction of and to the satisfaction of the Engineer.

Contact rail

Contact rail, for the supply of power to the trains, shall be installed throughout the length of all tracks shown. This rail shall be supported, installed and covered with an approved non-inflammable protection for the prevention of accidental contact therewith by workmen or other persons. In determining the location of this rail and in designing the details for this work, preference shall be given a construction which will permit exchange of equipment with existing subways.

All joints of contact rail shall be bonded by copper bonds or equivalent, which shall make the resistance of the joint substantially equivalent to the resistance of the same length of rail. This rail shall be operated upon a direct current line voltage which will permit the interchange of equipment with other existing subways, the return current being carried in part by the track structure.

Composition of rail

The composition and cross section of this rail, together with all details of construction, shall be as approved by the Engineer.

Feeder cables

Feeder cables shall be provided for the proper supply of current to the contact rail and for the return of said current from the track rails. These cables shall be installed of ample cross section and sufficient number to provide for the maximum service to be operated upon the Railroad. The return feeders shall be so arranged and of such resistance that, when operating upon said maximum schedule, the difference in potential between any two points of the structure of the Railroad or between said structure and any other metallic structure in its vicinity, shall be of an amount which shall not set up any appreciable electrolytic action due to the return current of the Railroad.

The direct current feeders shall be sufficient to provide, at all times and under all conditions, an operating potential suitable for the proper operation of the trains and shall be sufficient to give a reasonably steady illumination of the cars.

Other cables

All other cables required for power, lighting, heating or for any other purpose shall be of the highest quality and shall be installed in such numbers and in such manner as may be approved by the Engineer.

Signals

All main line tracks shall be equipped with an approved system of signals of the most reliable character and all signals shall be equipped with the necessary devices for automatically stopping any train attempting to pass a danger signal.

If, at any time during the life of this contract, additional signals are necessary, the same shall be promptly installed.

Interlocking

All switches and all signals controlling traffic over special work shall be interlocked in the most approved manner and controlled from power interlocking plants, suitably located and installed.

Emergency system

A system shall be installed throughout the underground sections of the Railroad, by means of which the power supplied to any section of contact rail can be quickly and certainly cut off in case of a wreck or other emergency.

A system shall also be installed and connected to all passenger stations of the line, by which all the ticket agents may be immediately notified in case of a blocked line. At least one sending and one recording device shall be located at each station of the Railroad.

Any other devices, apparatus or equipment, such as telephones, bells, etc., which in the opinion of the Commission are necessary to properly safeguard the operation of the Railroad shall be installed as a part of Equipment and any and all devices for emergency service shall be of the most reliable character.

At each sump and at such other points as may be necessary in order to keep the Railroad or any part thereof clear of water a pumping plant shall be installed. **Pumps**

Each of these plants shall be composed of not less than two (2) units, supplied from different sources of power, and each large enough to remove all water accumulating at that point under ordinary conditions. If, in the opinion of the Engineer, the local conditions require it, any of these plants shall, at his direction, be increased to take care of emergency conditions. This increase may be obtained by the addition of other pumps or the increase in size of the two pumps above called for; in either case the total capacity installed at any point shall not be less than that required by Engineer.

All pumps shall start and stop automatically with the variations in water level at the sumps which they drain, and shall be designed and installed to give the greatest possible reliability in service.

The delivery of these pumps shall be into the city sewers or elsewhere, as directed by the Engineer, and all piping, fittings and connections required therefor shall be installed as a part of Equipment.

Ejectors

At stations and at other points where the soil pipes cannot be connected directly to the sewer, the sewage shall be discharged into an approved sewage ejector. These ejectors, together with all necessary fittings, devices and connections necessary for the control or operation of the same, shall be furnished as a part of Equipment. The necessary pits or other permanent structures required for their installation, and all pipe work or other construction, built into and forming a part of the stations or other structures, which are required for the complete installation of the ejectors shall be a part of Construction.

The subway sections of the Railroad shall be supplied at all times with such quantities of pure air as may be necessary to maintain a standard of purity substantially equal to that of the street. Ventilation

The ventilation system shall also be so designed and operated as to maintain the summer temperature of the subway sections at as low a point as possible and, at points where a sufficient supply of ground water can be obtained, special cooling plants shall be installed, if so directed by the Commission.

The devices for ventilation must be of sufficient capacity to renew the air if so desired at least once every fifteen minutes.

In general, this shall be accomplished by exhausting the air at the ventilating chambers, hereinbefore described, at points between the stations, and supplying fresh air by an inflow through the gratings, and other openings, at the stations.

The air renewal is to be obtained as far as possible by the exhaling and inhaling action of the trains.

The renewal of the air by train action is to be effected by exhausting air through the movable valves or louvres or other approved devices, located in the ventilating chambers in the sidewalls or roof of the Railroad. These valves shall be so designed that air can only flow out through them into the chambers and thence through gratings to the street. The air thus exhausted at the chamber is renewed by fresh air entering the Railroad through the stairway openings and gratings at the stations.

Blowers

To augment this air supply, if necessary, and to provide at any time for the removal of smoke in case of fire, also to insure a supply at times of minimum operation of trains or entire stoppage thereof, motor-driven blowers of an approved pattern shall be provided. These blowers shall be of such capacity as may be necessary in order to provide for renewing the tunnel air once in every fifteen minutes independent of the action of trains.

The blowers shall each be provided with motors of adequate power to at all times operate the blowers to their full capacity; and these motors shall be so arranged that any group of blowers may be started simultaneously from some convenient point of control. The power lines supplying these blowers shall be independent of the local contact rails.

Toilet ventilation

All subway toilet rooms and such other rooms as the Engineer may indicate shall be equipped with motor driven exhaust fans, discharging into suitable air ducts leading to the outside air. All parts of this equipment built into the station, including the electric conduits, and portions of the air ducts are a part of Construction. The blower equipment, including the necessary brackets and supports, and all wiring, switches and other devices and all air flues connecting to the air ducts provided under Construction, shall be a part of Equipment. These blowers shall receive power from the local lighting boards and shall be self starting without the aid of external starting boxes.

Ducts

All tile duct construction, including the necessary manholes, required for the operation of the Railroad for any purpose whatsoever, not built along the line of the Railroad, as specified under Construction, shall be supplied and installed by and at the expense of the Contractor as a part of the Equipment.

Duct lines so constructed shall include all branches leading from the line of the Railroad to substations, power houses or to any other location off the line of the Railroad and all connecting lines between power houses and substations or between other points off the line of the Railroad.

This duct construction shall be ample as to size and number of ducts, and shall provide proper space for all cables required for the operation of the Railroad to its full capacity and a reasonable number of spare ducts shall be installed to provide for contingencies. The general construction of duct lines shall be as specified under Construction.

Conduit

All iron pipe conduit not installed in and forming part of the structures, as specified under Construction, shall be supplied and installed, complete with all outlet boxes, pull boxes and other details, by and at the expense of the Contractor as a part of the Equipment. This work shall be, in all respects, equal to conduit work called for under Construction.

Pipe conduit so installed shall include all runs, for any purpose whatsoever, installed upon the surface of any of the structures in a manner permitting its removal without seriously disfiguring the structure to which it is attached. In case any run of iron conduit has a part built into the structure and a part fastened to the surface thereof, such part as can be removed as above specified shall be Equipment and the remainder shall be Construction.

Lighting

All parts of the subway sections of the Railroad shall be illuminated by electric lights.

The lighting of the subway sections of the Railroad shall be of the most reliable character and shall be from an independent source from that supplying the power for the trains. It shall preferably be arranged to receive power from two different sources and arranged so that the light will automatically be maintained in case of the failure of either supply.

Fixtures and fittings shall be of substantial design and construction in all respects suitable for work of this character.

Tunnel lighting

Between stations sufficient light shall be provided at all points for the proper inspection of all parts of the Railroad. This illumination shall be not less than that supplied by one sixteen (16) candle power light to each forty (40) feet of single track. All lights in the line of vision and interfering with the view of signal lights shall be protected by a suitable shield, cutting off the light in the direction of the signal lights.

Station lighting

All points of the elevated or subway station platforms and the stairways and escalators leading thereto and all toilet rooms, ticket offices, news stands and other parts of the station shall have a general illumination at least equivalent to that provided by one sixteen (16) candle power light for each fifty (50) square feet of floor space. At all points within the station the light shall, however, be not less than one foot-candle at a point three feet above the floor and the arrangement of lights shall be such as to give this degree of illumination.

Upon stairways, ticket offices and at any other places where additional lights may be required, the same shall be installed as a part of the Equipment.

Heating

All ticket offices, toilet rooms, news stands, signal towers, store rooms, shops, and all similar rooms and offices in the subway sections shall be heated by electric heaters of ample capacity to maintain these rooms at a comfortable temperature under any conditions of outside temperature.

Suitable stoves shall be installed and connected for heating the waiting rooms of the elevated stations, and such other rooms upon the elevated structure as permit of this course. All rooms upon the elevated sections not conveniently heated by stoves shall be provided with electric heaters as specified for the subway.

Elevators and escalators

At all points indicated upon the plans and at any other points where these devices may be necessary, suitable elevators or moving stairways shall be installed of size and construction approved by the Commission.

All pits and permanent parts of the structure in which these devices are installed shall be a part of Construction, and all motors, machinery, cages, ropes and any other material or devices of a movable character shall be a part of Equipment.

Motive power

The motive power shall be electricity, supplied through cables to the contact rails and track, all as above specified. It shall be supplied at approximately 600 volts direct current or in such other manner as may be approved by the Commission.

The motive power shall be such as to permit an interchange of equipment with the existing subways and with other similar railroads now operating in the City.

Power stations

One or more power houses and the necessary sub-stations shall be located, designed and constructed to accommodate all of the generating and transforming equipment required for the full and complete operation of the Railroad to the limit of its capacity. These buildings shall be of the best fire-proof construction and of a design presenting an attractive appearance, in keeping with the magnitude of the work.

The equipment of the power houses and sub-stations shall be of the most modern construction and designed for the most economical operation. It shall be complete in all details, including boilers, stokers, pumps, engines, generators, switching devices, motors, rotary converters, transformers, and all other electrical or mechanical apparatus and devices required for the operation of the Railroad. In case the Contractor proposes to install a partial equipment for the initial operation, he shall obtain the approval of the Commission upon the equipment proposed, as required under the Operation Provisions.

The power and sub-stations complete, as above specified, together with all real estate required therefor, shall be provided as a part of Equipment.

Rolling stock

Cars for passenger service shall be provided in sufficient number and of proper design to operate the Railroad to the limit of its capacity as herein provided. However, should traffic require it and should it develop that more cars can be operated, the Contractor shall, under the instruction of the Commission, provide such additional cars and operate the same as a part of Equipment.

Should the Contractor, with the approval of the Commission, provide only a partial equipment of rolling stock for initial operation, such equipment shall at all times be of such an amount and of such a character as may be required by the Commission, as specified under the Operation Provisions.

Cars, freight or express cars or other rolling stock required for the operation of the road shall be provided complete as a part of Equipment.

Design of cars

Passenger cars shall be constructed only of steel or other fire-proof materials, unless specially authorized by the Engineer, and shall be designed and constructed to eliminate to the utmost all loose and rattling parts. Only the best workmanship and material shall enter into their construction.

They shall present an attractive appearance both from within and without, shall be provided with approved means for thorough ventilation, and shall be arranged to facilitate to the utmost the quick discharge and loading of passengers.

Cars shall be designed of such dimensions as can conveniently be operated in the subway.

All details of car design and construction shall be approved by the Commission.

Equipment of cars

Passenger cars shall be properly equipped in all details for the safe and rapid transportation of passengers over the line of the Railroad. All modern safety devices or appliances which are in use for service of this kind or which in the opinion of the Engineer will improve the service or increase the safety of operation, shall be included in the car equipment.

Brakes

All cars shall be equipped with approved pneumatic brakes, with special provisions for the stopping of long trains in emergencies without damage to any part of the Equipment. Suitable devices shall be applied to all cars which will automatically apply the brakes and bring the train to a stop in the shortest possible distance, in the event of the train passing a danger signal or in the event of an accident to the motorman.

Motors

The electrical equipment of the cars shall preferably be such that all cars are motor cars; other systems may, however, be submitted to the Commission for approval, but in any event shall have sufficient motor equipment to operate the schedules as hereinbefore provided.

Control The equipment for the control of the motors shall be of an approved automatic type, giving a smooth acceleration, and shall be provided with the necessary safety devices and so installed as to reduce to a minimum the possibility of a serious short circuit at any point above the floor of the car.

Lighting The cars shall be illuminated by electric lamps so arranged and of such candle power that passengers in any part of the car will at all times have ample light for reading. An approved method of emergency lighting shall be installed, which shall provide an illumination equivalent to at least five (5) four (4) candle power lamps per car for a period of not less than two hours in case of failure of the power lines from which the regular lighting is supplied.

Heating All cars shall be electrically heated. The heaters for this purpose shall be so arranged and connected that the heat shall be evenly distributed throughout the car and sufficient heat shall be provided to maintain the cars at a temperature not less than 40 degrees F. under any conditions of outside air. Heaters shall be divided into not less than three graduations and no heater shall attain a temperature in regular operation liable to injure the clothing of the passengers.

SCHEDULE OF STATIONS ON THE RAILROAD

In the Borough of Manhattan

In Battery Park. (*Express and Terminal Station.*)

On Church Street, at Rector Street.

On Church Street, between Cortlandt and Dey Streets.

On Broadway, between Murray and Warren Streets. (*Express Station.*)

On Centre Street, at Chambers Street.

On Centre Street, at Canal Street.

On Delancey Street, at the Bowery.

On Broadway, at Canal Street. (*Express Station. This Station also includes the Broadway Station of the Canal Street Route.*)

On Watts Street, at Washington Street.

On Canal Street, at West Broadway.

On Canal Street, at Broadway. (*This Station is included in the Canal Street Station of the Lexington Avenue Route.*)

On Broadway, at Prince Street.

On Broadway, at 8th Street.

On Irving Place, at East 14th Street.

On Lexington Avenue, at East 23d Street.

On Lexington Avenue, at East 28th Street.

On Lexington Avenue, at East 34th Street.

On Lexington Avenue, between East 42d and East 43d Streets. (*Express Station.*)

On Lexington Avenue, at East 51st Street.

On Lexington Avenue, at East 59th Street.

On Lexington Avenue, at East 68th Street.

On Lexington Avenue, at East 77th Street.

On Lexington Avenue, at East 86th Street. (*Express Station.*)

On Lexington Avenue, at East 96th Street.

On Lexington Avenue, at East 103d Street.

On Lexington Avenue, at East 110th Street.

On Lexington Avenue, at East 116th Street.

On Lexington Avenue, at East 125th Street. (*Express Station.*)

In the Borough of The Bronx

On Mott Avenue, at 138th Street.

On Mott Avenue, at 149th Street. (*Express Station.*)

On River Avenue, at 161st Street.

On River Avenue, at 167th Street.

On Jerome Avenue, at 170th Street.

On Jerome Avenue, at Belmont Street.

On Jerome Avenue, at 176th Street.

On Jerome Avenue, at Burnside Avenue. (*Express Station.*)

On Jerome Avenue, at 183d Street.

On Jerome Avenue, at Fordham Road.

On Jerome Avenue, at Kingsbridge Road.

Near Jerome Avenue, at 200th Street.

On Jerome Avenue, at Mosholu Parkway.

On Jerome Avenue, at Woodlawn Road. (*Express and Terminal Station.*)

On 138th Street, at Third Avenue. (*Express Station.*)

On 138th Street, at Brook Avenue.

On 138th Street, at Cypress Avenue.

On the Southern Boulevard, at St. Mary's Street.

On the Southern Boulevard, at 149th Street. (*Express Station.*)

On the Southern Boulevard, at Longwood Avenue.

On the Southern Boulevard, at Hunt's Point Road.

On Whitlock Avenue, near Westchester Avenue.

On Westchester Avenue, at Clason Point Road.

On Westchester Avenue, at St. Lawrence Avenue.

On Westchester Avenue, at 177th Street. (*Express Station.*)

On Westchester Avenue, at Castle Hill Avenue.

On Westchester Avenue, at Zerega Avenue.

On Westchester Avenue, at Westchester Square.

On Westchester Avenue, at Middletown Road.

On Westchester Avenue, at Buhre Avenue.

On Westchester Avenue, at Pelham Bay Park. (*Express and Terminal Station.*)

In the Borough of Brooklyn

On Flatbush Avenue Extension, at Gold Street.

On Flatbush Avenue Extension, at DeKalb Avenue.

On Lafayette Avenue, at South Portland Avenue.

On Lafayette Avenue, at Vanderbilt Avenue.

On Lafayette Avenue, at Ryerson Street.

On Lafayette Avenue, at Franklin Avenue.

On Lafayette Avenue, at Nostrand Avenue.

On Lafayette Avenue, at Tompkins Avenue.

On Lafayette Avenue, at Sumner Avenue.

On Kossuth Place, between Broadway and Bushwick Avenue.

On Broadway, at Marcy Avenue. (*Express Station.*)

On Broadway, at Lorimer Street.

On Broadway, at Flushing Avenue.

On Broadway, at Myrtle Avenue.

On Broadway, at Lafayette Avenue. (*Express Station.*)

On Fourth Avenue, at Pacific Street. (*Express Station.*)

On Fourth Avenue, at Union Street.

On Fourth Avenue, at 9th Street.

On Fourth Avenue, at Prospect Avenue.

On Fourth Avenue, at 25th Street.

On Fourth Avenue, at 36th Street. (*Express Station.*)

On Fourth Avenue, at 45th Street.

On Fourth Avenue, at 52nd Street.

On Fourth Avenue, at 60th street.

On Fourth Avenue, at Bay Ridge Avenue. (*Express Station.*)

On Fourth Avenue, at 77th Street.

On Fourth Avenue, at 86th Street.

On Fourth Avenue, at 92nd Street.

On Fourth Avenue, at 99th Street. (*Express Station.*)

On 40th Street, at Eighth Avenue.

On New Utrecht Avenue, at 43rd Street.

On New Utrecht Avenue, at 50th Street.

On New Utrecht Avenue, at 59th Street.

On New Utrecht Avenue, at 68th Street. (*Express Station.*)

On New Utrecht Avenue, at 79th Street.

On 86th Street, at Bay 22nd Street.

On 86th Street, at 22nd Avenue. (*Express Station.*)

On 86th Street, at 25th Avenue.

On Stillwell Avenue, at Bay 50th Street.

On Stillwell Avenue, near Surf Avenue. (*Express and Terminal Station.*)

Chapter III

OPERATION PROVISIONS

Subject and term of Operation Provisions

Article LXIII. The Contractor shall hold the right to the possession of the Railroad for a term of *

(*   ) years, and shall use the Railroad only for strictly railroad purposes and for such purposes as are hereinafter expressly mentioned.

Contractor to operate, etc.

Article LXIV. The Contractor hereby agrees to equip and to maintain and operate the Railroad during the whole of the said term in strict conformity with the provisions of this contract and the provisions of the Public Service Commissions Law. Should there be any apparent conflict between the provisions of this contract or the specifications thereof and the provisions of the Public Service Commissions Law the provisions of the Public Service Commissions Law shall in all cases govern. The provisions of this contract and of the specifications shall be without

*Fill in with term specified in Contractor's Proposal.

prejudice to the enforcement of the Public Service Commissions Law.

ARTICLE LXV. The term of the Operation Provisions shall begin on the date when any part of the Railroad is declared by the Commission to be completed and ready for operation as hereinafter provided. At the end of the said term or at the earlier termination of this contract, the Contractor shall surrender possession of the Railroad to the City or to a new contractor as hereinafter provided.

When term begins

ARTICLE LXVI. The Contractor shall keep all his accounts having to do in any way with the construction, equipment, maintenance or operation of the Railroad in accordance with the provisions of the Public Service Commissions Law and any uniform system of accounts now or hereafter established by the Commission thereunder.

How accounts shall be kept

In case the Public Service Commissions Law shall be repealed or modified so as to take from the Commission the power it now possesses to establish a uniform system of accounts such power shall devolve under and in pursuance of this contract as provided in Article XIX hereof.

From revenue to be deducted

ARTICLE LXVII. From any and all income and increase derived by the Contractor or on his behalf in any manner from the enterprise of constructing, equipping, maintaining and operating the Railroad (hereinafter in this article referred to as the "revenue") he shall at the end of each quarter year deduct:

Operating expenses

(1) All expenses actually and necessarily incurred in the administration, maintenance and operation of the Railroad.

Taxes

(2) All taxes, rates and assessments of whatsoever character (except special assessments, if any, for betterments which shall be paid by the

Contractor and treated as part of the cost of construction or equipment), save as provided in paragraphs (11) and (12) of Article VI.

(3) The Contractor shall, during the first three years of the term, pay all expenses of maintenance as a part of the expenses of operation referred to in paragraph (1) hereof. At the end of such period the Commission will prescribe an amount which the Contractor shall deduct and set aside in a separate fund for depreciation. The cost of all repairs, replacements and renewals to the Railroad and Equipment, due either to its wearing out or obsolesence, inadequacy or age, shall be chargeable to and payable from this fund. The cost of additions to the Railroad or to the Equipment shall not, however, be paid from this fund but shall be chargeable to and paid from the capital account and

Depreciation fund

treated in all respects as part of the cost of constructing and equipping the Railroad. The amount of such reserve for depreciation shall be subject to readjustment by the Commission from time to time. Any amounts in such fund not currently needed for the purposes herein specified shall be invested and reinvested and all accumulations and accretions added to such fund. If at any such time it be determined by the Commission that any part of such fund shall not have been needed for any of the purposes for which it shall have been set aside, such part shall be transferred to the contingent reserve fund mentioned in paragraph (6) of this article.

Amortization fund

(4) * (%) per centum of the cost of construction as determined according to the provisions of this contract for the quarter preceding

* To be filled in with percentage specified in Contractor's Proposal.

the date of payment, which shall be paid quarterly into a separate fund, and held in such fund and with interest and accretions securely invested and reinvested to amortize the cost of construction.

Fund to pay off discounts

(5) An amount, in the judgment of the Commission, sufficient with accrued interest, and any premiums which the Contractor may have received from the sale of stocks and bonds or other evidences of indebtedness, to pay off, within a period of ten years from the date when operation of any part of the Railroad shall actually begin (which period may be extended by the Commission), any discount on bonds or other evidences of indebtedness issued to pay the cost of construction and the cost of equipment. Any balance in this fund after the payment of such discount or any amount in excess of the sum needed shall be trans-

ferred to the contingent reserve fund hereinafter provided for.

Contingent reserve fund

(6) One quarter of one ($\frac{1}{4}$ of 1%) per centum of the revenue which with interest and accretions shall be securely invested and reinvested to provide a contingent reserve fund. When such fund with interest and accretions shall equal five per centum (5%) of the cost of construction and the cost of equipment, payments to such fund shall be suspended and interest thereon shall be included in the revenue. If thereafter such fund shall fall below such five per centum (5%), payments at the rate aforesaid shall be resumed until the fund with interest and accretions again equals said five per centum (5%). Such fund shall be used to meet deficits in the operation of the Railroad and in the amount available for the payment of the interest hereinafter in this article

provided for and for such other purposes as may from time to time be permitted by the Commission. At the end of the term or sooner termination of this contract as herein provided the balance then remaining of such fund shall be divided share and share alike between the City and the Contractor.

(7) * (%) per centum per annum, payable quarterly to the Contractor and to the City upon the investment of the Contractor and the City in the Railroad and Equipment, determined as in this contract provided, for the quarter year preceding the date of payment. Such investment shall mean, as to the Contractor, the cost of construction and the cost of equipment determined as herein provided, and as to the City (1) the cost of construction of the portion of the Railroad constructed or under construction by it (excluding the cost of constructing the bridges over the East River but including the cost of construction of the

Interest on cost

* To be filled in with percentage specified in Contractor's Proposal.

tracks and ties thereon); (2) the net cost of all real estate or interests therein acquired by the City for the portion of the Railroad (excluding such bridges) constructed or under construction by it; (3) the net cost to the City of all real estate or interests therein acquired by the City for the portion of the Railroad constructed by the Contractor; and (4) interest at the rate of four and one-half (4½) per centum per annum upon items (1), (2) and (3) prior to the beginning of operation. The amount of the City's investment shall be determined by a statement or statements of the Comptroller showing the amount of bonds issued by the City for such purposes. If the revenue after deducting the payments hereinbefore in this article required shall not equal the amount necessary for the payment of all the interest provided for in this paragraph due the City and the Contractor, the Contractor shall pay to each that proportion of the amount available that the investment of each bears to the combined investment of both. If in any quarter year the revenue, after deducting the payments hereinbefore in this article provided, shall not be sufficient to allow the payment to the City and to the Contractor of all the interest provided for in this paragraph, the division between the City and the Contractor hereinafter in this article provided for shall be deferred until the Railroad shall have earned such interest as remains unpaid.

(8) After making such payments, all amounts remaining shall be divided share and share alike between the Contractor and the City. The City's share shall be paid by the Contractor as hereinafter provided.

Division between City and Contractor

ARTICLE LXVIII. The first payments under Article LXVII shall be made on the first day of January, April, July or October succeeding the

When payable

date when any part of the Railroad shall be declared by the Commission to be completed and ready for operation. Thereafter such payments shall be made on the first days of January, April, July and October in each year during the term of the Operation Provisions. Interest and accruals to the Contractor from investments or otherwise shall be pro-rated and if necessary adjusted in the payments for the quarter succeeding the quarter in which they are actually paid to him. Any other readjustment of payments that in the opinion of the Commission is necesary shall be made (for the whole of the year preceding) upon the first day of July in any year.

Contractor to deliver statements of earnings

ARTICLE LXIX. The amounts payable to the City under paragraphs (7) and (8) of Article LXVII shall be paid to the Comptroller at the times specified in the last preceding article and the Contractor shall deliver to the Commission and to the Comptroller at the time of each payment a statement in the form and with details to be prescribed by the Commission showing the receipts and disbursements of the Contractor for the preceding quarter. Such statement shall be verified under oath by the Contractor or by the treasurer of the Contractor, or, in case of his absence or inability, then by its president, or other chief officer or manager.

Right of verification

ARTICLE LXX. The Comptroller and the Commission shall have the right to verify any of the said statements by an examination of the Contractor's and sub-Contractor's books, records and memoranda and the examination under oath of any of its officers or servants; and the Contractor hereby covenants that his officers and servants shall submit to such examination and produce such books, records and memoranda whenever and wherever they may be required by the Commission and the Comptroller.

Article LXXI. The Contractor shall hold the amortization fund provided for in paragraph (4) of Article LXVII in trust for the benefit of his bondholders and other creditors to whom he is indebted on account of the cost of construction. The Contractor covenants that such amortization fund shall be deemed to bear interest at the rate of* (%) compounded semi-annually and assumes the unqualified obligation—whether in fact the cost of construction shall actually be so paid or not—to discharge the cost of construction, including the cost of construction of all additions to or changes in the Railroad hereinafter provided for, at the rate that the percentage of the cost of construction specified in

*To be filled in with percentage specified in Contractor's Proposal.

paragraph (4) of Article LXVII, with interest at the rate specified in this Article compounded semi-annually, would discharge the cost of construction; and failure to so discharge the cost of construction shall be without prejudice to the City's rights hereunder and the City may take over the Railroad either at the end of the term or at any time after the expiration of ten years from the date when operation of any part of the Railroad shall actually begin whether the Contractor has actually discharged the cost of construction at the rate specified or not. For convenience an amortization table computed at such rates is here added and all payments that may be made by the City for construction shall be based thereon.†

†Before the contract is executed such amortization table will be here inserted.

Contractor to equip Railroad

Article LXXII. The Contractor shall, at his own expense, provide a complete equipment of the Railroad, and shall at all times during the term of this contract keep upon the Railroad cars, motors and other equipment, which shall be adequate to the requirements of the traveling public. The equipment so to be supplied shall include all such rolling stock, machinery, power houses, real estate and appliances or devices for various purposes as are or may be included in the definition of the word "Equipment" in Chapter I of this contract.

Construction of power houses, etc., may be deferred

The construction or completion of the power house or power houses and sub-stations for generation or furnishing of motive power may, with the consent of the Commission, be suspended during a period of ten years from the date when any part of the Railroad shall be declared by the Commission to be completed and ready for operation; provided that during such period there shall, when required, be available for use, in lieu of such power house or power houses and sub-stations, motive power furnished to the Contractor under and pursuant to the terms of a contract for the purchase of power, which contract shall, as to the parties thereto, the sureties thereon and the terms thereof, be first approved by the Commission. In case of the expiration or termination of this contract as hereinafter provided, any sub-contract for the furnishing of power may be terminated or taken over by the City without making any allowance or paying any amount to the Contractor for or on account of any unexpired term of such sub-contract.

Equipment to be ready before construction is completed

ARTICLE LXXIII. At a date not later than the time when one-half (½) in value of the work which the Contractor shall be bound to do, not including Equipment, shall have been finished and the Engineer shall so certify, the Contractor shall begin and shall thereafter diligently proceed with the provision of the Equipment of the Railroad, and such provision shall proceed at such rate that sufficient Equipment shall be completely ready to put any portion of the Railroad into immediate operation as soon as completed.

Motive power

ARTICLE LXXIV. The motive power shall be electricity, which shall be so used as to involve no combustion in the tunnels nor any injury to the purity of the air in the tunnels,—provided, however, that if in the future development of the railway art any method of generating or transmitting power superior to electricity and involving no injury to the purity of the air in the tunnels or in the cars shall be discovered to be practicable, then the Contractor shall have the right to adopt such different method if approved by the Commission, and the Commission shall have the right to require the adoption of such different method if in its opinion its adoption is necessary to insure safe and adequate service. If such different method shall be adopted then the Contractor shall provide and maintain equipment for the generation and transmission of power by such different method at least equal in completeness, efficiency and durability to the Equipment as provided to be used at the commencement of the term of the Operation Provisions. Any such change of motive power shall be made only upon general and detailed plans and specifications prepared by the Commission or prepared by the Contractor and approved by the Commission.

Character of equipment

ARTICLE LXXV. The cars, rolling stock and all other parts of the Equipment shall be of the best character known at the time to the art of intraurban railway operation. In case of any neglect to provide and maintain rolling stock in the amount and of the character above specified, the Commission may, upon notice, require the defect to be made good; and, if the defect shall not forthwith and upon such notice be made good, then the Commission shall be at liberty, in addition to the City's other remedies for a breach of this contract, either by contract or otherwise as it may see fit, to make good such defect; and for such purpose the Commission shall, so far and for such time as may be necessary or convenient, be entitled to enter upon or take possession of any part of the Railroad or Equipment. The Contractor shall forthwith repay to the City the cost to which it shall be put in making good any such defect.

Schedules of equipment to be filed

ARTICLE LXXVI. At the time that the Railroad is one-half completed, as certified by the certificate of the Commission, as provided in Article IX, the Contractor shall file with the Commission in duplicate a true schedule of the Equipment to be furnished by him for the initial operation of the Railroad. Such schedule shall be in detail and shall be prepared in such form as may be prescribed by the Commission. Such schedule shall be subject to the approval of the Commission, and if disapproved the Contractor shall make such additions thereto or changes therein as may be required by the Commission. After the operation of the Railroad shall have begun the Contractor shall within thirty days after the first day of January in each year file with the Commission a like schedule of the Equipment on such first day of January. Every such schedule shall be verified by the affidavit of the general manager or other officer of the Contractor who shall be in the general care and control of the Equipment, and who shall in such affidavit state that he is in such general care and control.

Equipment to be kept in good order

ARTICLE LXXVII. The Equipment of the Railroad shall be at all times kept by the Contractor in thoroughly good order and repair; and the Contractor hereby expressly covenants to and with the City that the Contractor will not at any time within three years before the end of the term of the Operation Provisions permit the Equipment to be less in quantity or inferior in quality to the Equipment as it shall have been at any prior time during the term of the Operation Provisions.

Article LXXVIII. The lien of the City upon the Equipment shall be applicable to all Equipment at any time provided by the Contractor during the term of the Operation Provisions in like manner as to the Equipment provided by the Contractor prior to the commencement of said term.

City's lien on equipment

Article LXXIX. The Commission reserves the right to permit other persons, firms and corporations and the City to use the tracks, structure and line equipment of the portion of the Seventh and Eighth avenue route included in this contract and referred to in Article III hereof. If the Commission determines that the use of such entire portion is necessary, such persons, firms or corporations or the City shall take over the same and shall pay the Contractor the cost of construction of the same and of the equipment

Reservation of trackage rights

thereof, such cost to be determined by the Engineer subject to review by arbitration in the manner prescribed herein for determining cost of construction and equipment. If the Commission determines that the use of less than such entire portion is necessary the conditions and compensation for such use shall be as hereinafter provided.

The Commission reserves the right to permit other persons, firms and corporations and the City to use the tracks, structure and line equipment of the Railroad, or any portion thereof, but, except as regards the portion referred to in the preceding paragraph, the Contractor shall not under the provisions hereof be deprived of any portion of the use of the Railroad that, in the opinion of the Commission, is necessary for his operations. Such persons, firms or corporations or the City shall pay to the Contractor at the end of each quarter year during such use, as compensation therefor, that proportion, determined by the Commission, of the payments the Contractor is then making under paragraphs (1) to (8) inclusive of Article LXVII that the use by such persons, firms or corporations or the City bears to the total use then made of the Railroad. Such amount when so paid shall be treated in all respects as part of the revenue referred to in said Article. Whenever and as often as the Commission shall deem such use by other persons, firms or corporations or the City necessary it shall prescribe such rules and regulations governing such use and the payment therefor as in its judgment are necessary.

Part of railroad may be put in operation

ARTICLE LXXX. In case the Contractor is of the opinion that any portion of the Railroad can be advantageously used before the whole is completed and fully equipped the Commission may, in its discretion, upon the request of the Contractor and not otherwise, declare such part of the Railroad to be ready for operation, and may fix a date from which operation shall begin, and give notice thereof to the Contractor. But no such declaration or notice shall operate as an extension of the time within which the Railroad must be entirely constructed and equipped, or as a waiver of the right of the City to damages for unexcused delay as above provided, or as a waiver of any other right of the City.

Contractor's assurance of character of railroad

ARTICLE LXXXI. The Contractor, by Chapter II of this contract, has agreed to construct the Railroad so that the same shall be an intra-urban railway of the very best character according to the highest modern standard, in respect of safety, speed and convenience and in all other respects.

The Contractor covenants to and with the City that at the time when the term of the Operation Provisions shall begin the portion of the Railroad constructed by him, so far as declared by the Commission ready for operation, shall be a complete railway of the character aforesaid ready for immediate and continuous operation, and that the same shall, at the time of the commencement of the said term, be a railway in all respects conforming to all and every of the requirements of this contract. The Contractor shall at no time and in no event be at liberty to object to the plans or specifications upon which such portion of the Railroad has been constructed, or the manner of its construction, maintenance or operation.

Contractor to observe highest standard of railway operation

ARTICLE LXXXII. The Contractor covenants to and with the City that the Contractor will, during the term hereof, operate the Railroad carefully and skillfully, according to the then highest known standards of railway operation, and the highest regard to the safety of the passengers and employees thereof and of all other persons. Mechanical and other devices for safety shall be of the then very best known character.

Safety

Facilities and services to be adequate

ARTICLE LXXXIII. The Contractor shall operate the Railroad as one complete system and shall afford such facilities and services as shall in all respects be adequate. Free transfers shall be given between all trains operated by the Contractor at the crossing at Canal street and Broadway in the Borough of Manhattan and at such other points, as may be required by the Commission, where the portions of the Railroad as constructed or as may hereafter be extended shall intersect other portions thereof.

ARTICLE LXXXIV. The Contractor hereby covenants to and with the City that it will save the City harmless of and from all claims of every nature arising from injuries to passengers, employees or other persons by reason of negligence on the part of the Contractor or of any of its employees, and all other claims by reason of the operation and maintenance of the Railroad, except those against which the City by this contract assures the Contractor, provided, however, that the provisions of this Article shall not prevent the Contractor from including any such damages in operating expenses .

City to be indemnified against claims for injuries, etc.

ARTICLE LXXXV. The Contractor shall run local trains and express trains, and if required by the Commission shall run trains part of the way as local and part of the way as express trains. The local trains shall be run at a speed on the average

Trains, their speed, frequency, etc.

(stops at stations included) of not less than fifteen miles an hour. The express trains shall be run at a speed on the average (stops at stations included) of not less than twenty-five miles an hour. The Contractor shall furnish such services and facilities as shall be safe and adequate and in all respects just and reasonable.

Fares

ARTICLE LXXXVI. The Contractor shall not during the term hereof charge for a single fare upon the Railroad to exceed the sum of five (5) cents unless otherwise permitted by the Commission.

Advertisements and trade prohibited

ARTICLE LXXXVII. No part of the Railroad or stations or other appurtenances constructed under this contract shall be used for advertising purposes, except that the Contractor may use the structure for posting necessary information for the public relative to the running of trains and to the operation of the Railroad; nor shall any trade, traffic or occupation, other than required for the operation of the Railroad, be permitted thereon or in the stations thereof, except such sale of newspapers and periodicals as may from time to time, always with the right of revocation, be permitted by the Commission.

Contractor to keep railroad in good condition

ARTICLE LXXXVIII. The Contractor shall keep the stations and cars, as also the tunnels and all other parts of the Railroad, clean and free from unnecessary dampness, and in that and in all other respects in thoroughly good order and condition. The Contractor shall promptly remove from the stations and their approaches, including the sidewalks immediately adjoining the approaches, all ice and snow and all other obstructions or hindrances.

To light and heat stations, cars, etc.

ARTICLE LXXXIX. The Contractor shall suitably and thoroughly light and heat the stations and cars of the Railroad; and they shall be so lighted that passengers may conveniently read therein. Such light and heat shall be provided by electricity or such other illuminating and heating agents as may be approved by the Commission.

Waiting rooms

ARTICLE XC. The Contractor shall keep the waiting-rooms, including toilets, in clean and comfortable condition and provide therein proper seating capacity and good drinking water.

Ventilation

ARTICLE XCI. The Contractor shall cause all tunnels, stations and cars of the Railroad to be thoroughly ventilated with pure air, using artificial ventilation when needed to supply pure or cooler air.

Tunnels to be lighted

ARTICLE XCII. The Contractor shall keep all tunnels sufficiently lighted at all times to permit the tracks and walls and roofs of the tunnels to be clearly visible for inspection.

Article XCIII. The Contractor shall at all times during the term of the Operation Provisions provide all reasonable conveniences for the inspection of the Railroad and Equipment and every part thereof by the Commission, its members, its engineers and subordinates. The members of the Commission, its engineers and subordinates shall at any time upon its authority have access to any part of the Railroad or Equipment or to any materials for the Equipment which may be in process of manufacture or assembling. Inspection

Article XCIV. The Contractor shall, under such rules and regulations as may from time to time be made by the Commission, carry free the members, engineers and subordinates of Provision for free transportation the Commission when necessary for the inspection of the Railroad or any part thereof.

Contractor to make necessary alterations

ARTICLE XCV. The Contractor shall not be relieved from the foregoing obligations of the Operation Provisions relative to the cleaning, lighting, ventilating and maintaining the tunnels and stations, by reason of anything contained in the plans or specifications upon which the Railroad has been constructed, but shall be bound (if any alterations in the structure are necessary in order to comply fully with the said obligations) to make all needful alterations at his own expense as part of the cost of construction, subject, however, in every case to the approval and consent of the Commission.

Repairs and replacements

ARTICLE XCVI. The Contractor shall during the term of the Operation Provisions keep the

Railroad and its Equipment and each and every part thereof in thorough repair, and shall restore and replace every part thereof which may wear out or cease to be useful, so that at all times and at the end or sooner termination of the Operation Provisions the Railroad shall be in thoroughly good and solid condition and fully and perfectly equipped presently ready for continuous and practical operation to the full limit of its capacity. If at any time the Commission or its Engineer shall notify the Contractor of any loss, wear, decay or defect in the Railroad or the Equipment, such loss, wear, decay or defect shall forthwith be completely remedied by the Contractor, so far as the same interferes or is inconsistent with the thoroughly good and solid condition of the Railroad or its Equipment as aforesaid, or with the continuous or practical operation thereof to its full limit as aforesaid. If the Contractor shall neglect or refuse to remedy such loss, wear, decay or defect, promptly and completely, the Commission may, in addition to the City's other remedies in such manner, whether by contract or otherwise, as it may deem proper, procure such loss, wear, decay or defect to be supplied and remedied, and for such purpose shall be entitled, so far as it shall deem necessary or convenient, to enter upon the Railroad; and the Contractor shall forthwith, upon the demand of the Commission, pay to the City the entire cost incurred by the City in supplying such loss or wear or in remedying such decay or defect.

Commission may order additions, changes, etc.

ARTICLE XCVII. The principal object of the City in making this contract is to secure for the public convenience an adequate, comfortable and rapid system of passenger traffic in the portions of New York that will be served by the Railroad. By the foregoing provisions of the Operation Provisions the Contractor has covenanted, among other things, to operate the Railroad carefully and skillfully, according to the highest known standards of railway operation at the time; to supply adequate rolling-stock; to run trains so as to meet reasonable requirements of the public; to use the best safety devices; to keep the stations and cars clean, dry, well lighted and warmed; to keep water-closets in sanitary condition; to cause all tunnels, stations and cars to be thoroughly ventilated; and to do other things, as hereinbefore set forth, for the convenience and accommodation of the public. These covenants on the part of the Contractor are among the principal considerations moving to the City in making this contract, and any breach thereof will entitle the City to the remedies provided in this contract or by the Rapid Transit Act. If the Commission shall at any time be of the opinion that any additions to the rolling stock or other equipment, or any additions to or changes in the Railroad are necessary, or that additional terminal or storage facilities or additional tracks are required, or that any change in the mode of operating the Railroad or conducting his business is necessary in order to carry out the purposes of the Operation Provisions or to promote the security, convenience and accommodation of the public, the Commission may direct the making of such additions, improvements or changes as the Commission deems proper. Such changes or additions shall be made to the satisfaction of the Commission and under such plans, specifications and directions as it may issue. If the Contractor shall neglect or refuse to comply with such directions, the Commission in addition to the City's other remedies for a breach of this contract may cause such changes or additions to be made at the expense of the Contractor or may treat such neglect or refusal as a breach of this contract.

Engineer to determine cost

ARTICLE XCVIII. The cost of construction of the additions to or changes in the Railroad, and the cost of additional Equipment provided for in Article XCVII, shall be determined as follows: The Engineer shall, on or about the first days of January, April, July and October during the course of the construction of such additions or changes or provision of additional equipment, render a determination in writing, in duplicate, to the Commission and to the Contractor, of the cost of construction of such additions or changes or of the cost of such additional equipment to the date of the last day of the last preceding quarter, including therein separately a determination of the cost of construction of such additions or changes or of the cost of such additional equipment during the quarter year immediately preceding the date of such determination. If either the Commission or the Contractor shall be dissatisfied with such separate determination or any item or items thereof, it or he shall within twenty (20) days after the receipt of such determination file with the Engineer a statement in writing of the item or items objected to and the reasons for such objection. If within such period of twenty (20) days the Commission or the Contractor shall fail to file such statement with the Engineer, such separate determination shall be final and conclusive upon the party so failing. The Engineer shall thereupon reconsider such determination, or any item or items thereof, so objected to and shall state his conclusions thereon in his determination for the quarter year succeeding the quarter year for which the determination so objected to was made. Such redetermination shall be final and conclusive unless the Commission or the Contractor shall within twenty (20) days after the receipt thereof appeal therefrom to the Board of Arbitration in this article provided for. The appeal shall be taken by a written notice addressed, if the Commission be the appellant, to the Contractor, or, if the Contractor be the appellant then to the Secretary of the Commission. The notice of appeal shall state the determination appealed from, the grounds of appeal, the precise award or redress desired, and shall include the appointment of a disinterested person as arbitrator on the part of the appellant, with a written acceptance by the arbi-

Subject to review by arbitration

trator of the appointment. Within twenty days after the receipt of such notice the party receiving the same shall name a disinterested person as an arbitrator and give written notice of such nomination to the other party, the notice to be accompanied by a written acceptance by the arbitrator of the appointment. If the party to whom the notice of arbitration is given shall not so nominate an arbitrator, who shall so accept, then the arbitrator named by the party giving the first notice shall be the sole arbitrator. Any vacancy in the office of an arbitrator so appointed shall be filled by the party which shall have appointed the last incumbent thereof within ten days after receiving from the other party written notice of the vacancy, during which ten days the running of other periods of time prescribed for or in course of the arbitration shall be suspended. If not so filled or if written notice of the appointment be not given within such ten days the remaining arbitrator shall be the sole arbitrator. The Commission and the Contractor shall select a disinterested person as the third arbitrator; but if they fail to agree upon such third arbitrator within ten days after the date of the appointment of the second arbitrator appointed, the third arbitrator (who shall be a disinterested person) shall be named by the Executive Committee for the time being of the Chamber of Commerce of the State of New York; or if within thirty days after being requested by either of the parties to make such nomination said Committee shall decline or fail to make a nomination then an arbitrator shall be named by the Executive Committee for the time being of the Association of the Bar of The City of New York. Any arbitrator appointed by the

Commission may at any time be removed by the Commission and likewise any arbitrator appointed by the Contractor may at any time be removed by the Contractor. The arbitrators shall hear the parties and their counsel or any statements or evidence which the parties, or either of them, desire to submit and may resort to any other sources of information in reference to the question submitted for determination. Within thirty days after the appointment of the third arbitrator, unless such time shall be extended for good cause by written order of the arbitrators, the arbitrators shall make their determination in duplicate, one to be delivered to the Commission and the other to the Contractor. In case any vacancy shall at any time occur by reason of the death, resignation or inability to serve of any arbitrator, a disinterested person shall be appointed to succeed him in the same manner as above provided in the original appointment of such arbitrator. Any determination by a majority of the arbitrators shall be final and conclusive. Every arbitrator shall be deemed employed by both the City and the Contractor but the fees and expenses of the arbitrators shall be borne and paid by the Contractor upon vouchers to be approved by the Commission and such fees and expenses shall be deemed a part of the cost of construction or of the cost of equipment as the case may be. Every such arbitrator shall before proceeding to consider the matter be sworn, as nearly as may be in the same manner as referees in actions at law are required to be sworn. Provided, however, that if in any case or for any reason an arbitration cannot validly be had as aforesaid then the City or the Contractor, if in no way responsible for the failure of the arbitration, may bring such action or suit as either of them may be advised for the purpose of determining any of the matters for which the arbitration is herein provided.

Remedies of City in case of Contractor's default

ARTICLE XCIX. In case of default of the Contractor in paying the rental herein provided or in case of the failure or neglect of the Contractor faithfully to observe, keep and fulfill any of the conditions, obligations and requirements of the Operation Provisions, the City, by the Commission, may:

City may take possession and as agent for the Contractor

(1) After notice to the Contractor of at least ten (10) days, take possession of the Railroad and Equipment, and, as the agent of the Contractor, either

operate the railroad

(*a*) Maintain and operate the Railroad and use thereon the Equipment (without commencing any proceeding for the enforcement of its lien thereon) for the full unexpired term of the Operation Provisions or such shorter period as the Commission may determine; or

(*b*) Enter into a new contract with some other person, firm or corporation for the maintenance and operation of the Railroad and use of the Equipment for any period of time not exceeding the unexpired term of the Operation Provisions. **or make a sub-contract**

In either of the above cases, the total annual income and increase payable to, or derived by, the City from the enterprise of the construction, equipment, maintenance and operation of the Railroad shall, after deducting the payments mentioned in paragraphs (1) to (6) inclusive of Article LXVII, and adequate compensation, to be determined by the Commission, to such new contractor, be deemed to be the net annual income. Out of such net annual income the City shall retain interest in full upon its investment at the rate specified in paragraph (7) of Article LXVII and, if there then be any balance, shall then pay to the Contractor interest upon his investment at the rate specified in paragraph (7) of

Article LXVII, or so much thereof as the amount available will permit. Any compensation made to such new contractor shall be deemed to be a payment on account to the Contractor of interest upon his investment under paragraph (7) of Article LXVII. All amounts then remaining shall be divided share and share alike between the Contractor and the City. If, however, such net annual income shall in any year be less than the interest in full upon the City's investment, at the rate specified in paragraph (7) of Article LXVII, then and in every such case the Contractor and the sureties on his Bond shall be and continue jointly and severally liable to the City, or any deposit of cash or securities held in lieu of a bond shall, as against the Contractor, be held for the amount of such deficiency until the end of the full term for which the Operation Provisions were originally made. Or

or may terminate contract

(2) The City may upon reasonable notice to the Contractor, and after reasonable notice to the Contractor to make good the default, terminate this contract; and thereupon upon such terms as to the Commission seem just and with such per-

sons or corporation as to the Commission may seem proper, make another operating contract for the residue of the term of the Contractor in default, including in such contract a provision as to a transfer to the new contractor of the lien and any other interest of the City on and in the Equipment, and in such case the Contractor shall be liable to the City for all damage by reason of such default. Or,

(3) The City may by the Commission or otherwise, bring such suit or proceeding as it may deem proper, to enforce its lien upon the Equipment or upon any cash, securities, bonds or surety obligations held, as provided in Chapter I of this contract, or for any other purpose. Or,

or may sue to enforce lien upon equipment

(4) The City may by the Commission or otherwise, but without suit, enforce by sale or otherwise its lien upon any cash, securities, bonds or securities or surety obligations held as aforesaid. Or,

or may sell securities

(5) The City may also bring any suit or proceeding for injunction or for specific performance

or may bring suit

or to recover damages or to forfeit the Operation Provisions or to obtain any relief or for any purpose proper under this contract.

or use other remedies

(6) Each and every remedy herein specifically given to the City shall be cumulative, and shall be in addition to every other remedy herein specifically given or now or hereafter existing at law or in equity or by statute, whether in the case of landlord or tenant or otherwise, and each and every remedy herein specifically given or otherwise so existing may be exercised from time to time and as often and in such order as may be deemed expedient by the Commission, and the exercise, or the beginning of the exercise, of one remedy shall not be deemed a waiver of the right to exercise, at the same time or thereafter, any other remedy, except that no two inconsistent remedies shall be exercised at the same time.

Enforcement of lien on equipment

In case the City shall become entitled to enforce its lien against the Equipment, then, at the time of beginning any suit or proceeding for the enforcement of such lien, whether by foreclosure or otherwise, or to any time thereafter, the City shall be entitled forthwith to enter into and take summary and complete possession of the Equipment, or any part thereof, it being the express intention of the contract that upon any default by the Contractor in construction, equipment or operation the City shall have the right forthwith to operate the Railroad so far as is then physically practicable (if at all), and to that end to have complete and immediate possession of all Equipment and of all other things necessary or convenient, or which may thereafter be necessary or convenient for the operation of the Railroad, which shall belong to the City or upon which the City shall have a lien as aforesaid.

In case the City shall avail itself of the provisions of this article for taking possession of the Railroad, or for making any new or other contract with respect thereto, no allowance shall be made to the Contractor by reason of any profits from operation over, or any increase of rental which the City shall reserve above the rental as specified in the Operation Provisions.

At the end of term

ARTICLE C. At the end of the term of the Operation Provisions, the City shall pay to the Contractor that percentage of the cost of construction of the additions to and changes in the Railroad, hereinbefore provided for, that at the rate specified in the amortization table forming a part of Article LXXI should remain unamortized, and shall also buy and the Contractor shall sell the equipment suitable to and used for the purposes of this contract. The right of the City so to buy shall be protected by its lien upon the equipment as aforesaid. Such purchase shall be at a reasonable price, due regard being had to the condition, wear and tear of the Equipment and its then value for railroad purposes, except that any real estate or interest therein forming part of the Equipment shall be purchased at an amount not exceeding actual cost of the same, and the purchase price of the rest of the Equipment shall not exceed the actual cost of the same plus fifteen per centum thereof. Such price for the Equipment may be fixed by agreement between the Commission and the Contractor; but if they shall not agree then such price shall be fixed by arbitration, or if the arbitration shall for any reason fail, then by appropriate suit or proceeding in the Supreme Court of the State of New York.

The City shall have the right at the termination of the Operation Provisions, whether or not the price shall have been ascertained or paid, to take possession of and use and operate all such property of the Contractor, but subject, however, to its liability to pay the value thereof to be ascertained as aforesaid with interest at the then legal rate from the time of taking possession.

Termination after ten years

ARTICLE CI. Upon giving one year's notice in writing to the Contractor the City, acting by the Commission, may terminate this contract at any time after the expiration of ten years from the date when operation of any part of the Railroad shall actually begin. Such right of termination shall, however, be upon condition as follows:

Equipment

(1) The equipment of the Railroad, suitable to and used for the purposes of this contract shall be purchased and taken by the City at an amount to be ascertained as provided in Article C.

(2) The City shall also pay to the Contractor that percentage of the cost of construction of the portion of the Railroad constructed by the Contractor, and of the cost of construction of the additions to and changes in the Railroad hereinbefore provided for (such percentage to be based upon the cost determined as herein provided to the end of the last preceding quarter year), that at the rate specified in Article LXXI should remain unamortized. In the event of the City taking over the Railroad at the expiration of ten (10) years from the date when operation of any part of the Railroad shall actually begin it shall pay in addition fifteen (15%) per centum of the cost of construction of the portion of the Railroad constructed by the Contractor (without deducting from such cost of construction any part thereof that according to the terms hereof should be amor- Construction

tized at that time) but for each year after such period of ten (10) years one fifteenth (1/15) of such fifteen (15%) per centum shall be deducted, and at and after the expiration of twenty-five (25) years from the date when operation of any part of the Railroad shall actually begin no part of such fifteen (15%) per centum shall be paid.

Title may be transferred to new contractor

ARTICLE CII. At the option of the City either at the expiration of the term of the grant or at the termination of the Contract, pursuant to notice as aforesaid, the Contractor may be required to transfer the title to and possession of the equipment and the right to the possession of the Railroad directly to a new contractor upon his paying the amount to the Contractor which the City would have been required to pay as aforesaid.

Payment

ARTICLE CIII. In case the City itself shall take over the equipment and the possession of the

Railroad such payment shall be made by a City warrant drawn by the Comptroller, or otherwise, as may then be provided by law. In case the Equipment and the right to the possession of the Railroad shall be taken over directly by a new contractor such payment shall be made by a certified check, drawn by such new contractor, to the order of the Contractor or by lawful money of the United States of America.

Article CIV. It is the intention of the parties that cost of construction, as hereinbefore defined, plus any percentage to be added, as hereinbefore provided, shall be the measure of any payments the City may be called upon to make hereunder, but if at any time in ascertaining the amount to be paid by the City as a condition of the termination, as hereinafter provided, or at the expiration of the full term, it shall be necessary, as in the case of Valuation

Equipment, that the valuation of any plant, property, equipment, construction or any investment in any thereof shall be determined, such valuation shall, in default of agreement, be determined by arbitration or by the Court.

If amounts not determined

ARTICLE CV. If the amounts to be paid to the Contractor at the end of the term or upon any such termination shall not have been finally determined or paid prior to or at the time when term is according to this contract to end or the termination is under the said notice given to take effect the title to and right of possession of the Equipment, and the right of possession of the Railroad shall nevertheless pass to the City or to a new contractor, free and clear of all liens or other incumbrances, in which event the City or such new contractor shall pay to the Contractor the amount so determined with interest from the date of taking possession, provided, however, that title to and possession of the Equipment and possession of the Railroad shall not pass to such new contractor in advance of payment as aforesaid unless such new contractor shall give the Contractor a bond to be approved by the Commission both as to amount and sureties conditioned for the payment of such amount.

ARTICLE CVI. Upon the expiration of the term of the Operation Provisions, or the termination by notice as aforesaid, the Contractor shall execute and deliver such instruments as may be either necessary or convenient to assure and perfect the title of the City or such new contractor in and to the Equipment free and clear of all liens and incumbrances as aforesaid. **Instruments of title**

Transportation over connecting lines

[ARTICLE CVII. The Contractor has by his proposal offered to the City, in case the latter should make this contract, that, upon completion of the Railroad and thereafter for the entire period of the Operation Provisions passengers over the same should have the right to transportation over certain connecting railways, and passengers over such connecting railways should have the right to transportation over the Railroad as follows:

Transportation without change of cars and for a single fare not exceeding five cents for one continuous trip over the Railroad and any of the connecting lines mentioned in List A forming part of the Contractor's Proposal, being as follows:

Transportation, with or without change of cars at the option of the Contractor, but for a single fare not exceeding five cents, for one continuous trip over the Railroad and any of the connecting lines mentioned in List B forming part of the Contractor's Proposal, being as follows:

Transportation, with or without change of cars at the option of the Contractor, over the Railroad and any of the connecting lines mentioned in List C forming part of the Contractor's Proposal and for fares for continuous trips not exceeding rates, as mentioned in said List C, being as follows:

The Contractor shall, therefore, procure to be executed and proved in form proper for record, and to be duly delivered in three identical originals, a passenger traffic agreement with all owners of each and every of the said connecting lines required by the Commission as follows: Each such agreement shall be between all such owners of the connecting line, as parties of one part, the Contractor as party of another part and the City acting by the Commission as party of the third part. Each such agreement shall recite this contract and shall effectually bind the Contractor and the owners of the connecting line as follows: the owners of such connecting line shall agree to furnish transportation over their line upon the terms above assured by the Contractor for every passenger coming to them over the Railroad; and the Contractor shall agree to furnish transportation over

Contractor to procure agreements with owners of connecting lines

the Railroad upon the terms above assured for every passenger coming to the Railroad over such connecting line. Each such agreement shall be in a form approved in writing by the Commission; shall contain such further provisions as the Commission shall deem necessary in order to effectually carry out the purpose and intent of this Contract; and shall be executed by such persons or corporations as owners or lessees or mortgagees, or otherwise, as the Commission shall require. The Contractor shall within ten days after the execution of this contract or such further time as shall be prescribed by the Commission, deliver to the Commission in duplicate a draft of the proposed agreements to be made with the owners (including the lessees or mortgagees and other lienors, if any, who or which the Commission shall require to join in the agreement) of every such connecting line, with a statement of ownership and title in sufficient detail to enable the Commission to know whether all necessary parties as owners or otherwise are proposed. The Commission within thirty days after receiving from the Contractor such draft and statement and evidence which shall be satisfactory to the Commission as to the power to enter into such contract possessed by the party or parties therein described as such owner or owners or lienors, shall return such draft to the Contractor either approved, or, if not approved, then with a memorandum of the changes (either in the form thereof or of the parties who are to execute the same) which in the opinion of the Commission ought to be made therein. If the Contractor shall not so deliver all such drafts required as aforesaid and furnish such information satisfactory as aforesaid as to ownership and title within such time limited as aforesaid, or if, after proposing any such draft, and within ten days after receiving the same back from the Commission either approved or with proposed amendments, he shall fail to procure the same as so approved or amended to be duly executed by all the parties named therein, then or in either of such cases the Commission may, in its discretion, by notice to the Contractor, terminate this contract, and the City shall thereupon have the same remedies against the Contractor for such default as are provided in Chapter I hereof in case of failure to complete the Construction of the Railroad.

Traffic agreements to be carried out

The Contractor covenants to and with the City that the terms of each and every passenger traffic agreement made or to be made with the owners of connecting lines as prescribed in this Article, shall be fully carried out.]*

* Article CVII in brackets above, referring to proposed traffic agreements, will be modified or omitted in the contract as executed so as to conform to the Contractor's bid.

Operation of extensions

ARTICLE CVIII. The Contractor further agrees (which agreement is one of the principal moving considerations to the City in making this contract) to equip, maintain and operate, or to provide rolling stock and operate the same through, any railroad or railroads constructed by or on behalf of the City which, in the opinion of the Commission, are proper extensions of the Railroad, upon terms and conditions to be specified by the Commission; provided, however, that the interest upon the Contractor's investment [provided for in paragraph (7) of Article LXVII] in the Railroad, including any extension or extensions, shall not by reason of the operation of such extension or extensions, be reduced below the rate therein provided for. If the Contractor shall, in advance of such equipment and operation, claim that the operation of the extension then to be made will reduce such interest below the rate in said paragraph provided the Contractor shall, nevertheless, upon the direction of the Commission, equip such extension Railroad and operate the same or provide rolling stock and operate through the same, for a period of one (1) year. If at the expiration of such period of one (1) year it be demonstrated to the satisfaction of the Commission that the operation of such extension does in fact reduce the interest upon the Contractor's investment in the Railroad, including such extension and extensions as are already made, below the rate provided for in said paragraph, the Contractor shall have the right, unless the Commission shall make such modifications of such terms and conditions as will increase such interest upon the Contractor's investment in the Railroad, including such extension and extensions as are already made, to the rate in said paragraph provided, to discontinue the operation of such extension and the City shall purchase from him the equipment provided by the Contractor for such extension upon the same terms and conditions as is provided herein for the purchase of the equipment of the Railroad as originally constructed.

ARTICLE CIX. The Operation Provisions shall not be assignable by the Contractor without the written consent of the Commission. Operation provisions, when assignable

In witness whereof, this contract has been executed for THE CITY OF NEW YORK by the PUBLIC SERVICE COMMISSION FOR THE FIRST DISTRICT, under and by the authority of a resolution duly adopted by the COMMISSION, and the seal of the COMMISSION has been hereto affixed and attested by its Secretary and these presents signed by the Chairman of the COMMISSION; and the CONTRACTOR has* caused its corporate seal to be hereto affixed and this contract to be witnessed by its President and Secretary the day and year first above written.

PUBLIC SERVICE COMMISSION FOR THE FIRST DISTRICT,

By

Chairman.

Attest:

Secretary.

* If the Contractor is not a corporation, the words following the asterisk will be stricken out and the words "hereto set his hand and seal" or other appropriate words, will be substituted.

STATE OF NEW YORK, }
County of New York, } *ss.:*

On the day of 19 , before me personally appeared William R. Willcox and Travis H. Whitney, to me known and known to me to be, the said William R. Willcox, the Chairman, and the said Travis H. Whitney, the secretary of the Public Service Commission for the First District; and the said William R. Willcox and Travis H. Whitney, being by me duly sworn, did depose and say, each for himself and not one for the other, the said William R. Willcox, that he resides in the Borough of Manhattan, in the City, County and State of New York, that he is the Chairman of the said Commission and that he subscribed his name to the foregoing contract by virtue of the authority hereof; and the said Travis H. Whitney, that he resides in the Borough of Brooklyn, in the City of New York, that he is the Secretary of the said Commission and that he subscribed his name thereto by like authority; and both the said William R. Willcox and Travis H. Whitney that they know the seal of the Commission and that the same was affixed to the foregoing instrument under and by the authority of a resolution duly adopted by the said Commission.

STATE OF NEW YORK, } ss.:
County of New York, }

On this day of , 1910, before me personally appeared
to me known, who, being by me first duly sworn, did depose and say: That he resided in
, in the State of
; that he is
of the
, the corporation described in and which executed the foregoing instrument; that he knew the corporate seal of said company; that one of the seals affixed to said contract was such corporate seal, and that it was affixed thereto by order of the Board of Directors of said company, and that he signed his name thereto by like authority.

STATE OF NEW YORK, }
County of New York, } *ss.:*

On this day of , 1910, before me personally came

to me known and known to me to be the individual described in and who executed the foregoing instrument, and he duly acknowledged to me that he executed the same.

CONTRACTOR'S PROPOSAL

(TRI-BOROUGH RAPID TRANSIT RAILROAD)

NOTICE.—*Sums of money must be written in words and also in figures. There must remain annexed hereto:*

Copy of Invitation to Contractors.

Copy of Form of Contract.

Form of Bond.

Lists A, B and C below, filled up or not at the bidder's option.

Schedule of Securities, filled up only if the bidder desires to deposit securities in lieu of cash.

To the

Public Service Commission for the First District:

1. The undersigned*

do hereby, in pursuance of the Invitation to Contractors, a copy of which is attached hereto, propose according to the terms thereof to enter into a contract with The City of New York in

*If the bid is submitted by a corporation, the full legal title must be given here and a certified copy of the certificate of incorporation must be submitted, together with an affidavit showing the amount of stock paid in in cash and the names and addresses of the directors and principal officers. If the bid is submitted by a firm, the above blank must be filled up in the following form, "the firm of A. B. & Co., composed of A. B., C. D., &c." (giving the names and addresses of all the partners).

the form referred to in said Invitation, and to construct, equip, maintain and operate the portion of the Railroad to be constructed by the Contractor wholly at expense and to equip, maintain and operate the portion of the Railroad constructed or under construction by the City, all as provided in such form of contract.

(2) do hereby propose that shall have the right to use, maintain and operate the Railroad subject to direction as provided in the form of contract, for the term of ( ) years from the date when operation of any part of the Railroad shall actually begin.

(3) The undersigned do further propose to set aside annually in quarterly payments per centum (%) of the cost of construction of the portion of the Railroad to be

constructed by the undersigned as an amortization fund.

(4) The undersigned do further propose that such amortization fund shall be deemed to bear interest at the rate of per centum (%) per annum compounded semi-annually.

(5) The undersigned do further propose and desire that the undersigned be allowed per centum (%) per annum, in quarterly payments, upon the cost to the undersigned of constructing and equipping the portion of the Railroad to be constructed and equipped by the undersigned and the cost of equipping the portion of the Railroad constructed or under construction by the City.

(6) The undersigned hereby selects type as the plan for the construction of the two tunnels under the Harlem River.

7. The undersigned do hereby propose to assure the City transportation facilities over railways connecting or intersecting or to connect or intersect this Railroad as specified in Lists A, B and C annexed to and forming a part of this proposal.

8. If this proposal is accepted, the undersigned will within ten days after delivery of notice, execute and deliver the contract with the City in the form aforesaid and at the same time will (a) deposit with the Comptroller of The City of New York, pursuant to the terms of the said contract the sum of two million dollars ($2,000,000) in cash or securities of the character of which a schedule is hereto annexed entitled "Schedule of Securities," (b) deliver to the said Comptroller a bond for the sum of two million dollars ($2,000,000) in the form hereto annexed entitled Bond

for Construction and Equipment and with the following named sureties;

and (c) deliver to the said Comptroller a bond in the sum of three million dollars ($3,000,000) in the form hereto annexed entitled " Bond for construction, equipment, maintenance and operation " with the following named sureties:

9. Your Commission may cause any notice intended for the undersigned to be delivered at Room No. on the floor of the building No. in the Borough of in the City of New York. Such delivery shall be sufficient notice to the undersigned.

10. At the time of delivering this proposal to your Commission the undersigned will separately deliver a certified check payable to the order of the Comptroller of The City of New York for the sum of one hundred thousand dollars ($100,000). If your Commission shall notify the undersigned that this Proposal is accepted and that the proposed contract is consented to by the Board of Estimate and Apportionment of The City of New York, then, if the undersigned shall fail within ten (10) days thereafter or within such longer period as may be prescribed by your Commission to make the deposit in cash or securities as aforesaid; or to procure the above described bonds to be duly executed and delivered; or if the

undersigned shall fail to procure the contract to be duly executed and delivered as aforesaid, then the Invitation to Contractors and this Proposal shall constitute a contract binding the undersigned to pay to the City the damages by it sustained by reason of such failure of the undersigned, as provided in said Invitation to Contractors. And the undersigned hereby assigns to the City the said sum so specially deposited by the delivery of such certified check, subject only to the condition that if this Proposal shall not be accepted, or, if it shall be accepted and the undersigned shall within ten (10) days after notice as aforesaid or any longer period prescribed by your Commission, execute the said contract and make the said deposit in cash or securities and procure the said bonds to be duly executed and delivered, then the amount of the said check so specially deposited shall be returned to the undersigned.

11. A notice of acceptance of this Proposal by your Commission addressed to the undersigned as aforesaid shall forthwith, at the option of your Commission, operate as against the undersigned as a complete making of a contract according to the form thereof as aforesaid, with the blanks therein contained filled in according to this Proposal.

12. There are no persons interested with the undersigned in this Proposal, except*

*Here insert the names and addresses of all persons interested with the bidder. If there are no such persons strike out the word "except." Any explanation of or addition to the bid may also be inserted in this blank space.

This Proposal is made without any connection with any other person making a proposal or bid for the same purpose, and is in all respects fair and without collusion or fraud. No member of the Board of Aldermen, head of department, chief of bureau, deputy thereof or clerk therein, or other officer of The City of New York, or any member or employee of the Public Service Commission for the First District, is interested directly or indirectly, as contracting party, partner, stockholder, or otherwise in or in the performance of the contract, or in the supplies, work or business to which it relates, or in any portion of the profits thereof.

Dated the day of , 1910.

Affidavit of Verification

STATE OF NEW YORK, } ss.:
City and County of New York, }

being duly

sworn, says: I am*

the proposing contractor above named. I have read the foregoing proposal. The same is in all respects true.

Sworn to before me this }
day of , 1910. }

*If the bidder is an individual do not fill this blank; if the bidder is a firm, here say "a member of the firm of "; if a corporation, say "the (President or other officer duly authorized) of the Company."

Acknowledgment for Individual or Firm

STATE OF NEW YORK, } *ss.:*
City and County of New York, }

On this day of ,
1910, before me personally came

to me known and known to me to be the person described in and who executed the foregoing proposal, and he acknowledged to me that he executed the same for the purposes therein mentioned.

Acknowledgment for Corporation

STATE OF NEW YORK, }
City and County of New York, } *ss.:*

On this day of , 1910, before me personally came to me known and known, who being by me duly sworn, did depose and say that he resides in in the State of ; that he is the of the corporation described in and which executed the foregoing proposal; that he knows the corporate seal of said Company; that the seal affixed to the foregoing instrument is such corporate seal; that it was so affixed by order of the Board of Directors of said Company, and that he signed his name thereto by like authority.

LIST A

Connecting lines over which the Contractor will assure to any passenger a continuous trip for a single fare not exceeding five cents without change of cars:

LIST B

Connecting lines over which the Contractor will assure to any passenger a continuous trip for a single fare not exceeding five cents with or without change of cars at the option of the Contractor:

LIST C

Connecting lines over which the Contractor will assure to any passenger a continuous trip with or without change of cars at the option of the Contractor, for fares exceeding five cents per trip but within limitations in this List specified:

Schedule of Construction Securities

(NOTE.—This schedule must give a description of all such securities as the bidder proposes to deposit in lieu of cash.

All securities when delivered must be payable to, or run in favor of, or be transferred to, the Comptroller of The City of New York.)

Schedule of Continuing Securities

(NOTE.—This schedule must give a description of all such securities as the bidder proposes to deposit in lieu of the bond for construction, equipment, maintenance and operation. All securities, when delivered, must be payable to, or run in favor of, or be transferred to, the Comptroller of The City of New York.)

FORM OF BOND FOR CONSTRUCTION AND EQUIPMENT

Know all Men by these Presents, That

of

hereinafter called the **Contractor** and

and

hereinafter called the **Sureties,** are held and firmly bound unto The City of New York, hereinafter called the **City,** in the sum of

dollars ($) lawful money of the United States of America, to be paid to the City, for which payment well and truly to be made the Contractor and the Sureties do hereby bind themselves and their, and each of

and assigns by these presents, as follows: The Contractor to be so held and bound for the full amount of the said dollars

($) and each of the said sureties to be so held and bound only for a portion of said sum as follows:

The said

for the sum of

dollars ($); the said

for the sum of

dollars ($); the said

for the sum of

dollars ($); the said

for the sum of

dollars ($).

In witness whereof, The Contractor and the Sureties have hereunto caused their respective seals to be hereto affixed and these presents to be attested by the proper officers of each of them which is a corporation, this

day of 1910.

Whereas, The City by the Public Service Commission for the First District (hereinafter called the **Commission**) is about to enter into a contract with the Contractor bearing even date herewith for the construction and equipment, and, after such construction and equipment shall be complete, then for the maintenance and operation of a Rapid Transit Railroad in the City of New York, more particularly described in the said contract; and

Whereas, The City is about to enter into such contract with the Contractor upon the condition, and not otherwise, that this bond shall be given to the City, and upon the faith thereof,

Now, therefore, the condition of the foregoing obligation is such that if the Contractor shall fully perform the said contract, so far as the same requires or shall require the construction and equipment of the Railroad and its appurtenances, then this obligation shall be null and void, but else it shall remain in full force and virtue.

It is expressly agreed, between the City and the Sureties (and it is upon such agreement that the City accepts this Bond) that the Sureties will and do waive any and every notice of default on the part of the Contractor; that they will and do permit the City to extend the time of the Contractor to make any payment or do any act; that no omission on the part of the City to give any notice of extension of time granted by or on behalf of the City shall be availed of by the Sureties or any of them as a defense upon this Bond; that the Sureties shall not set up or have any defense upon this Bond by reason of any alteration of the said contract unless such alteration shall be represented by a formal written instrument duly executed between the City and the Contractor which shall have been duly authorized by a vote of the Commission; and that in case of such alteration, however made, the same shall be a defense to the Sureties only to the extent of the actual injury or damage caused to the Sureties by said alteration.

And whereas, The Contractor has deposited with the City certain cash or securities and has filed another Bond as security for the performance by the Contractor of some of the acts or things, the performance of which is secured hereby;

Now, therefore It is further expressly agreed between the City and the Sureties that the City shall be at liberty in case of any default by the Contractor against which this Board is given as security, to collect the loss or damage to the

City, caused thereby either from the Sureties on this Bond or on the other Bond or out of the said deposit or out of all of such securities as the City may elect.

It is expressly agreed between the City and the Sureties that the Sureties hereby assume all the obligations prescribed for sureties upon bonds like this by the Rapid Transit Act (being chapter 4 of the Laws of 1891 as amended).

Note—The execution of the bond must be duly proved before delivery in the form essential to proof to entitle a deed to record in the State of New York. Full affidavits of justification of sureties must be added.

Bond for Construction, Equipment Maintenance and Operation

Know all Men by these Presents, that

of

hereinafter called the **Contractor** and

and

hereinafter called the **Sureties,** are held and firmly bound jointly and severally unto **The City of New York,** hereinafter called **the City,** in the sum of

dollars ($), lawful money of the United States of America, to be paid to the City, for which payment well and truly to be made the Contractor and the Sureties do hereby bind themselves and their and each of their

and assigns jointly and severally, firmly by these presents.

In witness whereof, the Contractor and the Sureties have hereunto caused their hands and seals to be set this day of , 1910.

Whereas, the City, by the Public Service Commission for the First District (hereinafter called the **Commission**) is about to enter into a contract with the Contractor bearing even date herewith for the construction and equipment, and, after such construction and equipment shall be complete, then for the maintenance and operation, of the rapid transit railroad in the City of New York more particularly described in the said contract; and

Whereas the City is about to enter into such contract with the Contractor upon the condition, and not otherwise, that this Bond shall be given to the City, and upon the faith thereof,—

Now, therefore, the condition of the foregoing obligation is such that if the Contractor shall fully perform the said contract so far as the same requires or shall require the construction and equipment of the Railroad and its appurtenances, and shall promptly pay the amount of the annual rental specified in the Operation Provisions included in said contract and shall faithfully perform all the conditions, covenants and requirements in the said contract specified and provided for, and in case of the default on the part of the Contractor, the Contractor shall pay the amount of the deficiency therein mentioned, as provided in section 29 of the Rapid Transit Act (being chapter 4 of the Laws of 1891, and the several acts amendatory thereof or supplemental thereto), then this obligation shall be null and void, but else it shall remain in full force and virtue.

It is expressly agreed between the City and the Sureties (and it is upon such agreement that the City accepts this Bond) that the Sureties will and do waive any and every notice of default on the part of the Contractor; that they will and do permit the City to extend the time of the Contractor to make any payment or do any act; that no omission on the part of the City or the Commission to give any notice or extension of time granted by or on behalf of the City shall be availed of by the Sureties or either of them as a defence upon this Bond; that the Sureties shall not set up or have any defence upon this Bond by reason of any alteration of the said contract unless such alteration shall be represented by a formal written instrument duly executed between the City and the Contractor which shall have been duly authorized by a vote of the Commission, and that in case of such alteration, however made, the same shall be a defence to the Sureties only to the extent of the actual injury or damage caused to the Sureties by such alteration. It is expressly agreed between the City and the Sureties that the Sureties hereby assume all the obligations prescribed for sureties upon bonds like this by the said Rapid Transit Act. This Bond shall be a continuing security to The City of New York for the entire term of years for which the Contractor has agreed to maintain and operate the Railroad, as prescribed in the said contract.

And whereas, the Contractor has deposited with the City certain cash or securities approved by the Commission and has filed another bond as security for the performance by the Contractor of some of the acts and things, the performance of which is secured hereby;

Now, therefore, it is further expressly agreed between the City and the Sureties that the City shall be at liberty in case of any default by the Contractor against which this Bond is given as security, to collect the loss or damage to the City caused thereby either from the Sureties on this Bond or on the other bond or out of the said deposit or out of all such securities as the City may elect.

NOTE.—The execution of the bond must be duly proved before delivery in the form essential to proof to entitle a deed to record in the State of New York. Full affidavits of justification of sureties must be added.

COPY

ROUTES AND GENERAL PLANS

Lexington Avenue Route.

WHEREAS, The Board of Rapid Transit Railroad Commissioners for The City of New York has determined that the rapid transit railway or railways for the conveyance and transportation of persons and property in addition to those already existing, authorized or proposed are necessary for the interest of the public and of The City of New York, and should be established therein as hereinafter provided; and

WHEREAS, This Board has duly made the inquest and investigation necessary or proper in the premises and all such inquests and investigations as are necessary or proper for such determination;

NOW, THEREFORE, This Board, by the concurrent votes of at least six members does hereby adopt the following route or routes for an additional rapid transit railway or railways in The City of New York, and does hereby determine and establish the said additional route or routes thereof as follows, and does hereby adopt a general plan of construction of the said railway or railways, the route or routes of which are herein provided, and does in such general plan hereby adopted show the general mode of operation and such details as to manner of construction as may be necessary to show the extent to which any street, avenue or other public place is to be encroached upon and the property abutting thereon affected.

This Board, in adopting the said route or routes and general plans, expressly reserves all the powers in relation to the construction of the said route or routes which are conferred upon it by section 34 of the Rapid Transit Act. In particular it reserves the right to contract for the construction of the whole road or all the roads provided for in the following plans in a single contract, or by separate contracts, executed from time to time, to provide for the construction of parts of said road or roads or for the construction at first of two or more tracks over a part or parts of such road or roads, and afterwards of one or more additional tracks over a part or parts of such road or roads, as the necessities of The City of New York and the increase of its population may in the judgment of this Board require.

ROUTES.

A route lying within the Boroughs of Manhattan and The Bronx and made up of several sections as hereinafter described. The said sections are as follows:

SECTION 5-O: A route the centre line of which shall begin in the Borough of Manhattan at or near the intersection of the southerly line of East One Hundred and Twenty-ninth street with the centre line of Lexington avenue; running thence southerly along Lexington avenue to a point about half-way between East Forty-second and East Forty-third streets.

SECTION 5-A: A route the centre line of which shall begin in the Borough of Manhattan at a point in Lexington avenue about half-way between East Forty-second and East Forty-third streets at the southerly end of Section 5-O, above described; running thence southwesterly in a curve under Lexington avenue and private property to East Forty-second street; thence westerly along East Forty-second street to a point near the intersection of the centre line of East Forty-second street with the centre line of Depew place produced; thence southwesterly in a curve under East Forty-second street and private property to Park avenue; and thence southwesterly and southerly under Park avenue to a point in Park avenue between East Thirty-eighth and East Forty-first street, at which a junction can conveniently be made with the subway constructed under resolutions of this Board, adopted January 14 and February 4, 1897.

SECTION 5-B: A route the centre line of which shall begin in the Borough of Manhattan at or near the intersection of the southerly line of East One Hundred and Twenty-ninth street with the centre line of Lexington avenue at the northerly end of Section 5-O, above described; running thence northerly and northeasterly in a curve under Lexington avenue and private property to and across East One Hundred and Thirtieth street; thence again under private property and East One Hundred and Thirty-first street and under the Harlem River to the Borough of The Bronx and to a point on the northeasterly side of the said Harlem River distant not less than two hundred feet northwesterly from the westerly side of Third avenue; thence running northeasterly under private property and East One Hundred and Thirty-fourth street and again under private property to Third avenue at or near the intersection of Third avenue with East One Hundred and Thirty-fifth street; thence running northeasterly under Third avenue and Morris avenue to a point at or near the intersection of Morris avenue and East One Hundred and Forty-eighth street; and thence running in a curve under Morris avenue, East One Hundred and Forty-eighth street and private property to a point in East One Hundred and Forty-ninth street between Morris avenue and Cortlandt avenue, at which a junction can conveniently be made with the subway constructed under resolutions of this Board adopted January 14 and February 4, 1897.

SECTION 5-C: A route, the centre line of which shall begin in the Borough of Manhattan at or near the intersection of the southerly line of East One Hundred and Twenty-ninth street with the centre line of Lexington avenue at the northerly end of Section 5-O above described; running thence northerly under Lexington avenue to the Harlem River and under and across the Harlem River to the Borough of The Bronx and to a point in the northeasterly side of the said river at or near the point where the said northeasterly side is intersected by the easterly side of Park avenue; thence curving northeasterly under private property into Park avenue and running northeasterly along Park avenue to a point at or near the intersection of East One Hundred and Thirty-fifth street, where the lines will diverge, one line continuing northeasterly along Park avenue to East One Hundred and Thirty-eighth street, near which point spurs or connections will be constructed as hereinafter stated, and thence still northeasterly and northerly along Park avenue and under East One Hundred and Forty-ninth street to the northerly side of said street, near which point a spur will be constructed as hereinafter stated; and thence still northerly and northeasterly along Park avenue to its intersection with East One Hundred and fifty-sixth street; and the other of said branches continuing northeasterly under Park avenue, private property and under the tracks of the New York Central and Hudson River Railroad Company and under East One Hundred and Thirty-eighth street and private property into Mott avenue; thence running along and under Mott avenue to a point between East One Hundred and Fiftieth street and East One Hundred and Fifty-first street; thence curving northwesterly into East One Hundred and Fifty-first street and continuing northwesterly under East One Hundred and Fifty-first street to a point between Walton avenue and Gerard avenue, curving thence northerly into Gerard avenue to a junction with a certain rapid transit route heretofore authorized and known as the Gerard Avenue Route. And also a spur beginning at a point in the Borough of The Bronx under private property in the centre line of the branch just described, situated about three hundred (300) feet south of East One Hundred and Thirty-eighth street, and curving thence northeasterly under private property, Mott avenue and private property into East One Hundred and Thirty-eighth street to a point near the intersection of East One Hundred and Thirty-eighth street and Park avenue; running thence easterly under East One Hundred and Thirty-eighth street to a point near Third avenue, where a connection can conveniently be made with a rapid transit route heretofore duly authorized and known as the Southern Boulevard and Westchester Avenue Route.

And also spurs, beginning as above stated, in the Borough of The Bronx, near the intersection of Park avenue with East One Hundred and Thirty-eighth street. One of the said spurs shall begin in Park avenue, south of East One Hundred and Thirty-eighth street, and thence curve northeasterly and easterly under Park avenue, private property and Canal street, west, and again under private property to East One Hundred and Thirty-eighth street. The other of said spurs shall begin in Park avenue north of East One Hundred and Thirty-eighth street, and thence curve southeasterly and easterly under Park avenue and private property to East One Hundred and Thirty-eighth street, where the said spur shall unite with the first spur above mentioned. The centre line of the said two spurs shall then run easterly along East One Hundred and Thirty-eighth street to a point about three hundred feet westerly from the intersection of East One Hundred and Thirty-eighth street with the westerly side of Third avenue.

And also a spur, beginning as above stated, in the Borough of The Bronx, at a point on the main line of the route of Section 5-C as above described, at or near its intersection with the northerly line of East One Hundred and Forty-ninth street; thence curving northerly under private property to Mott avenue; thence under and across Mott avenue and under and along East One Hundred and Fifty-third street and under and across One Hundred and Fifty-seventh street; thence under private property and under the bed of Cromwell Creek to Exterior street; thence under and along Exterior street and under the viaduct and Jerome avenue to a point near the northerly corner of Jerome avenue and Sedgwick avenue; thence running northeasterly in a curve under private property to Sedgwick avenue, and thence under and along Sedgwick avenue to the intersection of Sedgwick avenue and One Hundred and Sixty-fourth street.

And also a loop, beginning in the Borough of The Bronx, at a point on the main line of the route of Section 5-C, as hereinabove described, between East One Hundred and Fifty-first street and East One Hundred and Fifty-second street; running thence northwesterly and westerly under private property and connecting within private property with the spur of route 5-C last above described, near the point of where the centre line of said spur would intersect the northerly line of East One Hundred and Fifty-first street produced.

SECTION 5-D: A route the centre line of which shall begin in the Borough of Manhattan at a point in Lexington avenue about half-way between East Forty-second and East Forty-third streets, at the southerly end of Section 5-O, above described; running thence southerly along Lexington avenue to a point about half-way between East Thirty-sixth street and East Thirty-seventh street, at which point the tracks will diverge into two branches. The centre line of the route for one of such branches shall run thence in a curve southwesterly under Lexington avenue and private property to East Thirty-sixth street; thence westerly along East Thirty-sixth street to a point about one hundred feet easterly from the intersection of the centre line of East Thirty-sixth street with the easterly line of Fifth avenue; thence in a curve southwesterly under East Thirty-sixth street and private property to Fifth avenue, and thence southerly along Fifth avenue to a point between Thirty-fourth and Thirty-fifth streets, where it shall be rejoined by the second branch diverging as above stated. The centre line of the route for the said second branch shall run from the said point of divergence in Lexington avenue southerly under Lexington avenue to a point about half-way between East Thirty-fifth and East Thirty-sixth streets; thence in a curve southwesterly under Lexington avenue and private property to East Thirty-fifth street; thence westerly along East Thirty-fifth street to a point about one hundred feet easterly from the intersection of the centre line of East Thirty-fifth street with the easterly side of Fifth avenue; thence in a curve southwesterly under East Thirty-fifth street and private property to Fifth avenue, and thence in a curve under Fifth avenue and rejoining the branch first above described at a point between Thirty-fourth and Thirty-fifth street. From the last mentioned point the centre line of the route shall run southerly under Fifth avenue to a point about half-way between West Twenty-fourth and West Twenty-fifth streets produced; thence along Madison Square and into Broadway; thence southerly along Broadway, passing under Union Square, and still southerly under Broadway to Chambers street, at which point a loop will begin, as hereinafter stated; thence southerly along Broadway to a point between Vesey street and Barclay street; thence in a curve southwesterly under Broadway and private property to Vesey street; thence westerly along Vesey street to a point about one hundred feet easterly from the intersection of the centre line of Vesey street with the easterly side of Church street; thence in a curve southwesterly under Vesey street and private property to Church streeet; thence southerly along Church street and Trinity place and curving at the southerly end of Trinity place into Greenwich street, and thence southerly under Greenwich street and under and across Battery place, and under Battery Park to a suitable terminus therein.

SECTION 5-E: A route the centre line of which shall begin in the Borough of Manhattan at a point in Lexington avenue north of East Thirty-sixth street, where Section 5-D above described curves westerly into East Thirty-sixth and Thirty-fifth streets; thence running southerly along Lexington avenue to the intersection of Lexington avenue and Gramercy Park; thence southerly through and under Gramercy Park to its intersection with Irving place; thence still southerly along and under Irving place and crossing under East Fourteenth street, private property and East Thirteenth street to a point in private property between East Thirteenth street and East Twelfth street, curving thence southwesterly under private property, East Twelfth street, Fourth avenue and the present Rapid Transit Railway structure in Fourth avenue to a point in private property between Fourth avenue and Broadway at about East Eleventh street, curving thence southerly under private property into Broadway at a point near East Ninth street, at which a junction can be conveniently made with Section 5-D above described.

And also a loop the centre line of which shall begin as above stated in the Borough of Manhattan at or near the intersection of Broadway and Chambers street; running thence southeasterly in a curve under Broadway and the City Hall Park, recurving southerly and westerly under the City Hall Park and Broadway at a point about opposite the centre line of Murray street, and rejoining the main line at a suitable point in Broadway, between Murray street and Chambers street.

GENERAL PLAN OF CONSTRUCTION

The general plan of construction hereby adopted for the foregoing routes is as follows:

For the route running under Lexington avenue from about East Forty-third street to East One Hundred and Twenty-ninth street, known as Section 5-O, there shall be four tracks. For the route running westerly and southwesterly from the southerly end of route 5-O under East Forty-second street, and known as Section 5-A, there shall be four tracks. For the route running northerly from Lexington avenue and East One Hundred and Twenty-ninth street under the Harlem River, Third avenue and Morris avenue, known as Section 5-B, there shall be four tracks up to the point where the said route begins to curve in order to join the subway at East One Hundred and Forty-ninth street, and from that point there shall be two tracks. For the route running northerly from East One Hundred and Twenty-ninth street and Lexington avenue under the Harlem River and Park avenue and other streets to East One Hundred and Thirty-fifth street, where the lines diverge as above described, there shall be four tracks. For the branch of such road, running through Mott avenue to East One Hundred and Fiftieth street, there shall be four tracks, and for the remainder of such branch, through East One Hundred and Fifty-first street into Gerard avenue, and for the spur included in said branch, running easterly through East One Hundred and Thirty-eighth street to Third avenue, there shall be three tracks. For the branch of said route running northerly from East One Hundred and Thirty-fifth street and through Park avenue and other streets, including the various spurs above described, there shall be two tracks, except that in the loop north of East One Hundred and Fifty-second street there shall be one track. For the route running southerly from a point near East Forty-third street and Lexington avenue, known as Section 5-D above described, there shall be four tracks as far south as the point between East Thirty-sixth and East Thirty-seventh streets where the line diverges as above described; there shall be two tracks from the point of divergence through East Thirty-sixth street and Fifth avenue to the point where the lines reunite; and two tracks from the point of divergence through Lexington avenue and East Thirty-fifth street to the said point in Fifth avenue where the lines reunite; and for the remainder of the distance southerly under Fifth avenue and Broadway there shall be four tracks as far south as Chambers street. From Chambers street southerly under Broadway, Vesey street, Trinity place, and Greenwich street, there shall be two tracks. In the loop under the City Hall Park there shall be one track. There shall be as many additional tracks as may be needed for convenient operation of terminals under Battery place and Battery Park. For the portion of the route known as Section 5-E above described and running southerly through Lexington avenue, Gramercy Park and Irving place and private property to Broadway there shall be four tracks.

All of the above-mentioned tracks shall be placed in subway or tunnel substantially parallel with each other and on substantially the same level; except that wherever required by special necessities of surface or subsurface structures or other special or local necessities and except for the purpose of avoiding grade crossings at Lexington avenue and Thirty-fifth street, Lexington avenue and Thirty-sixth street, Lexington avenue and One Hundred and Twenty-ninth street, Third avenue and One Hundred and Thirty-eighth street, One Hundred and Forty-ninth street near Courtlandt avenue, Park avenue and One Hundred and Thirty-eighth street, or at the City Hall Park loop or elsewhere, any one or more of the tracks may be depressed below the level of the other track or tracks to a depth of not more than twenty feet; and except that the tracks upon the portion of the routes beginning at or near Houston street and thence extending northerly under Broadway to a point near East Ninth street, thence through private property to Irving place and thence northerly under Irving place, Gramercy Park and Lexington avenue to One Hundred and Third street and from One Hundred and Thirteenth street to the Harlem River shall be placed upon different levels—one set of tracks being constructed substantially on the same level near the surface and the other set of tracks being constructed substantially on the same level and at such distance below the first set of tracks as may be deemed most practicable and convenient, with the right, however, already reserved to vary the levels of the tracks of each set if required by special necessities or for the purpose of avoiding grade crossings.

The tracks shall be placed in general under the central part of the longitudinal streets of the route so far as may be practicable and convenient; except that in Morris avenue they shall be placed on the westerly side of said avenue; and except that in turning from Fifth avenue to Broadway, as described in Section 5-D above, the tracks may be placed as far easterly as necessary, or under the surface of Madison square; and wherever else required by special or local necessities, or for curves, the tracks or any one or more of them may be diverted as far as necessary to one side or the other of the longitudinal streets of the route or any of them. But in Fifth avenue and Broadway no wall of the tunnel or part thereof (except at stations, station approaches, points where the route passes from streets to private property, curves and places of access to sub-surface structures, as hereinafter provided) shall be within the distance of five feet of the exterior line or side of the longitudinal street of the route. In all other longitudinal streets of the route, any part of such streets may be occupied so far as the purposes of this general plan require.

The tracks under East Thirty-fifth street and East Thirty-sixth street may be constructed in and occupy the same tunnel as another subway to be built under the said streets between Third avenue and Eighth avenue, and the tracks for the spur under East One Hundred and Thirty-eighth street to Third avenue may be partly constructed in and occupy the same tunnels as another subway to be built under the said street as a part of another route.

The roof of the tunnels when under a street shall be as near the surface of the street as street conditions and grades will conveniently permit; except that under East Thirty-fifth and East Thirty-sixth streets and under Fourth avenue near East Twelfth street and under East One Hundred and Forty-ninth street and Park avenue, the tunnel shall be so constructed as to pass under the subway constructed under resolutions of this Board adopted January 14 and February 4, 1897; and except also that near the intersection of Third avenue and East One Hundred and Thirty-eighth street the tunnel may, if necessary, be depressed to a depth sufficient to allow other tunnels or subways to be constructed over and across it, and except also that for the portion of the routes between Houston street and the Harlem River where the tracks are to be constructed upon different levels the lower set of tracks may be depressed to such depth as may be deemed most practicable and convenient.

The tunnels above described shall in no case be less than thirteen feet in height in the clear.

The roof of the said tunnels shall be of iron or steel with brick or concrete arches, supported when necessary by iron or steel or masonry columns and resting upon masonry walls; or the roof shall be a masonry structure; or the whole of the lining may be of metal.

Adjacent tracks shall be connected by necessary and suitable switches and connections and an additional track for siding accommodations may be constructed not to exceed in length one quarter of a mile for each mile of roadway.

The tracks may at any point of the said route or of the spur or loops therein included be placed in the same tunnel; or there may be separate tunnels for one or more tracks as shall be most convenient.

The tracks shall be of standard gauge, that is to say, of the width of four feet and eight and a half inches between the rails. There shall be a width in the tunnels not exceeding fifteen feet for each track in addition to the thickness of the supporting walls, except that at stations, switches, turnouts, curves and crossovers the width may be increased.

Stations and station approaches shall, in general, be at the intersections of streets and shall be built under the streets and immediately adjoining private abutting property or through or under private property to be acquired for the purpose. The streets under which stations or station approaches shall be built may include cross streets, but no part of any cross street shall be used for a station approach at a distance greater than seventy-five feet from the exterior line or side of the longitudinal street of the route.

Wherever along any part of the routes above described it shall be necessary for the proper maintenance or accommodation of pipes, wires, sewers or other subsurface structures, the removal, construction or reconstruction of which shall be rendered necessary by the construction of the railway, the width of any tunnel or subway may be enlarged on either or both sides by an additional width on each side of the route, not to exceed fifteen feet on either side, provided always that the limits hereinbefore provided as to certain longitudinal streets of the route shall be observed. All or any pipes, wires, sewers or other subsurface structures may be placed in suitable galleries to be constructed within the additional widths hereinbefore permitted. At each cross street where accommodation for pipes, wires, sewers and other subsurface structures shall be those provided within the tunnels or subways, such tunnels or subways, in order to provide convenient access to the same, may have, within the limit of the sides or exterior lines of such cross streets or such lines produced, an additional width on each side of the routes not to exceed fifteen feet.

Pipes, wires, sewers and other subsurface structures at any part of the said routes shall be removed or disturbed only when necessary for the construction and operation of the railway above referred to, and if removed or disturbed shall be placed under the several streets in such manner and in such location that the use and service thereof shall not be impaired. Such pipes, wires, sewers and other subsurface structures shall be left or shall be so arranged as to give free access for their repair or alteration, or for the placing with them, so far as there may be space, of new pipes, wires, sewers and other like structures, and for making connections between the same and abutting buildings at any time.

The manner of construction shall be by tunneling or excavation under cover, except in places where this Board shall give express permission to construct by open excavation.

In parks, parkways, and public places under the jurisdiction of the Department of Parks, all trees injured or destroyed shall be replaced under the direction and to the satisfaction of the said Department.

MODE OF OPERATION.

The general mode of operation of the route or routes above described shall be by electricity or some other power not requiring combustion within the tunnels, and the motors shall be capable of moving trains at a speed of not less than forty miles per hour for long distances, exclusive of stops.

DEFINITIONS.

The word "street" wherever used herein, shall include an avenue or public place.

The words "Rapid Transit Act" wherever used herein shall be taken and held to mean chapter 4 of the Laws of 1891 as amended by chapter 752 of the Laws of 1894, and other acts of the Legislature.

MAPS AND DRAWINGS.

It is further

Resolved, That the twelve maps and drawings entitled "BOARD OF RAPID TRANSIT RAILROAD COMMISSIONERS of The City of New York—Route and General Plan," one of the said drawings being marked "Key Map No. 3 Borough of Manhattan," two of the said drawings being marked "Manhattan No. 3" sheets Nos. 1 and 3, one of the said drawings being marked "Manhattan Nos. 3 and 4," sheet No. 2, one of the said drawings being marked "Key Map, No. 4, Borough of Manhattan," five of the said drawings being marked "Manhattan No. 4" sheet No. 1 and sheets Nos. 3 to 6 inclusive, and two of the said drawings being marked "Manhattan, Nos. 4 and 2" sheets Nos. 7 and 8, are hereby adopted as showing the foregoing routes and general plans, for convenience merely, and that said maps and drawings are not to be deemed a part of the description of the routes or a part of the general plans, for any purposes whatever.

Note—The foregoing is a copy of the routes and general plans of construction of the Lexington Avenue Route as adopted by the Board of Rapid Transit Railroad Commissioners for The City of New York on May 12, 1905, and as since modified by resolutions adopted by the Public Service Commission for the First District on February 4, 1908, April 29, 1908, and May 21, 1909. These modifying resolutions of the Public Service Commission for the First District refer to certain maps as showing the modifications adopted. The portions of these modifying resolutions adopting such maps as showing such modifications are printed below for convenience, although such portions do not in terms modify the original resolutions.

[From the resolutions adopted by the Public Service Commission for the First District on February 4, 1908]:

Resolved, That the four maps entitled "Public Service Commission for the First District, Manhattan Key Map A, and Manhattan A—Sheet No. 3, Bronx Key Map A, and Bronx A—Sheet No. 1," are hereby adopted as showing the modifications as hereby adopted of the foregoing routes and general plan, for convenience merely, and that said maps are not to be deemed a part of the description of the routes, or a part of the general plan, for any purpose whatever.

[From the resolutions adopted by the Public Service Commission for the First District on April 29, 1908]:

Resolved, That the map entitled "Public Service Commission for the First District, Routes and General Plan, Manhattan A, Sheet No. 3-A," is hereby adopted as showing the modification, as hereby adopted, of the foregoing routes and general plan and of the modification of the said routes and general plan for convenience merely, and that said map is not to be deemed a part of the description of the routes or a part of the general plan for any purpose whatever.

[From the resolutions adopted by the Public Service Commission for the First District on May 21, 1909]:

RESOLVED, That the maps entitled "Board of Rapid Transit Railroad Commissioners of The City of New York, Routes and General Plan, Revised May 21, 1909, Manhattan No. 4, Sheet No. 6; Manhattan No. 3, Sheet No. 1; Manhattan No. 4, Sheet No. 1; Manhattan Nos. 3 and 4, Sheet No. 2; Manhattan No. 4, Sheet No. 3; Manhattan No. 3, Sheet No. 3"; and the maps entitled "Public Service Commission for the First District, Routes and General Plan, Revised May 21, 1909, Manhattan A, Sheet No. 3, and Manhattan A, Sheet No. 3-a," are hereby adopted as showing the foregoing modifications of the general plan of construction for convenience merely, and that said maps are not to be deemed a part of the description of the routes or a part of the general plan of construction for any purpose whatever.

Seventh and Eighth Avenue Route.

WHEREAS, The Board of Rapid Transit Railroad Commissioners for The City of New York has determined that a rapid transit railway or railways for the conveyance and transportation of persons and property in addition to those already existing authorized or proposed are necessary for the interest of the public and of The City of New York, and should be established therein as hereinafter provided; and

WHEREAS, This Board has duly made the inquest and investigation necessary or proper in the premises and all such inquests and investigations as are necessary or proper for such determination;

NOW, THEREFORE, This Board by the concurrent votes of at least six members does hereby adopt the following route or routes for an additional rapid transit railway or railways in The City of New York and does hereby determine and establish the said additional route or routes thereof as follows, and does hereby adopt a general plan of construction of the said railway or railways, the route or routes of which are herein provided, and does in such general plan hereby adopted show the general mode of operation and such details as to manner of construction as may be necessary to show the extent to which any street, avenue or other public place is to be encroached upon and the property abutting thereon affected.

This Board, in adopting the said route or routes and general plans expressly reserves all the powers in relation to the construction of the said route or routes which are conferred upon it by Section 34 of the Rapid Transit Act. In particular it reserves the right to contract for the construction of the whole road or all the roads provided for in the following plans in a single contract; or by separate contracts, executed from time to time, to provide for the construction of parts of the said road or roads or for the construction at first of two or more tracks over a part or parts of such road or roads, and afterwards of one or more additional tracks over a part or parts of such road or roads, as the necessities of The City of New York and the increase of its population may in the judgment of this Board require.

ROUTES.

A route lying wholly within the Borough of Manhattan and made up of several sections as hereinafter described. The said sections are as follows:

SECTION 4-O: A route the centre line of which shall begin at or near the intersection of the centre line of Seventh avenue with the northerly line of West Forty-third street; running thence southerly along Seventh avenue to a point about half way between West Twenty-fifth and West Twenty-sixth streets. And also a suitable connection extending under Seventh avenue and Broadway or Times Square to a point between West Forty-third street and West Forty-seventh street, so as to afford a junction with the existing subway constructed under resolutions of this Board adopted January 14 and February 4, 1897.

SECTION 4-A: A route the centre line of which shall begin at or near the intersection of the centre line of Seventh avenue with the northerly line of West Forty-third street at the northerly end of Section 4-O above described, and running thence northerly under Seventh avenue to the Central Park; and thence under the Central Park to Central Park West at or near the intersection of West Sixty-second street.

SECTION 4-AA: A route the centre line of which shall begin at a point under Central Park West at or near the intersection of West Sixty-second street at the northerly end of Section 4-A above described; running thence northerly under Central Park West and Eighth avenue to a point between West One Hundred and Forty-ninth street and West One Hundred and Fiftieth street; thence curving northeasterly and running under Macomb's lane to a point at or near the intersection of Macomb's lane with West One Hundred and Fifty-third street; thence in a curve northerly and westerly under Macomb's lane and private property to West One Hundred and Fifty-fourth street; thence westerly and southwesterly in a curve under One Hundred and Fifty-fourth street and private property to Eighth avenue; and thence southerly under Eighth avenue to a point where the centre line of the route as above described diverges northwesterly from Eighth avenue to pass under Macomb's lane. And also a spur running northerly along Eighth avenue from a suitable point north of West One Hundred and Forty-ninth street on the section last above described, to a point about half way between West One Hundred and Fifty-fourth street and West One Hundred and Fifty-fifth street, so as to afford a means for future connections or extensions northerly.

SECTION 4-H: A route the centre line of which shall begin at a point under Central Park West at or near the intersection of West Sixty-second street at the northerly end of Section 4-A above described; running thence southerly under Eighth avenue and Hudson street to a point at or near the intersection of

Hudson street, Chambers street and West Broadway upon the centre line of route 4-C hereinafter described.

And also a spur running from a point on the centre line of Section 4-H above described at or near the intersection of the centre line of Eighth avenue with the centre line of Greenwich avenue produced; running thence southeasterly along Greenwich avenue to a point at which a junction can be made with Section 4-B hereinafter described at or near the point of intersection of the centre line of Seventh avenue produced with the centre line of Greenwich avenue.

SECTION 4-B: A route the centre line of which shall begin at a point in Seventh avenue about half way between West Twenty-fifth street and West Twenty-sixth street at the southerly end of Section 4-O above described; running thence southerly under Seventh avenue to West Twelfth street; thence curving southeasterly under West Twelfth street, Seventh avenue and private property to West Eleventh street; thence still southeasterly under West Eleventh street and Greenwich avenue to, under and across Sixth avenue; thence running under private property and under Clinton place or Eighth street, and again under private property, to a point at or near the intersection of the northerly side of Waverly place with the easterly side of Macdougal street; thence still southeasterly under Macdougal street, Waverly place, Washington square and West Fourth street to a point in West Fourth street at or near the intersection of the centre line of West Fourth street with the centre line of West Broadway produced.

SECTION 4-C: A route the centre line of which begins at the southerly end of Section 4-B above described at or near the point of intersection of the centre line of West Fourth street with the centre line of West Broadway produced; running thence southerly under West Broadway to a point at or near the intersection of the centre line of Chambers street with the centre line of West Broadway.

SECTION 4-D: A route the centre line of which shall begin at the southerly end of Section 4-C above described at or near the point of intersection of the centre line of Chambers street with the centre line of West Broadway; running thence southerly under West Broadway to Murray street (near which point a loop may begin as hereinafter described); thence still southerly under West Broadway and Greenwich street crossing under Battery place into Battery Park, and thence curving easterly and northerly in a terminal loop under Battery Park to rejoin the main route in Greenwich street near the northerly side of Battery place. There may be also such additional terminal tracks lying under Battery place and Battery Park as may be necessary for convenient operation.

The centre line of the loop above mentioned as constituting a part of Section 4-D, shall begin under West Broadway at a point between Murray street and Warren street on the main line of said section as above described; curving thence southwesterly under private property, under Murray street, and again under private property in the block between Murray street and Park place, to a point near the intersection of the northerly side of Park place with the easterly side of Greenwich street; curving thence under Park place, under private property, under Greenwich street, and again under private property, to a point near the intersection of the westerly side of Greenwich street with the northerly side of Barclay street; thence curving easterly under Barclay street to a point near the intersection of the northerly side of Barclay street with the westerly side of West Broadway; and thence curving under private property and West Broadway and rejoining the main line in West Broadway at a convenient point between Barclay street and Park place.

SECTION 4-E: A route the centre line of which shall begin at a point in Seventh avenue about half way between West Twenty-fifth and West Twenty-sixth streets at the southerly end of Section 4-O above described; running thence southeasterly in a curve under Seventh avenue and private property to West Twenty-fifth street; thence easterly along West Twenty-fifth street to a point west of Broadway, but near the intersection of the southerly side of West Twenty-fifth street with the westerly side of Broadway; thence curving southeasterly under West Twenty-fifth street and private property to Broadway; thence under Broadway to a point between West Twenty-third and West Twenty-fourth streets; and thence curving into Fifth avenue and continuing southerly under Fifth avenue and Washington square to the southerly end of Route 4-B above described at or near the intersection of the centre line of West Fourth street with the centre line of West Broadway produced.

SECTION 4-F: A route the centre line of which shall begin at a point in Broadway between West Twenty-fourth street and West Twenty-fifth street, at which a junction can be made with the route described as Section 4-E above, and running thence northerly under Broadway to a point between West Forty-third street and West Forty-sixth street, at which a junction can be made with the subway constructed under resolutions of this Board adopted January 14th and February 7th, 1897.

PLAN OF CONSTRUCTION.

The general plan of construction hereby adopted for the foregoing routes is as follows:

For the route running under Seventh avenue between West Forty-third street and West Twenty-fifth street, known as Section 4-O, there shall be four tracks. For the route running northerly under Seventh avenue, Central Park West and Eighth avenue to West One Hundred and Forty-ninth street, known as Sections 4-A and 4-AA, there shall be four tracks; and on the loop at the extremity of section 4-AA under Macomb's lane, West One Hundred and Fifty-fourth street and Eighth avenue, there shall be two tracks. For the route under Seventh avenue, Greenwich avenue and Washington square, known as Section 4-B, there shall be four tracks. For the route under West Broadway from Fourth street to Chambers street, known as Section 4-C, there shall be four tracks. For the route running southerly from Chambers street under West Broadway and Greenwich street known as Section 4-D, there shall be four tracks; for the loop beginning near Murray street in West Broadway there shall be one track; for the terminal loop under Battery Park there shall be two tracks; and there may be constructed under Battery place and Battery Park as many additional terminal tracks as may be needed. For the route under Twenty-fifth street from Seventh avenue to Broadway, being a portion of Section 4-E, there shall be two tracks, and for the remaining portion of Section 4-E, from Twenty-fifth street and Broadway through Fifth avenue and Washington square, there shall be four tracks. For the route under Broadway between Twenty-fifth street and Forty-third street, being Section 4-F, there shall be four tracks. For the route under Eighth avenue and Hudson street, being Section 4-H, there shall be four tracks.

All of the above-mentioned tracks shall be placed in subway substantially parallel with each other and on substantially the same level, except that wherever required by special necessities of surface or sub-surface structures or other special or local necessities, and except for the purpose of avoiding grade crossings at Seventh avenue and West Twenty-fifth street and in the neighborhood of the junction of Seventh avenue and Broadway, and at the points where the loops above mentioned diverge from the main line of the route, or elsewhere, any one or more of the tracks may be depressed below the level of the other track or tracks to a depth of not more than twenty feet.

The tracks shall be placed in general under the central part of the longitudinal streets of the route so far as may be practicable and convenient, but wherever required by special or local necessities or for curves the tracks or any one or more of them may be diverted as far as necessary to one side or the other of such streets or any of them. But in Seventh avenue, Eighth avenue, West Twenty-fifth street, Broadway, West Broadway and Fifth avenue no wall of the tunnel or part thereof (except at stations, station approaches, points where the route passes from streets to private property, curves and places of access to subsurface structures as hereinafter provided) shall be within the distance of five feet of the exterior line or side of the longitudinal streets of the route. In all other longitudinal streets of the route any part of such streets may be occupied so far as the purposes of this general plan require.

The roof of the tunnels when under a street shall be as near the surface of the street as street conditions and grades will conveniently permit, except that in crossing Sixth avenue and West Twenty-fifth street the tunnel shall be depressed so as to pass under the subway heretofore authorized to be built along and under Sixth avenue; and except that in crossing the route of the subway constructed under resolutions of this Board adopted January 14, and February 4, 1897, the tunnel shall be depressed so as to pass under the said subway.

The tunnels above described shall in no case be less than thirteen feet in height in the clear.

The roof of the said tunnels shall be of iron or steel with brick or concrete arches, supported when necessary by iron or steel or masonry columns and resting upon masonry walls; or the roof shall be a masonry structure; or the whole of the lining may be of metal.

Adjacent tracks shall be connected by necessary and suitable switches and connections and an additional track for siding accommodations may be constructed not to exceed in length one-quarter of a mile for each mile of roadway.

The tracks may at any point of the said route or of the spur or loops therein included be placed in the same tunnel; or there may be separate tunnels for one or more tracks as shall be most convenient.

The tracks shall be of standard gauge, that is to say, of the width of four feet and eight and a half inches between the rails. There shall be a width in the tunnels not exceeding fifteen feet for each track in addition to the thickness of the supporting walls, except that at stations, switches, turnouts, curves and crossovers the width may be increased.

Stations and station approaches shall, in general, be at the intersections of streets and shall be built under the streets immediately adjoining private abutting property, or through or under private property to be acquired for the purpose. The streets under which stations or station approaches shall be built may include cross streets, but no part of any cross street shall be used for a station approach at a distance greater than seventy-five feet from the exterior line or side of the longitudinal street of the route.

Wherever along any part of the routes above described it shall be necessary for the proper maintenance or accommodation of pipes, wires, sewers or other subsurface structures, the width of any tunnel or subway may be enlarged on either or both sides by an additional width on each side of the route, not to exceed fifteen feet on either side, provided always that the limits hereinbefore provided as to certain longitudinal streets of the route shall be observed. All or any pipes, wires, sewers or other subsurface structures may be placed in suitable galleries to be constructed within the additional widths hereinbefore permitted. At each cross street where accommodation for pipes, wires, sewers and other subsurface structures shall be those provided within the tunnels or subways, such tunnels or subways, in order to provide convenient access to the same, may have, within the limit of the sides or exterior lines of such cross streets or such lines produced, an additional width on each side of the routes not to exceed fifteen feet.

Pipes, wires, sewers and other subsurface structures at any part of the said routes shall be removed or disturbed only when necessary for the construction and operation of the railway above referred to, and if removed or disturbed shall be placed under the several streets in such manner and in such location that the use and service thereof shall not be impaired. Such pipes, wires, sewers and other subsurface structures shall be left or shall be so arranged as to give free access for their repair or alteration, or for the placing with them, so far as there may be space, of new pipes, wires, sewers and other like structures, and for making connections between the same and abutting buildings at any time.

The manner of construction shall be by tunneling or excavation under cover, except in places where this Board shall give express permission to construct by open excavation.

In parks, parkways, and public places under the jurisdiction of the Department of Parks, all trees injured or destroyed in the course of construction shall be replaced under the direction and to the satisfaction of the said Department.

MODE OF OPERATION.

The general mode of operation of the route or routes above described shall be by electricity or some other power not requiring combustion within the tunnels, and the motors shall be capable of moving trains at a speed of not less than forty miles per hour for long distances, exclusive of stops.

DEFINITIONS.

The word "street" wherever used herein, shall include an avenue or public place.

The words "Rapid Transit Act" wherever used herein, shall be taken and held to mean Chapter 4 of the Laws of 1891 entitled "An Act to Provide for Rapid Transit Railroads in Cities of Over One Million Inhabitants" as amended by Chapter 752 of the Laws of 1894 and other acts of the Legislature.

MAPS AND DRAWINGS.

It is further

Resolved, That the fourteen maps and drawings entitled "BOARD OF RAPID TRANSIT RAILROAD COMMISSIONERS of The City of New York—Routes and General Plan," one of the said drawings being marked "Key Map No. 2" Borough of Manhattan," nine of the said drawings being marked "Manhattan No. 2" sheets numbers 10 to 18 inclusive, one of the said drawings being marked "Key Map No. 3 Borough of Manhattan," and three of the said drawings being marked "Manhattan No. 3" sheets Nos. 4, 5 and 6, are hereby adopted as showing the foregoing routes and general plans, for convenience merely, and that said maps and drawings are not to be deemed a part of the description of the routes or a part of the general plans, for any purpose whatever.

River Avenue Elevated Road.

WHEREAS, The Public Service Commission for the First District has determined that a rapid transit railway for the conveyance and transportation of persons and property, in addition to those already existing, authorized or proposed, is necessary for the interest of the public and of The City of New York and should be established therein as hereinafter provided; and

WHEREAS, This Commission has duly made the inquest and investigation necessary or proper in the premises and all such inquests and investigations as are necessary or proper for such determination;

NOW THEREFORE, This Commission does hereby adopt the following route for an additional rapid transit railway in The City of New York and does hereby determine and establish the said additional route thereof as follows, and does hereby adopt a general plan of construction of the said railway, the route of which is herein provided, and does in such general plan hereby adopted show the general mode of operation and such details as to manner of construction as may be necessary to show the extent to which any street, avenue or other public place is to be encroached upon and the property abutting thereon affected.

This Commission in adopting the said route and general plan, expressly reserves all the powers in relation to the construction of the said route which are conferred upon it by the Rapid Transit Act. In particular it reserves the right to contract for the construction of the whole road provided for in the following plan in a single contract, or by separate contracts executed from time to time, to provide for the construction of parts of said road or for the construction at first of two tracks over a part or parts of said road, and afterward of an additional track over a part or parts of said road, as the necessities of The City of New York and the increase of its population may in the judgment of this Commission require, or to provide in a contract for any part of such railroad that, at a future time, upon the requirement of this Commission the contractor shall construct the remainder or any part of the remainder of said road as the growth of the population or the interests of the city may, in the judgment of this Commission, require.

ROUTE.

A route lying wholly within the Borough of The Bronx, the centre line of which shall begin at a point in Mott avenue near East One Hundred and Fiftieth street, where a connection can conveniently be made with the Lexington avenue route, as modified, and running thence northerly under Mott avenue and crossing under the tracks of the New York Central and Hudson River Railroad Company and private property; thence curving in a

northwesterly direction under East One Hundred and Fifty-third street, Franz Sigel Park, Walton avenue, private property and Gerard avenue to a point in private property in the block bounded by Gerard avenue, River avenue, East One Hundred and Fifty-third street and East One Hundred and Fifty-seventh street; curving thence in a northerly direction through private property and East One Hundred and Fifty-seventh street into River avenue at a point near East One Hundred and Fifty-seventh street; thence continuing northerly along River avenue and Jerome avenue to a point in Jerome avenue at or near Clarke place, where a connection can conveniently be made with a proposed elevated railroad known as the Jerome avenue elevated route.

PLAN OF CONSTRUCTION.

The general plan of construction adopted for the route hereinbefore described is as follows:

For the whole of the said route there shall be three tracks.

All of the tracks shall be substantially parallel to each other and on substantially the same level, except that wherever required by special necessities of surface or subsurface structures or other special or local necessities and for the purpose of avoiding grade crossings, any one or more of the tracks may be elevated above or depressed below the level of the other track or tracks to the extent of not more than twenty feet.

The tracks from the point of beginning along Mott avenue, private property and the several cross streets to a point in the block bounded by Gerard avenue, River avenue, East One Hundred and Fifty-third street and East One Hundred and Fifty-seventh street, where the route begins to emerge from the ground shall be in subway or tunnel, and from the last mentioned point to the northerly terminus of the said road the tracks shall be carried upon a viaduct over and along River avenue and Jerome avenue.

The tracks shall be placed in general under or over the central part of the longitudinal streets which form a portion of the route above described, so far as may be practicable and convenient, but wherever required by special or local necessities or for curves the tracks or any one or more of them may be diverted as far as necessary to one side or the other of such streets or any of them. But no exterior line of the tunnel or viaduct (except at stations, station approaches, curves and places of access to subsurface structures as hereinafter provided) shall be within a distance of five feet of the exterior line or side of the longitudinal streets of the route.

Where the tracks change from tunnel to viaduct the change shall be so made as to involve the use of the surface to the least possible extent consistent with the proper gradient for the tracks.

Wherever necessary for the proper support of the surface of a street the roof of the tunnels shall be of iron or steel with brick or concrete arches supported when necessary by iron or steel or masonry columns and resting upon masonry walls; or the roof may be a masonry structure or the wall of the lining may be of metal.

The roof of the tunnel when under a street shall be as near the surface as street conditions and grades will conveniently permit.

The tunnel shall in no case be less than thirteen feet in height in the clear.

There shall be a width in the tunnel not exceeding fifteen feet for each track, in addition to the thickness of the supporting walls, except that at stations, switches, turnouts, curves and crossovers the width may be increased.

Viaducts shall be built with a width of thirteen feet for each track, except on curves or where greater width is required for special construction, and with an additional width of three feet on each side for outside foot-ways. Viaducts may be built of metal or of masonry or of both.

The tracks shall be of standard gauge, that is to say, of the width of four feet and eight and one-half inches between the gauge lines.

Adjacent tracks shall be connected by necessary and suitable switches and connections, and an additional track for siding accommodations may be constructed not to exceed in length one-quarter of a mile for each mile of roadway.

There shall be as many additional tracks as may be needed for convenient operation of terminals, if necessary, under Franz Sigel Park and contiguous private property, or under other adjacent streets or private property along this route.

The tracks wherever constructed below the surface may at any point of the route be placed in the same tunnel, or there may be separate tunnels for one or more tracks, as shall be most convenient.

Stations and station approaches shall in general be at the intersections of streets and shall be built under, or if the position of the tracks so require, over the streets, and immediately adjoining private abutting property, or through private property to be acquired for the purpose, or both under or over streets and through private property as aforesaid. The streets under or over which stations or station approaches shall be built may include cross streets, but no part of any cross street shall be used for a station approach at a distance greater than seventy-five feet from the exterior line or side of the longitudinal street of the route.

Wherever along any part of the route above described it shall be necessary for the proper maintenance or accommodation of pipes, wires, sewers or other subsurface structures, the removal, construction or reconstruction of which shall be rendered necessary by the construction of the railway, the width of any tunnel or subway may be enlarged on either or both sides by an additional width, not to exceed fifteen feet on each side, provided always that the limits hereinbefore provided as to the longitudinal streets of the route shall be observed. All or any pipes, wires, sewers or other subsurface structures may be placed in suitable galleries to be constructed within the additional widths hereinbefore permitted. At each cross street where accommodation for pipes, wires, sewers and other subsurface structures shall be thus provided within the tunnels or subways, such tunnels or subways, in order to provide convenient access to the same, may have, within the limit of the sides or exterior lines of such cross streets or such lines produced, an additional width on each side of the routes not to exceed fifteen feet.

Pipes, wires, sewers, street railway tracks, poles for electric wires and other surface and subsurface structures at any part of the said routes shall be removed or disturbed only when necessary for the construction and operation of the railway above referred to, and if removed or disturbed shall be placed over, upon or under the several streets in such manner and in such location that the use and service thereof shall not be impaired. All pipes, wires, sewers and other subsurface structures shall be left or shall be so arranged as to give free access for their repair or alteration, or for the placing with them, so far as there may be space, of new pipes, wires, sewers and other like structures, and for making connections between the same and abutting buildings at any time.

The manner of construction shall be by tunneling or open excavation. In parks, parkways and public places under the jurisdiction of the Department of Parks, all trees injured or destroyed in the course of construction shall be replaced under the direction and to the satisfaction of the said department.

MODE OF OPERATION.

The general mode of operation of the route or routes above described shall be by electricity or some other power not requiring combustion within the tunnels, and the motors shall be capable of moving trains at a speed of not less than forty miles per hour for long distances, exclusive of stops.

DEFINITIONS.

The word "street" wherever used herein shall include an avenue or public place.

The words "Rapid Transit Act" wherever used herein shall be taken and held to mean chapter 4 of the Laws of 1891, entitled "An Act to provide for Rapid Transit Railroads in cities of more than one million inhabitants," as amended by chapter 752 of the Laws of 1894, and chapter 429 of the Laws of 1907, and other acts of the Legislature.

MAPS AND DRAWINGS.

It is further

Resolved, That the map and drawing entitled "Public Service Commission for the First District, routes and general plan" and marked "Bronx A, Sheet No. 2-B" be and is hereby adopted as showing the foregoing route and general plan for convenience merely, and that the said map and drawing is not to be deemed a part of the description of the route or a part of the general plan for any purpose whatever.

Jerome Avenue Elevated Road.

WHEREAS, The Board of Rapid Transit Railroad Commissioners for The City of New York has determined that a rapid transit railway for the conveyance and transportation of persons and property, in addition to those already existing, authorized or proposed, is necessary for the interest of the public and of The City of New York, and should be established therein as hereinafter provided; and

WHEREAS, This Board has duly made the inquest and investigation necessary or proper in the premises and all such inquests and investigations as are necessary or proper for such determination;

NOW THEREFORE This Board by the concurrent votes of at least six members does hereby adopt the following route for an additional rapid transit railway in The City of New York and does hereby determine and establish the said additional route thereof as follows, and does hereby adopt a general plan of construction of the said railway, the route of which is herein provided, and does in such general plan hereby adopted show the general mode of operation and such details as to manner of construction as may be necessary to show the extent to which any street, avenue or other public place is to be encroached upon and the property abutting thereon affected.

This Board, in adopting the said route and general plans, expressly reserves all the powers in relation to the construction of the said route which are conferred upon it by Section 34 of the Rapid Transit Act. In particular it reserves the right to contract for the construction of the whole road provided for in the following plans in a single contract; or by separate contracts, executed from time to time, to provide for the construction of parts of said road or for the construction at first of two or more tracks over a part or parts of such road, and afterwards of one or more additional tracks over a part or parts of such road, as the necessities of The City of New York and the increase of its population may in the judgment of this Board require; or to provide in a contract for any part of such railroad that, at a future time, upon the requirement of this Board, the contractor shall construct the remainder or any part of the remainder of said road as the growth of the population or the interests of the City may, in the judgment of this Board, require.

ROUTE.

A route lying wholly within The Borough of The Bronx, the centre line of which shall begin at a point on Jerome avenue at or near the intersection of Jerome avenue with Clarke place, near the point where Gerard avenue joins Jerome avenue, at which point a connection can be made with a rapid transit elevated railway to be hereafter constructed, running southerly from the same point along Jerome avenue, and at which point a connection can also be conveniently made with a rapid transit subway to be hereafter constructed along Gerard avenue; and shall run thence northerly along and over Jerome avenue from the point of beginning to the point of junction of Jerome avenue with Woodlawn road, opposite the Woodlawn Cemetery.

SECTION A. Beginning at a point in Jerome avenue about one hundred and twenty (120) feet north of the northerly side of East One Hundred and Ninety-eighth street projected, where a connection can conveniently be made with the route above described in Jerome avenue and extending thence northerly over Jerome avenue and property on the west side of Jerome avenue to a point in Jerome avenue about one hundred and fifty (150) feet south of East Two Hundred and Fourth street, where a connection can conveniently be made with the route above described in Jerome avenue.

PLAN OF CONSTRUCTION.

The general plan of construction hereby adopted for the foregoing route, including Section A, is as follows:

There shall be three tracks, all placed on an elevated structure or viaduct, except on Section A above described where they may be on an elevated structure or viaduct or in open cut and on embankment, all substantially parallel with each other and on substantially the same level.

The tracks shall be of standard gauge, that is to say, of a width of four feet eight and one-half inches between the rails. The tracks along Jerome avenue shall be placed in general over the central part of the said Jerome avenue so far as may be practicable and convenient, except that where required by special or local necessities or for curves the tracks or any one or more of them may be diverted as far as necessary to one side or the other of said street; but no part of the viaduct structure (except at stations, station approaches and curves and where Section A above described enters property on the west side of Jerome avenue) shall be within a distance of five feet from the exterior line or side of said Jerome avenue.

The viaduct shall be built with a width of twelve and one-half feet for each track, except on curves or where greater width is required for special construction, and with an additional width of three feet on each side for outside footways. The said viaduct may be built of metal or masonry or both.

Adjacent tracks shall be connected by necessary and suitable switches and connections, and an additional track for siding accommodations may be constructed not to exceed one-quarter of a mile for each mile of roadway.

Stations and station approaches shall in general be at the intersection of streets, and shall be built over the streets and immediately adjoining private abutting property, or over private property to be acquired for the purpose, or both over streets and private property as aforesaid or on Section A above described through property on the west side of Jerome avenue. The streets over which stations or station approaches shall be built may include cross streets, but no part of any cross street shall be used for a station or station approach at a distance greater than seventy-five feet from the exterior line or side of said Jerome avenue.

Pipes, wires, sewers, street railway tracks, poles for electric wires and other surface and sub-surface structures at any part of the route shall be removed or disturbed only when necessary for the construction and operation of the railway above referred to, and if removed or disturbed shall be placed upon, over or under the several streets in such manner and in such location that the use and service thereof shall not be impaired.

MODE OF OPERATION.

The general mode of operation of the route above described shall be by electricity or some other power not requiring combustion upon the viaduct, and the motors shall be capable of moving trains at a speed of not less than forty miles per hour for long distances, exclusive of stops.

DEFINITIONS.

The word "street," wherever used herein, shall include an avenue or public place.

The words "Rapid Transit Act," wherever used herein, shall be taken and held to mean chapter 4 of the Laws of 1891, entitled "An Act to provide for rapid transit railroads in cities of more than one million inhabitants," as amended by chapter 752 of the Laws of 1894 and other acts of the Legislature.

MAPS AND DRAWINGS.

It is further

Resolved, that the maps and drawings entitled "Board of Rapid Transit Railroad Commissioners of The City of New York —Routes and General Plan," one of the said drawings being marked "Key Map No. 1, Borough of The Bronx," and four of the said drawings being marked "The Bronx No. 1," sheets 7, 8, 9 and 10, be and they are hereby adopted as showing the foregoing routes and general plans for convenience merely, and that said maps and drawings are not to be deemed a part of the description of the routes or a part of the general plans for any purpose whatever.

Southern Boulevard and Whitlock Avenue Route.

WHEREAS, The Public Service Commission for the First District has determined that a rapid transit railway for the conveyance and transportation of persons and property, in addition to those already existing, authorized or proposed, is necessary for the interest of the public and of The City of New York and should be established therein as hereinafter provided; and

WHEREAS, This Commission has duly made the inquest and investigation necessary or proper in the premises and all such inquests and investigations as are necessary or proper for such determination;

NOW THEREFORE, This Commission does hereby adopt the following route for an additional rapid transit railway in The City of New York and does hereby determine and establish the said additional route thereof as follows, and does hereby adopt a general plan of construction of the said railway, the route of which is herein provided, and does in such general plan hereby adopted show the general mode of operation and such details as to manner of construction as may be necessary to show the extent to which any street, avenue or other public place is to be encroached upon and the property abutting thereon affected.

This Commission in adopting the said route and general plan, expressly reserves all the powers in relation to the construction of the said route which are conferred upon it by the Rapid Transit Act. In particular it reserves the right to contract for the construction of the whole road provided for in the following plan in a single contract, or by separate contracts executed from time to time, to provide for the construction of parts of said road or for the construction at first of two tracks over a part or parts of said road, and afterward of an additional track over a part or parts of said road, as the necessities of The City of New York and the increase of its population may in the judgment of this Commission require, or to provide in a contract for any part of such railroad that, at a future time, upon the requirement of this Commission the contractor shall construct the remainder or any part of the remainder of said road as the growth of the population or the interests of the city may, in the judgment of this Commission, require.

ROUTE.

A route lying within the Borough of The Bronx, the centre line of which shall begin at a point under East One Hundred and Thirty-eighth street near Cypress avenue, where a connection can conveniently be made with the Southern Boulevard and Westchester avenue route, heretofore adopted by the Board of Rapid Transit Railroad Commissioners for The City of New York, and extending thence easterly under East One Hundred and Thirty-eighth street to a point near Robbins avenue; curving thence in a northerly direction under East One Hundred and Thirty-eighth street and private property to and under the Southern Boulevard, continuing thence northerly under the Southern Boulevard to a point between Barretto street and Hunts Point road, where it curves to the northeast under the Southern Boulevard, private property, Hunts Point road and the public park to and under Whitlock avenue, continuing thence in a general northerly direction under Whitlock avenue, private property and Aldus street to a point in private property where it emerges from the ground to an elevated structure, and continues thence northerly over private property and Whitlock avenue to a point near Westchester avenue where it curves to the east over Whitlock avenue and private property, to and over Westchester avenue where a connection can conveniently be made with the said Southern Boulevard and Westchester avenue route.

PLAN OF CONSTRUCTION.

The general plan of construction adopted for the route hereinbefore described is as follows:

For the whole of the said route there shall be three tracks.

All of the tracks shall be substantially parallel to each other and on substantially the same level, except that wherever required by special necessities of surface or subsurface structures or other special or local necessities and for the purpose of avoiding grade crossings, any one or more of the tracks may be elevated above or depressed below the level of the other track or tracks to the extent that may be necessary.

The tracks from the point of beginning along East One Hundred and Thirty-eighth street, the Southern Boulevard, Whitlock avenue, private property and the several cross streets to a point in the block bounded by Aldus street, Longfellow avenue, Bancroft street and Whitlock avenue, where the route begins to emerge from the ground shall be in subway or tunnel, and from the last-mentioned point to the northerly terminus of the said road the tracks shall be carried upon a viaduct over and along Whitlock avenue and Westchester avenue.

The tracks shall be placed in general under or over the central part of the longitudinal streets which form a portion of the route above described, so far as may be practicable and convenient, but wherever required by special or local necessities or for curves the tracks or any one or more of them may be diverted as far as necessary to one side or the other of such streets or any of them. On the portion of the route under ground the entire width of the street may be used so far as necessary for the purposes of this general plan.

Where the tracks change from tunnel to viaduct the change shall be so made as to involve the use of the surface to the least possible extent consistent with the proper gradient for the tracks.

Wherever necessary for the proper support of the surface of a street the roof of the tunnels shall be of iron or steel with brick or concrete arches supported when necessary by iron or steel or masonry columns and resting upon masonry walls; or the roof may be a masonry structure or the wall or the lining may be of metal.

The roof of the tunnel when under a street shall be as near the surface as street conditions and grades will conveniently permit.

The tunnel shall in no case be less than thirteen feet in height in the clear.

There shall be a width in the tunnel not exceeding fifteen feet for each track, in addition to the thickness of the supporting walls, except that at stations, switches, turnouts, curves and crossovers the width may be increased.

Viaducts shall be built with a width of thirteen feet for each track, except on curves or where greater width is required for special construction, and with an additional width of three feet on each side for outside footways. Viaducts may be built of metal or of masonry or of both.

The tracks shall be of standard gauge, that is to say, of the width of four feet and eight and one-half inches between the gauge lines.

Adjacent tracks shall be connected by necessary and suitable switches and connections, and an additional track for siding accommodations may be constructed not to exceed in length one-quarter of a mile for each mile of roadway.

There shall be as many additional tracks as may be needed for convenient operation of terminals, if necessary, under the Southern Boulevard and Whitlock avenue and contiguous private property.

The tracks wherever constructed below the surface may at any point of the route be placed in the same tunnel, or there may be separate tunnels for one or more tracks, as shall be most convenient.

Stations and station approaches shall in general be at the intersections of streets and shall be built under, or, if the position of the tracks so require, over the streets, and immediately adjoining private abutting property, or through private property to be acquired for the purpose or both under or over streets and through private property as aforesaid. The streets under or over which stations or station approaches shall be built may include cross streets, but no part of any cross street shall be used for a station approach at a distance greater than seventy-five feet from the exterior line or side of the longitudinal street of the route.

Wherever along any part of the route above described it shall be necessary for the proper maintenance or accommodation of pipes, wires, sewers or other subsurface structures, the removal, construction or reconstruction of which shall be rendered necessary by the construction of the railway, the width of any tunnel or subway may be enlarged on either or both sides by an additional width, not to exceed fifteen feet on each side All or any pipes, wires, sewers or other subsurface structures may be placed in suitable galleries to be constructed within the additional widths hereinbefore permitted. At each cross street where accommodation for pipes, wires, sewers and other subsurface structures shall be thus provided within the tunnels or subways, such tunnels or subways, in order to provide convenient access to the same, may have, within the limit of the sides or exterior lines of such cross streets or such lines produced, an additional width on each side of the routes not to exceed fifteen feet.

Pipes, wires, sewers, street railway tracks, poles for electric wires and other surface and subsurface structures at any part of the said routes shall be removed or disturbed only when necessary for the construction and operation of the railway above referred to, and if removed or disturbed shall be placed over, upon or under the several streets in such manner and in such location that the use and service thereof shall not be impaired. All pipes, wires, sewers and other sub-surface structures shall be left or shall be so arranged as to give free access for their repair or alteration, or for the placing with them, so far as there may be space, of new pipes, wires, sewers and other like structures, and for making connections between the same and abutting buildings at any time.

The manner of construction shall be by tunneling or open excavation. In parks, parkways and public places under the jurisdiction of the Department of Parks, all trees injured or destroyed in the course of construction shall, so far as possible, be replaced under the direction and to the satisfaction of the said department.

MODE OF OPERATION.

The general mode of operation of the route or routes above described shall be by electricity or some other power not requiring combustion within the tunnels, as shall be capable of furnishing transportation at a speed of not less than forty miles per hour for long distances, exclusive of stops.

DEFINITIONS.

The word "street" wherever used herein shall include an avenue or public place.

The words "Rapid Transit Act" wherever used herein shall be taken and held to mean Chapter 4 of the Laws of 1891, entitled "An Act to provide for Rapid Transit Railroads in cities of more than one million inhabitants," as amended by Chapter 752 of the Laws of 1894, and Chapter 429 of the Laws of 1907, and other acts of the Legislature.

MAPS AND DRAWINGS.

It is further

Resolved, That the maps and drawings entitled "Public Service Commission for the First District, Routes and General Plan" and marked "Bronx Key Map C, Bronx C, Street No. 22-1 and Bronx C, Sheet No. 22-2" be and are hereby adopted as showing the foregoing route and general plan for convenience merely, and that the said maps and drawings are not to be deemed a part of the description of the route or a part of the general plan for any purpose whatever.

Southern Boulevard and Westchester Avenue Route.

WHEREAS, The Board of Rapid Transit Railroad Commissioners for The City of New York has determined that a rapid transit railway for the conveyance and transportation of persons and property in addition to those already existing, authorized or proposed, is necessary for the interest of the public and of The City of New York, and should be established therein as hereinafter provided; and

WHEREAS, This Board has duly made the inquest and investigation necessary or proper in the premises and all such inquests and investigations as are necessary or proper for such determination;

NOW, THEREFORE, This Board by the concurrent votes of at least six members does hereby adopt the following route for an additional rapid transit railway in the City of New York and does hereby determine and establish the said additional route thereof as follows, and does hereby adopt a general plan of construction of the said railway, the route of which is herein provided, and does in such general plan hereby adopted show the general mode of operation and such details as to manner of construction as may be necessary to show the extent to which any street, avenue or other public place is to be encroached upon and the property abutting thereon affected.

This Board, in adopting the said route and general plans, expressly reserves all the powers in relation to the construction of the said route which are conferred upon it by Section 34 of the Rapid Transit Act. In particular it reserves the right to contract for the construction of the whole road provided for in the following plans in a single contract; or by separate contracts, executed from time to time, to provide for the construction of parts of said road or for the construction at first of two or more tracks over a part or parts of such road, and afterwards of one or more additional tracks over a part or parts of such road, as the necessities of The City of New York and the increase of its population may, in the judgment of this Board, require; or to provide in a contract for any part of such railroad that, at a future time, upon the requirement of this Board, the contractor shall construct the remainder or any part of the remainder of said road as the growth of the population or the interests of the City may, in the judgment of this Board, require.

ROUTE.

A route lying wholly within the Borough of The Bronx and beginning at a point in East One Hundred and Thirty-eighth street about three hundred (300) feet easterly from the easterly side of Lincoln avenue at which point a connection can conveniently be made with a spur from a subway to be hereafter constructed under Lincoln avenue and Morris avenue; and running thence westerly under and along East One Hundred and Thirty-eighth street to a point near the intersection of the easterly side of Cypress avenue with the centre line of East One Hundred and Thirty-eighth street, at which point the route herein described shall begin to emerge from the ground and shall thence continue in an open cut or upon a viaduct to and across Robbins avenue; and there curving into the Southern Boulevard shall continue upon a viaduct or elevated structure over and along the Southern Boulevard northeasterly to the intersection of the Southern Boulevard with the southerly side of Westchester avenue; and curving easterly and running thence over and along Westchester avenue and Westchester turnpike upon a viaduct or elevated structure to Williamsbridge road, in the former Village of Westchester.

PLAN OF CONSTRUCTION.

The general plan of construction adopted for the route hereinabove described is as follows:

For the whole of the said route there shall be three tracks.

All of the tracks shall be substantially parallel to each other and on substantially the same level, except that wherever required by special necessities of surface or sub-surface structures or other special or local necessities, and for the purpose of avoiding grade crossings, any one or more of the tracks may be elevated above or depressed below the level of the other track or tracks to the extent of not more than twenty feet.

The tracks from the point of beginning along East One Hundred and Thirty-eighth street to the point near Cypress avenue where the route begins to emerge from the ground, shall be in subway or tunnel; and from the said last mentioned point to the easterly end of the said road in the former Village of Westchester, the tracks shall be carried upon a viaduct over and along the Southern Boulevard and Westchester avenue.

The tracks shall be placed in general under the central part of the longitudinal streets forming a portion of the route above described so far as may be practicable and convenient, but wherever required by special or local necessities or for curves, the tracks or any one or more of them may be diverted as far as necessary to one side or the other of such streets or any of them. But no wall of the tunnel or viaduct or any part thereof (except at stations, station approaches, curves and places of access to sub-surface structures as hereinafter provided) shall be within a distance of five feet of the exterior line or side of the longitudinal streets of the route.

Where the tracks change from tunnel to viaduct, the change shall be so made as to involve the use of the surface to the least possible extent consistent with the proper gradient for the tracks.

Wherever necessary for the proper support of the surface of a street, the roof of the tunnels shall be of iron or steel, with brick or concrete arches, supported when necessary by iron or steel or masonry columns and resting upon masonry walls; or the roof shall be a masonry structure; or the whole of the lining may be of metal.

The roof of the tunnel when under a street shall be as near the surface as street conditions and grades will conveniently permit.

The tunnel shall in no case be less than thirteen feet in height in the clear.

There shall be a width in the tunnel not exceeding fifteen feet for each track, in addition to the thickness of the supporting walls, except that at stations, switches, turnouts, curves and crossovers the width may be increased.

Viaducts shall be built with a width of twelve and one-half feet for each track, except on curves or where greater width is required for special construction, and with an additional width of three feet on each side for outside footways. Viaducts may be built of metal or of masonry or of both.

The tracks shall be of standard gauge; that is to say, of the width of four feet and eight and a half inches between the rails.

Adjacent tracks shall be connected by necessary and suitable switches and connections, and an additional track for siding accommodations may be constructed not to exceed in length one-quarter of a mile for each mile of roadway.

The tracks wherever constructed below the surface, may at any point of the route be placed in the same tunnel; or there may be separate tunnels for one or more tracks as shall be most convenient.

Stations and station approaches shall in general be at the intersections of streets and shall be built under or, if the position of the tracks so require, over the streets and immediately adjoining private abutting property, or through private property to be acquired for the purpose, or both under or over streets and through private property as aforesaid. The streets under which stations or station approaches shall be built may include cross streets, but no part of any cross street shall be used for a station approach at a distance greater than seventy-five feet from the exterior line or side of the longitudinal street of the route.

Wherever along any part of the routes above described it shall be necessary for the proper maintenance or accommodation of pipes, wires, sewers or other sub-surface structures, the removal, construction or reconstruction of which shall be rendered necessary by the construction of the railway, the width of any tunnel or subway may be enlarged on either or both sides by an additional width on each side of the route, not to exceed fifteen feet on either side, provided always that the limits hereinbefore provided as to the longitudinal streets of the route shall be observed. All or any pipes, wires, sewers or other sub-surface structures may be placed in suitable galleries to be constructed within the additional widths hereinbefore permitted. At each cross street where accommodation for pipes, wires, sewers and other subsurface structures shall be those provided within the tunnels or subways, such tunnels or subways, in order to provide convenient access to the same, may have, within the limit of the sides or exterior lines of such cross streets or such lines produced, an additional width on each side of the routes not to exceed fifteen feet.

Pipes, wires, sewers, street railway tracks, poles for electric wires and other surface and sub-surface structures at any part of the said routes shall be removed or disturbed only when necessary for the construction and operation of the railway above referred to, and if removed or disturbed shall be placed over, upon or under the several streets in such manner and in such location that the use and service thereof shall not be impaired. All pipes, wires, sewers and other sub-surface structures shall be left or shall be so arranged as to give free access for their repair or alteration, or for the placing with them, so far as there may be space, of new pipes, wires, sewers and other like structures, and for making connections between the same and abutting buildings at any time.

The manner of construction shall be by tunnelling or open excavation.

In parks, parkways and public places under the jurisdiction of the Department of Parks, all trees injured or destroyed in the course of construction shall be replaced under the direction and to the satisfaction of said Department.

MODE OF OPERATION.

The general mode of operation of the route or routes above described shall be by electricity or some other power not requiring combustion within the tunnels, and the motors shall be capable of moving trains at a speed of not less than forty miles per hour for long distances, exclusive of stops.

DEFINITIONS.

The word "street," wherever used herein, shall include an avenue or public place.

The words "Rapid Transit Act," wherever used herein, shall be taken and held to mean Chapter 4 of the Laws of 1891 as amended by Chapter 752 of the Laws of 1894 and other acts of the Legislature.

MAPS AND DRAWINGS.

It is further

Resolved, that the maps and drawings, entitled "BOARD OF RAPID TRANSIT RAILROAD COMMISSIONERS of the City of New York—Routes and General Plan," one of said drawings being marked "Key Map No. 1, Borough of The Bronx," and three of the said drawings being marked "Bronx No. 1," sheets Nos. 16, 17 and 18, be and they are hereby adopted as showing the foregoing routes and general plans, for convenience merely, and that said maps and drawings are not to be deemed a part of the description of the routes or a part of the general plans, for any purpose whatever.

Canal Street Route.

WHEREAS, The Public Service Commission for the First District has determined that a rapid transit railway or railways for the conveyance and transportation of persons and property, in addition to those already existing, authorized or proposed, are necessary for the interest of the public and of The City of New York and should be established therein as hereinafter provided; and

WHEREAS, This Commission has duly made the inquest and investigation necessary or proper in the premises, and all such inquests and investigations as are necessary or proper for such determination,

NOW, THEREFORE, This Commission does hereby adopt the following route or routes for an additional rapid transit railway or railways in The City of New York, and does hereby determine and establish the said additional route or routes thereof as follows, and does hereby adopt a general plan of construction of the said railway or railways, the route or routes of which are herein provided, and does in such general plan hereby adopted show the general mode of operation and such details as to manner of construction as may be necessary to show the extent to which any street, avenue or other public place is to be encroached upon and the property abutting thereon affected.

This Commission in adopting the said route or routes and general plans expressly reserves all the powers in relation to the construction of the said route or routes which are conferred upon it by section 34 of the Rapid Transit Act. In particular, it reserves the right to contract for the construction of the whole road or all the roads provided for in the following plans in a single contract; or by separate contracts executed from time to time, to provide for the construction of parts of said road or roads or for the construction at first of two or more tracks over a part or parts of such road or roads and afterwards of one or more additional tracks over a part of such road or roads as the necessities of The City of New York and the increase of its population may in the judgment of this Board require; or to provide in a contract for any part of such railroad that at a future time upon the requirement of this Commission the Contractor shall construct the remainder or any part of the remainder of said road as the growth of the population or the interests of the City may, in the judgment of this Commission, require.

ROUTE.

A route lying wholly within the Borough of Manhattan, the centre line of which shall begin at a suitable point in Canal street at or near Centre street at which a connection or connections can be made with a route running over the Manhattan Bridge, thence running westerly through and under Canal street to Hudson street; thence continuing westerly under Canal street to Washington street; thence in a loop curving southerly under Canal street, public park and private property to West street; thence southerly under West street and curving easterly under private property to Watts street; thence easterly under Watts street to Canal street and at or near the intersection of Canal and Hudson streets joining the line on Canal street described above. Also two spurs connecting the route hereby described with a rapid transit railroad to be constructed under Broadway. One of such spurs to begin at a point in Canal street at or near Lafayette street; running thence westerly along and under Canal street, on the northerly side thereof to a point between Lafayette street and Broadway, where it curves in a northwesterly direction under private property to Broadway, connecting with the said rapid transit railroad under Broadway at about Grand street. The other of such spurs to begin at a point in Canal street at or near Lafayette street; running thence westerly along and under Canal street, on the southerly side thereof, to a point between Lafayette street and Broadway, where it curves in a southwesterly direction under private property to Broadway, connecting with the said rapid transit railroad under Broadway at about White street.

GENERAL PLAN OF CONSTRUCTION.

The general plan of construction hereby adopted for the foregoing route is as follows:

For the part of the route from Centre street to Hudson street there shall be four tracks; for the entire remainder of the route, including the spurs above described, there shall be two tracks. There shall be as many additional tracks as may be needed for convenient operation of terminals under the public park and streets at Canal, Hoboken and West streets.

All of the above-mentioned tracks shall be placed in subway or tunnel substantially parallel with each other and on substantially the same level; except that wherever required by special necessities of surface or subsurface structures or other special or local necessities, or for the purpose of avoiding grade crossings, any one or more of the tracks may be depressed below the level of the other track or tracks so far as may be necessary.

The tracks shall be placed in general under the central part of the longitudinal streets of the route so far as may be practicable and convenient, except that wherever required by special or local necessities or for curves the tracks or any one or more of them may be diverted as far as necessary to one side or the other of the longitudinal streets of the route or any of them. In all such longitudinal streets of the route any part of such streets may be occupied so far as the purposes of this general plan require.

The roof of the tunnels shall be as near the surface of the street as street conditions and grades and rapid transit railroads heretofore proposed or constructed will conveniently permit.

The tunnels above described shall in no case be less than thirteen (13) feet in height in the clear.

The roof of the said tunnels shall be of iron or steel with brick or concrete arches, supported when necessary by iron or steel or masonry columns and resting upon masonry walls; or the roof shall be a masonry structure, or the whole of the lining may be of metal.

Adjacent tracks shall be connected by necessary and suitable switches and connections, and additional track for siding accommodations may be constructed not to exceed in length one-fourth of a mile for each mile of roadway.

The tracks from Wooster street to Centre street may be partly constructed in and occupy the same tunnels as other subways to be built under part of Canal street as portions of other rapid transit routes adopted by the Board of Rapid Transit Railroad Commissioners for The City of New York.

The tracks may at any point of the said route or of the loop therein included be placed in the same tunnel; or there may be separate tunnels for one or more tracks as shall be most convenient.

The tracks shall be of standard gauge, that is to say, of the width of four (4) feet and eight and one-half (8½) inches between the rails. There shall be a width in the tunnels not exceeding fifteen (15) feet for each track in addition to the thickness of the supporting walls, unless it shall be necessary to tunnel by the shield method, in which event the tracks may be placed in tubes not exceeding twenty (20) feet in diameter and driven or placed along such part of the street or streets as shall be most convenient, except that at stations, switches, turnouts, curves and crossovers, the width or diameter may be increased.

Stations and station approaches shall in general be at the intersection of streets and shall be built under the streets and immediately adjoining private abutting property or through or under private property to be acquired for the purpose or both under streets and through private property as aforesaid. The streets under which stations or station approaches shall be built may include cross streets, but no part of any cross street shall be used for a station approach at a distance greater than seventy-five (75) feet from the exterior line or side of the longitudinal street of the route.

Wherever along any part of the routes above described it shall be necessary for the proper maintenance or accommodation of pipes, wires, sewers or other subsurface structures, the removal, construction or reconstruction of which shall be rendered necessary by the construction of the railway, any tunnel or subway may be enlarged on either or both sides by an additional width not to exceed (15) feet on each side of the route. All or any pipes, wires, sewers or other subsurface structures may be placed in suitable galleries to be constructed within the additional width hereinbefore permitted. At each cross street where accommodation for pipes, wires, sewers and other subsurface structures shall be thus provided within the tunnels or subways, such tunnels or subways, in order to provide convenient access to the same, may have, within the limit of the sides or exterior lines of such cross streets or such lines produced, an additional width on each side of the route not to exceed fifteen (15) feet.

Pipes, wires, sewers and other subsurface structures at any part of the said route shall be removed or disturbed only when necessary for the construction and operation of the railway above referred to, and if removed or disturbed shall be placed under the several streets in such manner and in such location that the use and the service thereof shall not be impaired. Such pipes, wires, sewers and other subsurface structures shall be left or shall be so arranged as to give free access for their repair or alteration, or for the placing with them, so far as there may be space, of new pipes, wires, sewers and other like structures, and for making connections between the same and abutting building at any time.

The manner of construction shall be by tunneling or excavation under cover, except in places where this Commission shall give express permission to construct by open excavation.

In parks, parkways and public places under the jurisdiction of the Department of Parks, all trees injured or destroyed shall be replaced under the direction and to the satisfaction of the said Department.

MODE OF OPERATION.

The general mode of operation of the route above described shall be by electricity or some other power not requiring combustion within the tunnels, and the motors shall be capable of moving trains at a speed of not less than forty (40) miles per hour for long distances, exclusive of stops.

DEFINITIONS.

The word "street" wherever used herein shall include an avenue or public place.

The words "Rapid Transit Act" wherever used herein shall be taken and held to mean Chapter 4 of the Laws of 1891 as amended by Chapter 752 of the Laws of 1894, and by other Acts of the Legislature.

MAPS AND DRAWINGS.

IT IS FURTHER RESOLVED, That the maps and drawings entitled "Public Service Commission for the First District, Manhattan Key Map A and Manhattan A—Sheet No. 1," are hereby adopted as showing the foregoing routes and general plans, for convenience merely, and that said maps and drawings are not to be deemed a part of the description of the route or a part of the general plans, for any purpose whatever.

Manhattan Bridge Route (Revised).

WHEREAS, The Board of Rapid Transit Railroad Commissioners for the City of New York has determined that a rapid transit railway or railways for the conveyance and transportation of persons and property, in addition to those already existing, authorized or proposed, are necessary for the interest of the public and of the City of New York, and should be established therein as hereinafter provided; and

WHEREAS, This Board has duly made the inquest and investigation necessary or proper in the premises and all such inquests and investigations as are necessary or proper for such determination;

NOW, THEREFORE, This Board, by the concurrent votes of at least six members, does hereby adopt the following route or routes for an additional rapid transit railway or railways in the City of New York, and does hereby determine and establish the said additional route or routes thereof as follows, and does hereby adopt a general plan of construction of the said railway or railways, the route or routes of which are herein provided, and does in such general plan hereby adopted show the general mode of operation and such details as to manner of construction as may be necessary to show the extent to which any street, avenue or other public place is to be encroached upon and the property abutting thereon affected.

This Board, in adopting the said route or routes and general plans, expressly reserves all the powers in relation to the construction of the said route or routes which are conferred upon it by Section 34 of the Rapid Transit Act. In particular it reserves the right to contract for the construction of the whole road or all the roads provided for in the following plans in a single contract; or by separate contracts, executed from time to time, to provide for the construction of parts of said road or roads or for the construction at first of two or more tracks over a part or parts of such road or roads, and afterwards of one or more additional tracks over a part or parts of such road or roads, as the necessities of the City of New York and the increase of its population may, in the judgment of this Board, require; or to provide in a contract for any part of such railroad that, at a future time, upon the requirement of this Board, the contractor shall construct the remainder or any part of the remainder of said road as the growth of the population or the interests of the city may, in the judgment of this Board, require.

ROUTE.

A route lying within the Boroughs of Brooklyn and Manhattan, the centre line of which shall begin at or near the intersection of the centre line of Willoughby street with the centre line of Flatbush avenue as the same has been extended; running thence under said Flatbush avenue extension and the easterly Manhattan Bridge approach to a point near the intersection of Nassau street, and there emerging to the surface and continuing northwesterly in an open approach and along the easterly Manhattan Bridge approach and along and across the Manhattan Bridge, and the westerly Manhattan Bridge approach over and across the East River and the Borough of Manhattan to a point at or near the intersection with the centre line of the Manhattan Bridge prolonged with the centre line of Chrystie street prolonged. Near the said last mentioned point the tracks will diverge, making two spurs. The centre line of the southerly one of the said spurs will continue in a southwesterly direction, curving under the Manhattan Bridge approach or plaza into the Bowery, and continuing southerly along the Bowery to a point at or near the intersection of Doyers street with the Bowery, at which connections can conveniently be made with a subway proposed to be constructed running northerly and southerly under the Bowery. From the above-mentioned point near the intersection of the centre line of the Manhattan Bridge prolonged with the centre line of Chrystie street prolonged, the second spur will diverge in a westerly and northwesterly direction, continuing to a point near the intersection of the centre line of Canal street with the easterly line of the Bowery. At this point the said spur will again branch, with two tracks curving northwesterly into the Bowery and two tracks continuing westerly under Canal street. The two tracks curving northwesterly into the Bowery will continue under and along the Bowery to a point about half way between Hester street and Grand street, at which a connection can conveniently be made with a subway to be constructed running northerly and southerly under the Bowery. The two tracks continuing westerly under Canal street as above mentioned, will run along the northerly side of Canal street as far as Mulberry street, and then along the middle of Canal street, passing under the proposed subway in Centre street and the existing subway in Elm street to a point in Canal street between Broadway and Elm street where a connection can conveniently be made with a proposed subway to be constructed running under Canal street, Wooster street, University Place and other streets.

The said route shall also include a suitable spur or connection in the Borough of Brooklyn, the centre line of which shall begin at or near the point of beginning above mentioned near the intersection of the centre line of Willoughby street with the centre line of Flatbush avenue extension; and running thence southeasterly under the said Flatbush avenue extension and under and across Fulton street to a possible connection with the subway now being constructed under Flatbush avenue pursuant to resolutions of this Board adopted January 24, 1901, and April 13, 1905.

The said last mentioned spur may be partly constructed in the same tunnels as a subway to be hereafter constructed under Willoughby street, the Flatbush avenue extension and

Fulton street, and may include suitable tracks to afford a means of connection with the said proposed subway last mentioned.

PLAN OF CONSTRUCTION.

The general plan of construction hereby adopted for the foregoing route is as follows:

There shall be four tracks throughout the whole of the said route from Willoughby street in Brooklyn to the line of Chrystie street in Manhattan. There shall be two tracks in each of the spurs connecting the said route with the proposed subway under the Bowery and two tracks in the spur or branch running westerly under Canal street to connect with the proposed subway under that street, as above described. There shall also be such additional tracks, not more than four in number, southeasterly from Willoughby street, as may be requisite to make proper connections with other subways near that point.

All of the above-mentioned tracks shall be placed in subway or tunnel; except that upon the Manhattan Bridge and the approaches thereto the tracks shall be such and so many of those to be constructed by the City as a part of the bridge structure as may be hereafter determined; and except that between the ends of the bridge tracks and the tunnel or tunnels the tracks of the railway hereby established shall be placed in open cuts or upon viaducts or otherwise, as may be necessary for efficient operation.

All of the tracks will be substantially parallel with each other and on substantially the same levels, except that wherever required by special necessities of surface or subsurface structures or other special or local necessities, and except for the purpose of avoiding grade crossings near the intersection of the Flatbush avenue extension with Willoughby street and the various connections at and near the westerly end of the Manhattan Bridge, and for the purpose of passing under and connecting with the proposed subway in the Bowery, and for the purpose of passing under the present subway, any one or more of the tracks may be depressed below the level of the other track or tracks to a depth of not more than twenty feet.

The tracks shall be placed in general along the central part of the Manhattan Bridge and the longitudinal streets of the route so far as may be practicable or convenient, except, as above provided, they shall be on the northerly side of Canal street, from the Bowery to Mulberry street, and except that wherever required by special or local necessities the tracks, or any one or more of them, may be diverted as far as necessary to one side or the other of the said bridge and the said longitudinal streets or any of them.

The roof of the tunnel shall be as near the surface as street conditions and grades will conveniently permit, except that wherever necessary to cross the line of other subways or proposed subways the tracks may be so depressed as to avoid grade crossings.

Wherever the tracks change from tunnel to viaduct the change shall be so made as to occupy or obstruct the surface of the street or bridge approach to the least possible extent consistent with the proper gradient for the tracks.

The tunnels above described shall in no case be less than thirteen feet in height in the clear.

The roof of the said tunnels shall be of iron or steel, with brick or concrete arches, supported when necessary by iron or steel or masonry columns, and resting upon masonry walls; or the roof shall be a masonry structure; or the whole of the lining may be of metal.

Viaducts shall be built with a width of 12½ feet for each track and with an additional width of 3 feet on each side for outside footways. Viaducts may be built of metal, or of masonry, or both.

The tracks may at any point of the said route or of the spur therein included be placed in the same tunnel; or there may be separate tunnels for one or more tracks, as shall be most convenient.

The tracks shall be of standard gauge; that is to say, of the width of 4 feet and 8½ inches between the rails. There shall be a width in the tunnels not exceeding 15 feet for each track in addition to the thickness of the supporting walls, except that at stations, switches, turnouts, curves and crossovers the width may be increased.

Adjacent tracks shall be connected by necessary and suitable switches and connections and an additional track for siding accommodations may be constructed not to exceed in length one-quarter of a mile for each mile of roadway.

Stations and station approaches shall, in general, be at the intersection of streets and shall be built under or, if the position of the tracks so requires, over the streets and immediately adjoining private abutting property, or through private property to be acquired for the purpose, or both under or over streets and through private property as aforesaid. The streets under which stations or station approaches shall be built may include cross streets, but no part of any cross street shall be used for a station approach at a distance greater than seventy-five feet from the exterior line or side of the longitudinal street of the route.

Wherever along any part of the routes above described it shall be necessary for the proper maintenance or accommodation of pipes, wires, sewers or other subsurface structures the removal, construction or reconstruction of which shall be rendered necessary by the construction of the railway, the width of any tunnel or subway may be enlarged on either or both sides by an additional width on each side of the route, not to exceed fifteen feet on either side, provided always that the limits hereinbefore provided as to certain longitudinal streets of the route shall be observed. All or any pipes, wires, sewers or other subsurface structures may be placed in suitable galleries to be constructed within the additional widths hereinbefore permitted. At each cross street where accommodation for pipes, wires, sewers and other subsurface structures shall be those provided within the tunnels or subways, such tunnels or subways, in order to provide convenient access to the same, may have, within the limit of the sides or exterior lines of such cross streets or such lines produced, an additional width on each side of the routes not to exceed fifteen feet.

Pipes, wires, sewers and other subsurface structures at any part of the said routes shall be removed or disturbed only when necessary for the construction and operation of the railway above referred to, and if removed or disturbed shall be placed under the several streets in such manner and in such location that the use and service thereof shall not be impaired. Such pipes, wires, sewers and other subsurface structures shall be left or shall be so arranged as to give free access for their repair or alteration, or for the placing with them, so far as there may be space, of new pipes, wires, sewers and other like structures, and for making connections between the same and abutting buildings at any time.

The manner of construction under the Flatbush avenue extension shall be by tunneling or excavation under cover, except in places where and at times when the Board shall give express permission to construct by open excavation.

Upon or along the Manhattan Bridge and the approaches thereto all work of construction shall be subject to the requirements of the Commissioner of Bridges. In the Borough of Manhattan at all points west of the Manhattan Bridge approach or other places under the jurisdiction of the Department of Bridges, the work shall be done by excavation under cover, except that the Board reserves the right to permit open excavation in Canal street west of the westerly side of the Bowery, in such places and during such times as it may direct.

In parks, parkways and public places under the jurisdiction of the Department of Parks, all trees injured or destroyed in the course of construction shall be replaced under the direction and to the satisfaction of said department.

MODE OF OPERATION.

The general mode of operation of the route or routes above described shall be by electricity or some other power not requiring combustion within the tunnels, and the motors shall be capable of moving trains at a speed of not less than forty miles per hour for long distances, exclusive of stops.

DEFINITIONS.

The word "street," wherever used herein, shall include an avenue or public place.

The words "Rapid Transit Act," wherever used herein, shall be taken and held to mean chapter 4 of the Laws of 1891 as amended by chapter 752 of the Laws of 1894 and other acts of the Legislature.

MAPS AND DRAWINGS.

It is further

Resolved, That the maps and drawings entitled "Board of Rapid Transit Railroad Commissioners of The City of New York —Routes and General Plan," one of the said drawings being marked "Key Map No. 7, Boroughs of Manhattan and Brooklyn" and four drawings marked "Manhattan and Brooklyn 7, Sheets Nos. 1 to 4, inclusive," be and they are hereby adopted as showing the foregoing routes and general plan for convenience merely, and that said maps and drawings are not to be deemed a part of the description of the route or a part of the general plan for any purpose whatsoever.

Brooklyn and Manhattan Loop Lines.

WHEREAS, The Board of Rapid Transit Railroad Commissioners for The City of New York has determined that a rapid transit railway or railways for the conveyance and transportation of persons and property, in addition to those already existing authorized or proposed, are necessary for the interest of the public and of The City of New York, and should be established therein as hereinafter provided; and

WHEREAS, This Board has duly made the inquest and investigation necessary or proper in the premises, and all such inquests and investigations as are necessary or proper for such determination;

NOW, THEREFORE, This Board, by the concurrent votes of at least six members, does hereby adopt the following route or routes for an additional rapid transit railway or railways in the City of New York, and does hereby determine and establish the said additional route or routes thereof as follows, and does hereby adopt a general plan of construction of the said railway or railways, the route or routes of which are herein provided, and does in such general plan hereby adopted show the general mode of operation, and such details as to manner of construction as may be necessary to show the extent to which any street, avenue or other public place is to be encroached upon and the property abutting thereon affected.

This Board, in adopting the said route or routes and general plans, expressly reserves all the powers in relation to the construction of the said route or routes which are conferred upon it by Section 34 of the Rapid Transit Act. In particular it reserves the right to contract for the construction of the whole road or all the roads provided for in the following plans in a single contract; or by separate contracts, executed from time to time, to provide for the construction of parts of the said road or roads or for the construction at first of two or more tracks over a part or parts of such road or roads, and afterwards of one or more additional tracks over a part or parts of such road or roads as the necessities of The City of New York and the increase of its population may, in the judgment of this Board, require; or to provide in a contract for any part of such railroad that, at a future time, upon the requirement of this Board, the contractor shall construct the remainder or any part of the remainder of said road as the growth of the population or the interests of the City may, in the judgment of this Board, require.

ROUTE.

A route or routes lying within the Boroughs of Brooklyn and Manhattan and made up of several sections as hereinafter described. The said sections are as follows:

SECTION 9-O: A route the centre line of which shall begin at a point in the Borough of Brooklyn, at the easterly end of the Williamsburgh Bridge approach, where a connection can conveniently be made with a rapid transit railway or rapid transit railways to be hereafter constructed under Broadway and Bedford avenue or other streets; and thence continuing over and along the Williamsburgh Bridge and over and across the East River to the Borough of Manhattan, and over and across the Williamsburgh Bridge plaza in Manhattan, and over and along Delancey street to a suitable point east of Norfolk street, where the said line shall descend below the surface; running thence westerly under and along Delancey street to the Bowery, and under and across the Bowery; thence continuing still westerly and parallel or nearly so with Broome street under private property, Elizabeth street, private property, Mott street and private property to a point in Mulberry street about half way between Broome street and Spring street; thence curving southwesterly under Mulberry street and private property to a point near the intersection of the easterly line of Marion street with the northerly line of Broome street; thence under and across Broome street to Centre street, and under and along Centre street to Grand street, where spurs will begin to run westerly under Grand street as hereinafter stated; thence still southerly and along Centre street to Walker street, where spurs will begin to run easterly under Walker street as hereinafter stated; thence still southerly under and along Centre street to its intersection with Duane street; and thence curving southeasterly and terminating at a suitable point under the proposed new terminal of the Brooklyn Bridge.

Also spurs beginning as above mentioned near the intersection of Centre street and Grand street. The said spurs may be two in number, subsequently uniting in a single spur as hereinafter stated. The centre line of the northerly one of said spurs shall begin at a suitable point in Centre street, near Broome street; running thence southerly under Centre street and curving westerly under Centre street and private property to a point in Grand street, between Centre street and Elm or Lafayette street, where it will unite with the centre line of the southerly spur hereinafter next described. The said southerly spur shall begin at a suitable point in Centre street, near its intersection with Howard street; running thence northerly and northwesterly under Centre street and private property to a point in Grand street, between Centre street and Elm or Lafayette street, to a point where it will unite with the centre line of the northerly spur above mentioned. From the said point of junction the centre line of the said spur shall run westerly under Grand street to a point between Thompson street and Sullivan street; thence curving under Grand street and private property and continuing westerly under and across Varick street; thence under private property to Canal street at a point between Canal street and Hudson street; thence diagonally under and across Canal street and under private property to a point in Hudson street about seventy-five feet southerly from the intersection of the easterly side of Hudson street with the southwesterly side of Canal street, and opposite to Desbrosses street; thence under and across Hudson street, and under and along Desbrosses street to its intersection with the marginal wharf built along the Hudson or North River.

Also spurs beginning as above mentioned near the intersection of Centre street and Walker street. Said spurs may be two in number, subsequently uniting in a single spur as hereinafter stated. The northerly one of said spurs shall begin at a suitable point in Centre street, between Canal street and Grand street; running thence southerly under and along Centre street and under and across Canal street to a point near the intersection of the southerly line of Canal street with the easterly line of Centre street; thence curving southeasterly under private property to a point in Walker street, between Centre street and Baxter street, where it will unite with the centre line of the southerly spur hereinafter next described. This said southerly spur shall begin at a suitable point in Centre street near its intersection with Franklin street; running thence northerly and northeasterly under Centre street and private property near the intersection of the easterly line of Centre street with the southerly line of Walker street, and there curving into Walker street and uniting at a point between Centre street and Baxter street with the said northerly spur. From the said point of junction the centre line of the said spur shall run easterly under and along Walker street and under and across Baxter street and under Harry Howard square and Canal street to a point near the intersection of Canal street with Christie street at which a connection can conveniently be made with a rapid transit railway to be hereafter constructed running from Brooklyn over and across the Manhattan Bridge.

Also a spur the centre line of which shall begin at the end of route 9-O above described under the proposed new terminal of the Brooklyn Bridge, and running thence southerly under the said Brooklyn Bridge Terminal and under and across Park row to William street and under and along William street to its intersection with Beekman street.

SECTION 9-A—A route the centre line of which shall begin at a point in the Borough of Brooklyn at or near the intersection of the centre line of Bedford avenue with the centre line of Lafayette avenue; running thence northerly under and along Bedford avenue to its intersection with Heyward street; thence under and across Heyward street to a point at or near the intersection of the northerly side of Heyward street with the easterly side of Bedford avenue; thence in a straight line under private property, Rutledge street, private property, Penn street, private property, Hewes street and private property to a point in the westerly side of Lee avenue about half-way between Hewes street and Hooper street; thence diagonally under and across Lee avenue to a point at or near the intersection of the northerly side of Hooper street with the easterly side of Lee avenue; thence in a straight line under private property, Keap street, private property, Rodney street, private property, Ross street and private property to a point in the southerly side of Division avenue about one hundred and twenty-five feet easterly from the intersection of the said southerly side of Division avenue with the southeasterly side of Wilson street; thence under and across Division avenue, private property, South Ninth street and private property again to a point at or near the intersection of the easterly side of Havemeyer street with the southerly side of Broadway; thence northerly and westerly under and over the Williamsburgh Bridge plaza to the Williamsburgh Bridge approach, at which a connection can be made with Section 9-O above described.

The said section shall also include suitable means of connection near the intersection of Lafayette avenue with Bedford avenue so as to unite with Section 9-F hereinafter described, which is to run under and along Lafayette avenue. Also suitable means of connection to unite with a subway to be hereafter constructed and which is to run northerly from the Williamsburgh Bridge plaza under Driggs avenue and other streets to the Borough of Queens.

SECTION 9-A1—A route the centre line of which shall begin at a point in the Borough of Manhattan at or near the intersection of the centre line of William street with the centre line of Beekman street at the southern end of the spur running from Section 9-O, as above described; running thence southerly under and along William street, and under and across Exchange place and Beaver street, and curving easterly to Old Slip; thence easterly under Old Slip and private property and under and across the East River and private property to the Borough of Brooklyn at a point in said borough near the intersection of Furman street with Montague street; and thence easterly under and along Montague street to a point near its intersection with Court street. Said section shall include suitable connections with other subways to be hereafter constructed near the intersection of William street and Maiden Lane, in the Borough of Manhattan.

SECTION 9-A3—A route the centre line of which shall begin at a point in the Borough of Brooklyn near the intersection of the centre line of Broadway with the centre line of Lafayette avenue produced, at which a connection can conveniently be made with a subway to be hereafter constructed under and along Lafayette avenue; running thence northwesterly under and along Broadway to a point near the junction of Throop avenue and Broadway, at which a spur to connect with a subway to be hereafter constructed under Union avenue may begin; thence still northwesterly under and along Broadway to a point about half-way between Marcy avenue and the Williamsburgh Bridge plaza; thence curving under Broadway, private property and the Williamsburgh Bridge plaza to a point opposite the centre line of the Williamsburgh Bridge and emerging from the ground at a suitable point in the Williamsburgh Bridge plaza, and running thence westerly under and over the Williamsburgh Bridge plaza to the Williamsburgh Bridge approach at which a connection can be made with Section 9-O above described.

SECTION 9-B—A route the centre line of which shall begin at a point in the Borough of Brooklyn in Fulton street, opposite the Borough Hall Park, at which a connection can conveniently be made with Section 9-C hereinafter described; and running thence northwesterly under and along Fulton street to a point about two hundred feet southerly from the intersection of the centre line of Fulton street with the southerly line of Myrtle avenue produced, at which point the section here described shall diverge into two separate branches. One of the said branches shall curve westerly under and across Court street to a point in Montague street west of Court street, at which a convenient connection can be made with Section 9-A1 in Montague street aforesaid. The other one of said branches shall continue northwesterly under Fulton street to a point near Myrtle avenue at which a convenient connection can be made with Section 9-E2 hereinafter described.

Also a suitable spur or connection from a point on the said Section 9-B, opposite the Borough Hall Park, running southeasterly under Fulton street to a possible connection with the subway to be constructed under Fulton street, by resolutions of this Board adopted January 24, 1901, as modified by resolutions of this Board adopted April 13, 1905.

SECTION 9-C—A route the centre line of which shall begin at a point in the Borough of Brooklyn under Lafayette avenue at or near its intersection with Fulton street at the point of beginning of Sections 9-D1 and 9-F hereinafter described; running thence northwesterly under Fulton street to a point near the beginning of the proposed extension of Flatbush avenue; thence curving and running northwesterly under the proposed extension of Flatbush avenue to a point about half way between DeKalb avenue and Willoughby street; thence curving westerly under private property near the intersection of the southerly line of Willoughby street with the westerly line of Prince street, to a point in Willoughby street about half way between Prince street and Gold street; thence westerly under and along Willoughby street to a point at or near the intersection of the centre line of Willoughby street with the easterly line of Adams street produced; and thence curving northwesterly and passing under private property in the angle between Adams street and Fulton street, and turning into Fulton street opposite the Borough Hall Park to the point of beginning of Section 9-B above described.

A part of the said Section 9-C may be constructed in the same tunnel as a subway to be hereafter constructed running from the Manhattan Bridge to the junction of Fulton street and Flatbush avenue, and may include suitable tracks to afford a means of connection with the said proposed subway.

SECTION 9-D1—A route the centre line of which shall begin at a point in the Borough of Brooklyn under Lafayette avenue at or near its intersection with Fulton street at the point of beginning of Section 9-C above described and of Section 9-F hereinafter described, and running thence westerly under and along Lafayette avenue to Flatbush avenue to a possible connection with the subway to be constructed under Flatbush avenue by resolutions of this Board adopted January 24, 1901, as modified by resolutions of this Board adopted April 13, 1905.

SECTION 9-E—A route the centre line of which shall begin at a point in the Borough of Manhattan, at or near the intersection of the centre line of William street with the centre line of Beekman street; running thence southeasterly under Beekman street and under and across the East River and private property to the Borough of Brooklyn and to a point in said Borough of Brooklyn at or near the intersection of Furman street and Cranberry street; thence easterly under and along Cranberry street to a point in Cranberry street, near Fulton street; thence curving southeasterly under private property into Fulton street and running southerly under and along Fulton street to a point about half way between Pineapple street and Clark street.

Also a spur beginning at or near the intersection of the centre line of William street with the centre line of Beekman street, in the Borough of Manhattan, the point of beginning of said Section 9-E, above described, and running thence westerly under and along William street and under and across Park Row and the City Hall Park to a point in said park at which a connection can conveniently be made with the City Hall loop of the subway heretofore constructed under resolutions of this Board adopted January 14 and February 4, 1897.

SECTION 9-E1—A route, the centre line of which shall begin at a point in the Borough of Manhattan, near the intersection of William street with Liberty street, at which a connection can conveniently be made with a subway to be hereafter constructed under Liberty street; and running from the said point of beginning southeasterly under and along Liberty street and under and along Maiden lane and under and across the East River and private property to the Borough of Brooklyn, to a point in said borough near the intersection of Furman street and Pineapple street; thence running easterly under and along Pineapple street to a point in Pineapple street, between Henry street and Fulton street; and thence curving southerly under Pineapple street and private property to a point in Fulton street about half way between Pineapple street and Clark street, where the said centre line will unite with the centre line of route 9-E, above described.

SECTION 9-E2—A route the centre line of which shall begin at a point in the Borough of Brooklyn, under Fulton street, about half way between Pineapple street and Clark street, at the end or point of junction of Sections 9-E and 9-E1, above described; and shall run thence southeasterly under and along Fulton street to a point at or near the intersection of Fulton street, Myrtle avenue and Court street, at which a connection or connections can conveniently be made with Section 9-B above described.

Section 9-F—A route, the centre line of which shall begin at a point in the Borough of Brooklyn, under Lafayette avenue, at or near its intersection with Fulton street, at the point of beginning of Sections 9-C and 9-D1, above described; running thence easterly under and along Lafayette avenue to a point at or near its intersection with Bedford avenue at which a connection can conveniently be made with Section 9-A, above described.

The said section shall also include suitable spurs or connections near the intersection of Lafayette avenue and Bedford avenue. The said spurs or connections shall be two in number, one curving northerly into Bedford avenue and the other curving southerly into Bedford avenue. The northerly one of the said spurs shall begin at a suitable point in Lafayette avenue near its intersection with Franklin avenue; running thence easterly under Lafayette avenue and curving northerly under Lafayette avenue and private property into Bedford avenue to a point at which a connection can conveniently be made with Section 9-A above described. The southerly one of said spurs shall begin at a suitable point in Lafayette avenue near its intersection with Franklin avenue; running thence easterly under Lafayette avenue and curving southerly under Lafayette avenue and private property to a point at or near the intersection of the westerly side of Bedford avenue with the northerly side of Clifton place, and thence under and along Bedford avenue to a point near Clifton place, at which a connection can conveniently be made with Section 9-K hereinafter described.

Section 9-G—A route the centre line of which shall begin at a point in the Borough of Brooklyn, under Lafayette avenue near the intersection of Lafayette avenue and Bedford avenue at which a connection can conveniently be made with Section 9-F above described; running thence easterly under Lafayette avenue to a point between Lewis avenue and Stuyvesant avenue at which connections can conveniently be made with subways, to be hereafter constructed, running easterly under Lafayette avenue and northerly under Stuyvesant avenue.

SECTION 9-H—A route the centre line of which shall begin at a point in the Borough of Brooklyn, at or near the intersection of Lafayette avenue and Broadway at the point of beginning of Section 9-A3 above described; running thence southeasterly under and along Broadway to a point at or near the intersection of Broadway, Fulton street and Jamaica avenue, at which a connection or connections can conveniently be made with a subway running southerly under Georgia avenue and a subway running northeasterly under Jamaica avenue.

SECTION 9-I—A route the centre line of which shall begin at a point in the Borough of Brooklyn at or near the intersection of Bedford avenue and Quincy street at the southerly end of Section 9-K hereinafter described; running thence southeasterly in a curve under Bedford avenue and private property to Gates avenue at a point between Bedford avenue and Nostrand avenue; thence easterly under and along Gates avenue to Broadway; and thence curving into Broadway at a point southeasterly from the intersection of Broadway and Gates avenue, at which a connection can conveniently be made with Section 9-H above described.

SECTION 9-K—A route the centre line of which shall begin at a point in the Borough of Brooklyn at the point of beginning of Section 9-G above described, at or near the intersection of Bedford avenue and Lafayette avenue; running thence southerly under and along Bedford avenue to a point at or near the intersection of Bedford avenue and Quincy street at the northerly end of Section 9-I above described.

This section shall also include a suitable spur or connection to unite with Section 9-F above described.

SECTION 9-K1—A route the centre line of which shall begin at a point in the Borough of Brooklyn near the intersection of Bedford avenue and Quincy street, at the southerly end of Section 9-K above described; running thence southerly under and along Bedford avenue to a point near the intersection of Bedford avenue and Eastern Parkway, at which a connection can conveniently be made by means of spurs with a subway to be hereafter constructed under and along said Eastern Parkway.

PLAN OF CONSTRUCTION.

The general plan of construction hereby adopted for the foregoing route is as follows:

For the part of Section 9-O above described across the Williamsburgh Bridge and its approaches there shall be two or more tracks as shall be hereafter determined by the Commissioner of Bridges. For the part of Section 9-O under Delancey street and Centre street to the new Brooklyn Bridge terminal there shall be four tracks. For the spur under Walker and Canal streets to the Manhattan Bridge there shall be two tracks. For the spur under Grand street and Desbrosses street there shall be two tracks. For the spur from the Brooklyn Bridge terminal under William street to Beekman street there shall be two tracks. For the whole of Section 9-A under Bedford avenue and Bedford avenue extended to the Williamsburgh Bridge plaza there shall be four tracks, except that between Division avenue and Broadway there may be two additional tracks in order to afford suitable connections near that point with other subways. For Section 9-A1, under William street and Old Slip in Manhattan, the East River and Montague street in Brooklyn, there shall be two tracks. For Section 9-A3 under Broadway there shall be four tracks. For Sections 9-B and 9-C under Fulton street, Willoughby street and other streets, there shall be four tracks. For Section 9-D1 under Lafayette avenue, between Fulton street and Flatbush avenue, there shall be two tracks. For Section 9-E under Beekman street in Manhattan, the East River, and Cranberry street and Fulton street in Brooklyn there shall be two tracks. For the spur running through Beekman street to the City Hall loop of the present subway there shall be two tracks. For Section 9-E1 under Liberty street and Maiden lane in Manhattan, the East River, and Pineapple street and Fulton street in Brooklyn, there shall be two tracks. For Section 9-E2 under Fulton street, between Pineapple street and Court street, there shall be two tracks. For Section 9-F under Lafayette avenue, from Fulton street to Bedford avenue, there shall be four tracks. For Section 9-G under Lafayette avenue, from Bedford avenue to Stuyvesant avenue, there shall be four tracks. For Section 9-H under Broadway, from Lafayette avenue to Fulton street, there shall be four tracks. For Section 9-I under Gates avenue, from Bedford avenue to Broadway, there shall be two tracks. For Section 9-K under Bedford avenue, between Lafayette avenue and Gates avenue, there shall be two tracks. For Section 9-K1 under Bedford avenue, between Gates avenue and the Eastern Parkway, there shall be two tracks. The several spurs or connections uniting the above sections with each other or with other subways to be hereafter constructed shall have no more than two tracks.

All of the above-mentioned tracks shall be placed in subway or tunnel, except that upon the Williamsburgh Bridge and the approaches thereto the tracks shall be two or more of those constructed by the City as a part of the bridge structure, and except that between the ends of the bridge tracks and the tunnel or tunnels, the tracks of the railway hereby established shall be placed in open cuts and on viaducts or otherwise, as may be necessary for efficient operation.

All of the tracks of the routes hereby established shall be substantially parallel with each other, and on substantially the same levels, except that wherever required by special necessities of surface or sub-surface structures or other special or local necessities and except for the purpose of avoiding grade crossings at the intersections of the several sections with each other or with spurs, branches or connections, or elsewhere, any one or more of the tracks may be depressed below the level of the other track or tracks to such depth as may be necessary; but this limitation as to the level of the tracks shall not apply to the portions of the route passing in tunnel under the East River.

The tracks shall be placed in general under the central part of the longitudinal streets of the route so far as may be practicable and convenient, but wherever required by special or local necessities or for curves the tracks or any one or more of them may be diverted as far as necessary to one side or the other of such longitudinal streets or any of them.

The roof of the tunnels when under a street shall be as near the surface as street conditions and grades will conveniently permit, except that in the approaches to the East River tunnels the depth shall be such as will conform to the grades of such river tunnels, and except that in passing under Water street, Pearl street, Nassau street, Broadway, Church street, Elm or Lafayette street, Wooster street, West Broadway, Hudson street and Washington street, in the Borough of Manhattan, and at intersections with other proposed rapid transit railway routes in the Borough of Brooklyn, such tunnels or subways may be depressed to such a depth under subways constructed or to be hereafter constructed as may be necessary for proper construction and operation.

Wherever the tracks change from tunnel to viaduct, or from viaduct to tunnel, the changes shall be so made as to occupy or obstruct the surface of the street to the least possible extent consistent with the proper gradient for the tracks.

The tunnels above described shall in no case be less than thirteen feet in height in the clear.

The roof of the said tunnels shall be of iron or steel with brick or concrete arches, supported when necessary by iron or steel or masonry columns and resting upon masonry walls; or the roof shall be a masonry structure; or the whole of the lining may be of metal.

Viaducts shall be built with a width of twelve and one-half feet for each track and with an additional width of three feet on each side for outside footways. Viaducts may be built of metal, or of masonry, or of both.

Adjacent tracks shall be connected by necessary and suitable switches and connections and an additional track for siding accommodations may be constructed not to exceed in length one-quarter of a mile for each mile of roadway.

The tracks may at any point of the said routes or of the spurs therein included be placed in the same tunnel; or there may be separate tunnels for one or more tracks, as shall be most convenient.

The tracks shall be of standard gauge, that is to say, of the width of four feet and eight and a half inches between the rails. There shall be a width in the tunnels not exceeding fifteen feet for each track in addition to the thickness of the supporting walls, except that at stations, switches, turnouts, curves and crossovers the width may be increased.

Stations and station approaches shall, in general, be at the intersections of streets and shall be built under or, if the position of the tracks so require, over the streets and immediately adjoining private abutting property, or through private property to be acquired for the purpose, or both under or over streets and through private property as aforesaid.

The streets under which stations or station approaches shall be built may include cross streets, but no part of any cross street shall be used for a station approach at a distance greater than seventy-five feet from the exterior line or side of the longitudinal street of the route.

Wherever along any part of the routes above described it shall be necessary for the proper maintenance or accommodation of pipes, wires, sewers or other sub-surface structures, the width of any tunnel or subway may be enlarged on either or both sides by an additional width on each side of the route, not to exceed fifteen feet on either side. All or any pipes, wires, sewers, or other sub-surface structures may be placed in suitable galleries to be constructed within the additional widths hereinbefore permitted. At each cross street where accommodation for pipes, wires, sewers and other sub-surface structures shall be those provided within the tunnels or subways, such tunnels or subways, in order to provide convenient access to the same, may have, within the limit of the sides or exterior lines of such cross streets or such lines produced, an additional width on each side of the routes not to exceed fifteen feet.

Pipes, wires, sewers and other sub-surface structures at any part of the said routes shall be removed or disturbed only when necessary for the construction and operation of the railway above referred to, and if removed or disturbed shall be placed under the several streets in such manner and in such location that the use and service thereof shall not be impaired. Such pipes, wires, sewers and other sub-surface structures shall be left or shall be so arranged as to give free access for their repair or alteration, or for the placing with them, so far as there may be space, of new pipes, wires, sewers and other like structures, and for making connections between the same and abutting buildings at any time.

The manner of construction shall in general be by tunneling, except in places where the Board shall give express permission to construct by open excavation; but upon or along the Williamsburgh Bridge and the approaches thereto, all work of construction shall be subject to the requirements of the Commissioner of Bridges.

In parks, parkways and public places under the jurisdiction of the Department of Parks, all trees injured or destroyed in the course of construction shall be replaced under the direction and to the satisfaction of said Department.

MODE OF OPERATION.

The general mode of operation of the route or routes above described shall be by electricity or some other power not requiring combustion within the tunnels, and the motors shall be capable of moving trains at a speed of not less than forty miles per hour for long distances, exclusive of stops.

DEFINITIONS.

The word "street," wherever used herein, shall include an avenue or public place.

The words "Rapid Transit Act," wherever used herein, shall be taken and meant to mean chapter 4 of the Laws of 1891 entitled "An Act to provide for Rapid Transit Railroads in Cities of over one million Inhabitants," as amended by chapter 752 of the Laws of 1894 and other acts of the Legislature.

MAPS AND DRAWINGS.

It is further

Resolved, that the maps and drawings entitled "Board of Rapid Transit Railroad Commissioners of The City of New York —Routes and General Plan," one of the said drawings being marked "Key Map, No. 5, Borough of Manhattan," four drawings being marked "Manhattan, No. 5," sheets Nos. 1, 2, 3 and 4, one drawing being marked "Key Map, No. 6, Borough of Manhattan," one drawing being marked "Manhattan No. 6," sheet No. 1, one drawing being marked "Key Map, No. 1, Borough of Brooklyn," and eight drawings being marked "Brooklyn, No. 1," sheets Nos. 1 to 8, inclusive, be and they are hereby adopted as showing the foregoing routes and general plans, for convenience merely, and that said maps and drawings are not to be deemed a part of the description of the routes or a part of the general plans, for any purpose whatever.

Brooklyn, Manhattan, and Long Island City Route.

WHEREAS, The Board of Rapid Transit Railroad Commissioners for The City of New York has determined that a rapid transit railway or railways for the conveyance and transportation of persons and property, in addition to those already existing, authorized or proposed, are necessary for the interest of the public and of The City of New York, and should be established therein as hereinafter provided; and

WHEREAS, This Board has duly made the inquest and investigation necessary or proper in the premises and all such inquests and investigations as are necessary or proper for such determination; NOW THEREFORE,

This Board, by the concurrent votes of at least six members, does hereby adopt the following route or routes for an additional rapid transit railway or railways in the City of New

York and does hereby determine and establish the said additional route or routes thereof, as follows, and does hereby adopt a general plan of construction of the said railway or railways, the route or routes of which are herein provided, and does, in such general plan hereby adopted, show the general mode of operation and such details as to manner of construction as may be necessary to show the extent to which any street, avenue or other public place is to be encroached upon and the property abutting thereon affected.

This Board, in adopting the said route or routes and general plans, expressly reserves all the powers in relation to the construction of the said route or routes which are conferred upon it by section 34 of the Rapid Transit Act. In particular it reserves the right to contract for the construction of the whole road or all the roads provided for in the following plans in a single contract, or by separate contracts, executed from time to time, to provide for the construction of parts of the said road or roads or for the construction at first of two or more tracks over a part or parts of such road or roads, and afterwards of one or more additional tracks over a part or parts of such road or roads, as the necessities of the City of New York and the increase of its population may, in the judgment of this Board, require; or to provide in a contract for any part of such railroad that, at a future time, upon the requirement of this Board, the contractor shall construct the remainder or any part of the remainder of said road, as the growth of the population or the interests of the City may, in the judgment of this Board, require.

ROUTES.

A route lying within the Boroughs of Brooklyn, Manhattan and Queens and made up of several sections as hereinafter described. The said sections are as follows:

Section 10-O—A route the centre of which shall begin at a point in the Borough of Brooklyn, under North Seventh street, distant about two hundred feet northwesterly from the intersection of the centre line of Union avenue with the centre line of Metropolitan avenue, at the northwesterly end of Section 10-D, hereinafter described; thence running northwesterly under and along North Seventh street to a point about half way between Driggs avenue and Bedford avenue, at which point spurs, running northerly and southerly to a connection with the subway to be constructed under Driggs avenue, known as Section 10-C hereinafter described, will begin; thence still northwesterly under North Seventh street and private property to the East River, and under the East River to the Borough of Manhattan and to a point on the westerly side of the East River between Thirteenth and Fourteenth streets; thence passing under private property to a point at or near the intersection of East Fourteenth street and Avenue D; and thence westerly under East Fourteenth street to a point about half way between Avenue B and Avenue C, where a connection can conveniently be made with a subway to be hereafter constructed under East Fourteenth street.

SECTION 10-A—A route the centre line of which shall begin at a point in the Borough of Brooklyn in Stuyvesant avenue at or near the intersection of the centre line of said avenue with the southerly line of Kosciusko street; running thence northerly under Stuyvesant avenue to its intersection with Broadway; thence continuing northerly under Broadway and private property to Myrtle avenue; thence still northerly under Myrtle avenue and private property, Jefferson street and private property, Melrose street and private property to a point at or near the intersection of the southeasterly side of Arion place and the southwesterly side of Bushwick avenue; thence northwesterly and northerly under and along Bushwick avenue to a point about half way between Devoe street and Metropolitan avenue; thence curving northwesterly and westerly under Bushwick avenue and private property into Metropolitan avenue; thence westerly under and along Metropolitan avenue to a point near its intersection with Union avenue, and thence curving westerly under Metropolitan avenue and Union avenue into North Seventh street and under North Seventh street to the easterly end of Section 10-O above described.

And also a spur beginning at or near the intersection of the centre line of Stuyvesant avenue and Kosciusko street, the place of beginning of Section 10-A above described, and curving thence southwesterly under Stuyvesant avenue and private property to Lafayette avenue, and thence under Lafayette avenue to a point about one hundred and fifty feet westerly from the westerly side of Stuyvesant avenue at the point of beginning of Section 10-B, hereinafter described.

SECTION 10-B—A route the centre line of which shall begin in the Borough of Brooklyn at a point in the centre line of Lafayette avenue distant about one hundred and fifty feet westerly from the intersection of the centre line of said Lafayette avenue with the westerly side of Stuyvesant avenue, being at the terminus of the spur running from Section 10-A above described; running thence easterly under Lafayette avenue to Patchen avenue, at which point a spur shall begin curving southeasterly under and along Broadway to a point about seventy-five feet southerly from the intersection of Lafayette avenue and Broadway where a connection can conveniently be made with another subway to be built under Broadway. The main line of Section 10-B, from the above mentioned point near the intersection of Broadway, Lafayette avenue and Patchen avenue, shall curve northeasterly under and across Broadway to Kossuth street; running thence northeasterly along Kossuth street to a point about one hundred feet southwesterly from the intersection of Kossuth street and Bushwick avenue; thence curving northerly under Kossuth street and private property to Bushwick avenue; thence under and across Bushwick avenue to Stanhope street; thence northeasterly under and along Stanhope street to a point about one hundred and fifty feet northerly from the intersection of the centre line of Stanhope street with the northerly line of St. Nicholas avenue; thence curving easterly and southeasterly under Stanhope street and private property to Cypress avenue at a point near the intersection of the southwesterly side of Cypress avenue with the northwesterly line of Himrod street, and thence southeasterly under and along Cypress avenue to a point at or near the intersection of the centre line of Cypress avenue with the centre line of Palmetto street.

Section 10-C—A route, the centre line of which shall begin at a point in the Borough of Brooklyn, near the intersection of the southerly side of Broadway with the easterly side of Havemeyer street, at which a connection can conveniently be made with a railway to be hereafter constructed under Bedford avenue and Bedford avenue extended or under and over private property and the Williamsburgh Bridge; running thence northeasterly under Broadway and the Williamsburgh Bridge plaza to a point at or near the intersection of the centre line of Driggs avenue with the northerly line of South Fourth street; thence running northerly under Driggs avenue and crossing under Section 10-O at the intersection of North Seventh street and Driggs avenue, and with spurs or connections near that point to unite with the said Section 10-O on North Seventh street; and still northerly under Driggs avenue and Williamsburgh Park to a point in the southwesterly side of Lorimer street distant about four hundred and ninety feet from the intersection of the said southwesterly side of Lorimer street with the southeasterly side of Nassau street; thence running under and across Lorimer street and curving under private property to a point in Manhattan avenue about half way between Nassau street and Driggs avenue; thence curving and running westerly and northwesterly under Manhattan avenue to a point about half way between Dupont street and Clay street; thence curving and running under private property, Clay street, private property, Box street, and private property to Ash street at a point about one hundred and fifty feet easterly from the intersection of the southerly side of Ash street with the easterly side of Manhattan avenue; thence still northerly and under Ash street and private property to Newtown Creek; thence under Newtown Creek to the Borough of Queens and to a point on the northerly side of said Newtown Creek distant about one hundred and eighty feet easterly from the intersection of the said northerly side of Newtown Creek with the northerly side of Manhattan avenue; thence still northerly and parallel, or nearly so, with Manhattan avenue, under private property, Borden avenue and private property again to a point in the southerly side of Third street about twenty-five feet easterly from the intersection of the southerly side of Third street with the southeasterly side of Jackson avenue; thence curving northeasterly under Third street and Jackson avenue and running northeasterly under and along Jackson avenue to a point in Jackson avenue about half way between Rogers street and Skillman avenue, where a connection can conveniently be made with a railway to be hereafter constructed over the Blackwell's Island Bridge.

Connecting Spurs.—The spurs connecting Sections 10-O and 10-C above described shall be two in number, diverging from a point in the centre line of North Seventh street about half-way between Driggs avenue and Bedford avenue. The centre line of the southerly one of such spurs shall curve from said point easterly and southerly under North Seventh street and private property to a point on the westerly side of Driggs avenue about seventy-five feet southerly from the intersection of the said westerly side of Driggs avenue with the southerly side of North Seventh street, and thence still southerly under Driggs avenue to a convenient point of connection with Section 10-C above described between North Seventh street and North Second street.

The centre line of the northerly one of such spurs shall curve from the point of beginning above described under North Seventh street and private property to a point in the westerly side of Driggs avenue about half-way between North Seventh street and North Eighth street, and thence under and along Driggs avenue to a convenient point of connection with Section 10-C above described between North Seventh street and North Twelfth street.

SECTION 10-D—A route the centre line of which shall begin at a point in the Borough of Brooklyn near the intersection of Union avenue and Broadway at which a connection can conveniently be made with a subway to be hereafter constructed under Broadway; running thence northerly through Union avenue to a point about half way between Devoe street and Metropolitan avenue; thence curving northwesterly under Metropolitan avenue into North Seventh street; and thence running northwesterly under and along North Seventh street to the easterly end of Section 10-O hereinbefore described.

PLAN OF CONSTRUCTION.

The general plan of construction hereby adopted for the foregoing routes is as follows:

For the whole of Section 10-O there shall be four tracks. For the whole of Section 10-A, including the spur or connection from Stuyvesant avenue into Lafayette avenue, there shall be four tracks. For the whole of Section 10-B, under Stuyvesant avenue, Kossuth street, Stanhope street and Cypress avenue, there shall be two tracks, with a third track between Reid avenue and Broadway to permit of convenient connection with the spur near that point. For Section 10-C, under Williamsburgh Bridge Plaza and Driggs avenue to a point between North Seventh street and North Twelfth street, where the northerly spur above described connecting with Section 10-O unites with the main portion of Section 10-C, there shall be four tracks; and from the said point northerly to the terminus of Section 10-C, in the Borough of Queens there shall be two tracks. For the whole of Section 10-D, under Union avenue and other streets, there shall be four tracks. There may also be in Section 10-O, between Driggs avenue and the East River two additional tracks, if required, for making convenient connections between Sections 10-O and 10-C above described. There may also be in Section 10-O, between Union avenue and Driggs avenue, two additional tracks if required for making convenient connections between said Section 10-O and Sections 10-A and 10-D above described.

All of the above-mentioned tracks shall be placed in subway or tunnel substantially parallel with each other and substantially on the same level except that wherever required by special necessities of surface or subsurface structures or other special or local necessities and except for the purposes of avoiding grade crossings near the intersection of Stuyvesant avenue and Lafayette avenue, Lafayette avenue and Broadway, and Driggs avenue and North Seventh street, all in the Borough of Brooklyn, or elsewhere, any one or more of the tracks may be depressed below the level of the other track or tracks to a depth of not more than twenty feet; but the limitation as to the level of the tracks shall not apply to the portion of the route under the East River.

The tracks shall be placed in general under the central part of the longitudinal streets of the route so far as may be practicable and convenient; but wherever required by special or local necessities or for curves, the tracks or any one or more of them may be diverted as far as necessary to one side or the other of such longitudinal streets or any of them.

The roof of the tunnels when under a street shall be as near the surface as street conditions and grades will conveniently permit, except that Section 10-C along Driggs avenue shall be depressed so as to pass under the line of Section 10-O, running under North Seventh street; and said Section 10-C may be depressed under the Williamsburgh Bridge Plaza, in the Borough of Brooklyn, so as to permit another rapid transit railway or other rapid transit railways to be constructed over it.

The tunnels above described shall in no case be less than thirteen feet in height in the clear.

The roof of the said tunnels shall be of iron or steel with brick or concrete arches, supported when necessary by iron or steel or masonry columns and resting upon masonry walls; or the roof shall be a masonry structure; or the whole of the lining may be of metal.

Adjacent tracks shall be connected by necessary and suitable switches and connections and an additional track for siding accommodations may be constructed not to exceed in length one-quarter of a mile for each mile of roadway.

The tracks may at any point of the said route or of the spur or loops therein included be placed in the same tunnel; or there may be separate tunnels for one or more tracks as shall be most convenient.

The tracks shall be of standard gauge, that is to say, of the width of four feet and eight and a half inches between the rails. There shall be a width in the tunnels not exceeding fifteen feet for each track in addition to the thickness of the supporting walls, except that at stations, switches, turnouts, curves and crossovers the width may be increased.

Stations and station approaches shall, in general, be at the intersections of streets and shall be built under the streets and immediately adjoining private abutting property, or through or under private property to be acquired for the purpose.

The streets under which stations or station approaches shall be built may include cross streets, but no part of any cross street shall be used for a station approach at a distance greater than seventy-five feet from the exterior line or side of the longitudinal street of the route.

Wherever along any part of the routes above described it shall be necessary for the proper maintenance or accommodation of pipes, wires, sewers or other subsurface structures, the removal, construction or reconstruction of which shall be rendered necessary by the construction of the railway, the width of any tunnel or subway may be enlarged on either or both sides by an additional width on each side of the route, not to exceed fifteen feet on either side. All or any pipes, wires, sewers or other subsurface structures may be placed in suitable galleries to be constructed within the additional widths hereinbefore permitted. At each cross street where accommodation for pipes, wires, sewers and other subsurface structures shall be those provided within the tunnels or subways, such tunnels or subways, in order to provide convenient access to the same, may have, within the limit of the sides or exterior lines of such cross streets or such lines produced, an additional width on each side of the routes not to exceed fifteen feet.

Pipes, wires, sewers and other sub-surface structures at any part of the said routes shall be removed or disturbed only when necessary for the construction and operation of the railway above referred to, and if removed or disturbed shall be placed under the several streets in such manner and in such location that the use and service thereof shall not be impaired. Such pipes, wires, sewers and other sub-surface structures shall be left or shall be so arranged as to give free access for their repair or alteration, or for the placing with them, so far as there may be space, of new pipes, wires, sewers and other like structures, and for making connections between the same and abutting buildings at any time.

The manner of construction shall be by tunneling or excavation under cover, except in places where the Board shall give express permission to construct by open excavation.

In parks, parkways and public places under the jurisdiction of the Department of Parks, all trees injured or destroyed in the course of construction shall be replaced under the direction and to the satisfaction of said Department.

MODE OF OPERATION.

The general mode of operation of the route or routes above described shall be by electricity or some other power not requiring combustion within the tunnels, and the motors shall be capable of moving trains at a speed of not less than forty miles per hour for long distances, exclusive of stops.

DEFINITIONS.

The word "street" wherever used herein shall include an avenue or public place.

The words "Rapid Transit Act" wherever used herein, shall be taken and held to mean chapter 4 of the Laws of 1891, entitled 'An Act to provide for Rapid Transit Railroads in Cities of over one million Inhabitants" as amended by chapter 752 of the Laws of 1894 and other acts of the Legislature.

MAPS AND DRAWINGS.

It is further

Resolved, That the maps and drawings entitled "BOARD OF RAPID TRANSIT RAILROAD COMMISSIONERS of The City of New York—Routes and General Plans," one of the said drawings being marked "Key Map, No. 5, Borough of Manhattan," one drawing being marked "Manhattan, No. 5, sheet No. 7," one drawing being marked "Key Map, No. 2, Borough of Brooklyn," and six drawings being marked "Brooklyn, No. 2," sheets Nos. 1 to 6, inclusive, be and they are hereby adopted as showing the foregoing routes and general plans, for conveniences merely, and that said maps and drawings are not to be deemed a part of the description of the routes or a part of the general plans, for any purpose whatever.

Fourth Avenue Route.

WHEREAS, The Board of Rapid Transit Railroad Commissioners for The City of New York has determined that a rapid transit railway or railways for the conveyance and transportation of persons and property, in addition to those already existing, authorized or proposed are necessary for the interest of the public and of The City of New York, and should be established therein as hereinafter provided; and

WHEREAS, This Board has duly made the inquest and investigation necessary or proper in the premises, and all such inquests and investigations as are necessary or proper for such determination; NOW, THEREFORE,

This Board, by the concurrent votes of at least six members, does hereby adopt the following route or routes for an additional rapid transit railway or railways in the City of New York, and does hereby determine and establish the said additional route or routes thereof as follows, and does hereby adopt a general plan of construction of the said railway or railways, the route or routes of which are herein provided, and does in such general plan hereby adopted show the general mode of operation and such details as to manner of construction as may be necessary to show the extent to which any street, avenue or other public place is to be encroached upon and the property abutting thereon affected.

This Board, in adopting the said route or routes and general plans, expressly reserves all the powers in relation to the construction of the said route or routes which are conferred upon it by Section 34 of the Rapid Transit Act. In particular it reserves the right to contract for the construction of the whole road or all the roads provided for in the following plans in a single contract; or by separate contracts, executed from time to time, to provide for the construction of parts of said road or roads or for the construction at first of two or more tracks over a part or parts of such road or roads, and afterwards of one or more additional tracks over a part or parts of such road or roads, as the necessities of The City of New York and the increase of its population may in the judgment of this Board require; or to provide in a contract for any part of such railroad that, at a future time, upon the requirement of this Board, the contractor shall construct the remainder, or any part of the remainder of said road as the growth of the population or the interests of the City may, in the judgment of this Board, require.

ROUTES.

A route lying wholly within the Borough of Brooklyn, and divided into several sections as hereinafter described. Said sections are as follows:

SECTION 11-A—A route the centre line of which shall begin at a point in the Borough of Brooklyn at or near the intersection of the centre line of Fourth avenue with the southerly line of Dean street; running thence southerly under Fourth avenue to a point at or near the intersection of the centre line of Fourth avenue with the centre line of Thirty-seventh street, where a spur will begin as hereinafter stated; thence still southerly under Fourth avenue to a point about half way between Sixty-third street and Sixty-fourth street, where another spur will begin as hereinafter stated; and thence still southerly under Fourth avenue to a point at or near the intersection of the centre line of Fourth avenue with the centre line of Sixty-fifth street.

The said Section 11-A shall include three spurs or connections as follows:

A spur or connection from the point of beginning of Section 11-A above described at or near the intersection of the centre line of Fourth avenue with the southerly line of Dean street, and running thence northerly under Fourth avenue and under and across Atlantic avenue to a possible connection with the subway to be constructed under Flatbush avenue by resolutions of this Board adopted January 24, 1901, as modified by resolutions of this Board adopted April 13, 1905.

Also a spur or connection beginning at a point near the intersection of the centre line of Fourth avenue with the centre line of Thirty-seventh street; thence curving southeasterly under Fourth avenue to a point in the easterly side thereof near the intersection of the said easterly side of Fourth avenue with the northerly side of Thirty-eighth street; thence still southeasterly under private property and Thirty-eighth street to a point in the southerly side of Thirty-eighth street not more than two hundred feet easterly from the easterly side of Fourth avenue, and thence under private property to a point about three hundred feet easterly from the easterly side of Fourth avenue, where a connection can conveniently be made with the South Brooklyn Railway.

And also a spur beginning at a point under Fourth avenue about half way between Sixty-third and Sixty-fourth streets; thence curving southeasterly under Fourth avenue to a point near the intersection of the easterly side thereof with the northerly side of Sixty-fourth street; thence still southerly under private property and Sixty-fourth street to a point in the southerly side of Sixty-fourth street not more than two hundred feet easterly from the easterly side of Fourth avenue, and thence under private property to a point in the block between Sixty-fourth street and Sixty-fifth street about four hundred feet easterly from the easterly side of Fourth avenue, where a connection can conveniently be made with the Sea Beach Railway.

SECTION 11-B—A route the centre line of which shall begin at a point in the Borough of Brooklyn at or near the intersection of the centre line of Fourth avenue with the centre line of Sixty-fifth street at the southerly end of Section 11-A above described; running thence southerly under Fourth avenue to a point about two hundred and fifty feet southerly from the intersection of the centre line of Fourth avenue with the southerly side of One Hundredth street produced.

SECTION 11-D—A route the centre line of which shall begin at a point in the Borough of Brooklyn at or near the intersection of the centre line of Fourth avenue with the southerly line of Dean street at the northerly end of Section 11-A above described; running thence in a curve under Fourth avenue to a point in the westerly side thereof between Pacific street and Atlantic avenue, and thence under private property to a point in the southerly side of Atlantic avenue distant about one hundred feet westerly from the intersection of the said southerly side of Atlantic avenue with the westerly side of Fourth avenue; running thence westerly under Atlantic avenue to a point about one hundred feet westerly from the intersection of the centre line of Atlantic avenue with the westerly side of Boerum place; curving thence northwesterly under Atlantic avenue and private property to a point at or near the intersection of the southerly side of State street with the easterly side of Court street; thence northerly under Court street to a point at or near the intersection of the centre line of Court street with the northerly side of Remsen street produced; and thence curving northerly and westerly under Court street and private property to a point in Montague street west of Court street at which a convenient connection can be made with a subway to be hereafter constructed in Montague street aforesaid.

And also a spur or connection to unite Section 11-D, above described, with a subway to be hereafter constructed under Fulton street northwesterly from Myrtle avenue. The centre line of the said spur shall begin at or near the intersection of the centre line of Court street with the northerly side of Remsen street produced; and shall run thence northerly under Court street and Fulton street to a point northwest of Myrtle avenue, at which a suitable connection can be made with said subway to be hereafter constructed.

And also a spur or connection to unite section 11-D above described with the subway to be hereafter constructed under Flatbush avenue in accordance with the resolutions of this Board adopted March 24, 1904. The centre line of the said spur shall begin at a point in Atlantic avenue about half way between Third avenue and Fourth avenue running thence easterly under Atlantic avenue to a point in the southerly side thereof, about half way between Fourth avenue and Flatbush avenue curving thence southeasterly under private property and Flatbush avenue and running to a suitable point in Flatbush avenue between Atlantic avenue and the Prospect Park plaza, at which a connection can conveniently be made with the said subway to be constructed under the said resolutions of March 24, 1904.

SECTION 11-E1—A route the centre line of which shall begin at a point in the Borough of Brooklyn at the northerly end of Section 11-A above described at or near the intersection of the centre line of Fourth avenue with the southerly line of Dean street; running thence northerly under Fourth avenue and for a part of the way in the same tunnel with, but at a different level from Section 11-D and the spur connecting with the Flatbush avenue subway as above described; and under and across Atlantic avenue and Flatbush avenue and curving under and across Hanson Place into Ashland Place; thence under and along Ashland Place to a point near Lafayette avenue, at which point a spur will begin, as hereinafter stated, to afford a connection with a subway to be hereafter constructed in Lafayette avenue; thence under and across Lafayette avenue and under and along Ashland Place to a point between Lafayette avenue and Fulton street, where a connection can conveniently be made by a suitable spur with a subway to be hereafter constructed under Fulton street.

And also suitable spurs or connections curving from Fourth avenue easterly under Dean street and Pacific street to connect with subways to be constructed in said last-mentioned streets between Flatbush and Atlantic avenues.

And also the said spur or connection to unite Section 11-E1 above described with a subway to be hereafter constructed under Lafayette avenue. The centre line of the said spur shall begin at a point at or near the intersection of Lafayette avenue and South Elliott Place, and shall run thence southwesterly under and along Lafayette avenue to a point at or near the intersection of the centre line of Lafayette avenue with the centre line of St. Felix street; thence curving southerly under Lafayette avenue and private property to Ashland place; and thence along Ashland place to a convenient point of connection with Section 11-E1 above described.

The railway to be constructed in Section 11-E1, including the spur or connection with Lafayette avenue, may, if necessary, occupy private property, to be acquired for the purpose on either or both sides of Ashland place.

PLAN OF CONSTRUCTION.

The general plan of construction hereby adopted for the foregoing routes is as follows:

For the route running under Fourth avenue, from Dean street to a point south of One Hundredth street, known as Sections 11-A and 11-B, there shall be four tracks. For the route running under Atlantic avenue and Court street, known as section 11-D, there shall be four tracks. For Section 11-E1 there shall be four tracks. For the branches or spurs from Fourth avenue through Dean street and Pacific street there shall be one track each; and for the several branches or spurs above described, running respectively from Lafayette avenue to Fourth avenue, from Court street to Fulton street, from Atlantic avenue to Flatbush avenue, and from Fourth avenue to the South Brooklyn Railway and the Sea Beach Railway there shall be two tracks each.

All of the above mentioned tracks shall be placed in subway or tunnel substantially parallel with each other. If there are two or more tracks in a tunnel, such tracks shall be on substantially the same levels, except that wherever required by special necessities of surface or sub-surface structures or other special or local necessities, and except for the purpose of avoiding grade crossings at various points between the intersection of Fourth avenue with Dean street and Ashland place, near Fulton street, and near the intersection of Flatbush avenue with Atlantic avenue, and of Court street with Montague street, and at points where spurs or connections begin, or elsewhere, any one or more of the tracks may be depressed below the level of the other track or tracks to such a depth as may be required for proper construction and operation, of not more than twenty feet.

The tracks shall be placed in general under the central part of the longitudinal streets of the route so far as may be practicable and convenient, except that wherever required by special or local necessities or for curves the tracks or any one or more of them may be diverted as far as necessary to one side or the other of the longitudinal streets or any of them. But in Fourth avenue no wall of the tunnel or part thereof (except at stations, station approaches, points where the route passes from streets to private property, curves and places of access to subsurface structures, as hereinafter provided) shall be within the distance of five feet of the exterior line or side of the said Fourth avenue. In all other longitudinal streets of the route any part of such streets may be occupied so far as the purposes of this general plan require.

The roof of a tunnel when under a street shall be as near the surface as street conditions and grades will conveniently permit; except in Ashland place, where the tracks shall be so far depressed as to pass under the subway heretofore authorized in Flatbush avenue and the spurs connecting with the subway to be hereafter constructed in Lafayette avenue.

The tunnels above described shall in no case be less than thirteen feet in height in the clear.

The roof of the said tunnels shall be of iron or steel with brick or concrete arches, supported when necessary by iron or steel or masonry columns and resting upon masonry walls; or the roof shall be a masonry structure; or the whole of the lining may be of metal.

Adjacent tracks shall be connected by necessary and suitable switches and connections, and an additional track for siding accommodations may be constructed, not to exceed in length one-quarter of a mile for each mile of roadway.

The tracks may at any point of the said route or of the spurs therein included be placed in the same tunnel; or there may be separate tunnels for one or more tracks, as shall be most convenient.

The tracks shall be of standard gauge, that is to say, of the width of four feet and eight and a half inches between the rails. There shall be a width in the tunnels not exceeding fifteen feet for each track, in addition to the thickness of the supporting walls, except that at stations, switches, turnouts, curves and crossovers the width may be increased.

Stations and station approaches shall, in general, be at the intersections of streets and shall be built under the streets and immediately adjoining private abutting property, or through or under private property to be acquired for the purpose. The streets under which stations or station approaches shall be built may include cross streets, but no part of any cross street shall be used for a station approach at a distance greater than seventy-five feet from the exterior line or side of the longitudinal street of the route.

Wherever along any part of the routes above described it shall be necessary for the proper maintenance or accommodation of pipes, wires, sewers or other sub-surface structures, the removal, construction or reconstruction of which shall be rendered necessary by the construction of the railway, the width of any tunnel or subway may be enlarged on either or both sides by an additional width on each side of the route, not to exceed fifteen feet on either side, provided always that the limits hereinbefore provided as to certain longitudinal streets of the route shall be observed. All or any pipes, wires, sewers or other sub-surface structures may be placed in suitable galleries, to be constructed within the additional widths hereinbefore permitted. At each cross street where accommodation for pipes, wires, sewers and other sub-surface structures shall be those provided within the tunnels or subways, such tunnels or subways, in order to provide convenient access to the same, may have, within the limit of the sides or exterior lines of such cross streets or such lines produced, an additional width on each side of the routes not to exceed fifteen feet.

Pipes, wires, sewers and other sub-surface structures at any part of the said routes shall be removed or disturbed only when necessary for the construction and operation of the railway above referred to, and if removed or disturbed shall be placed under the several streets in such manner and in such location that the use and service thereof shall not be impaired. Such pipes, wires, sewers and other sub-surface structures shall be left or shall be so arranged as to give free access for their repair or alteration, or for the placing with them, so far as there may be space, of new pipes, wires, sewers and other like structures, and for making connections between the same and abutting buildings at any time.

The manner of construction shall be by tunneling or excavation under cover, except in places where the Board shall give express permission to construct by open excavation.

In parks, parkways, and public places under the jurisdiction of the Department of Parks, all trees injured or destroyed in the course of construction shall be replaced under the direction and to the satisfaction of said Department.

MODE OF OPERATION.

The general mode of operation of the route or routes above described shall be by electricity or some other power not requiring combustion within the tunnels, and the motors shall be capable of moving trains at a speed of not less than forty miles per hour for long distances, exclusive of stops.

DEFINITIONS.

The word "street" wherever used herein, shall include an avenue or public place.

The words "Rapid Transit Act," whenever used herein, shall be taken and held to mean chapter 4 of the Laws of 1891 as amended by chapter 752 of the Laws of 1894 and other acts of the Legislature.

MAPS AND DRAWINGS.

It is further

Resolved, that the maps and drawings entitled "BOARD OF RAPID TRANSIT RAILROAD COMMISSIONERS of the City of New York—Routes and General Plan," one of the said drawings being marked "Key Map No. 3, Borough of Brooklyn," and five of the said drawings being marked "Brooklyn No. 3," sheets Nos.

1 to 5, inclusive, be and they are hereby adopted as showing the foregoing routes and general plans, for convenience merely, and that said maps and drawings are not to be deemed a part of the description of the routes or a part of the general plans, for any purpose whatever.

Bensonhurst, Bath Beach and Coney Island Route.

WHEREAS, This Board has determined that a rapid transit railway for the conveyance and transportation of persons and property in addition to those already existing, authorized or proposed, is necessary for the interest of the public and The City of New York, and should be established as hereinafter provided.

NOW, THEREFORE, This Board does hereby adopt the following route for a rapid transit railway in the City of New York, and does hereby determine and establish the said route thereof as follows, and does hereby adopt a general plan of construction of the said railway the route of which is herein provided, and does in such general plan hereby adopted show the general mode of operation and such details as to manner of construction as may be necessary to show the extent to which any street, avenue or other public place is to be encroached upon and the property abutting thereon affected.

This Board, in adopting the said route and general plans, expressly reserves all the powers in relation to the construction of the said road which are conferred upon it by section 34 of the Rapid Transit Act. In particular, it reserves the right to contract for the construction of the whole road provided for in the following plans in a single contract; or by separate contracts, executed from time to time, to provide for the construction of parts of said road or for the construction at first of two or more tracks over a part or parts of such road, and afterwards of one or more additional tracks over a part or parts of said road, as the necessities of The City of New York and the increase of its population may in the judgment of this Board require; or to provide in a contract for any part of such railroad that, at a future time, upon the requirement of this Board, the contractor shall construct the remainder or any part of the remainder of said road as the growth of the population or the interests of the City may, in the judgment of this Board, require.

ROUTE.

A route the centre line of which shall begin in the Borough of Brooklyn at a point at or near the intersection of Fourth avenue and Thirty-sixth street at which connections can conveniently be made with another subway or other subways to be hereafter constructed running southerly under Fourth avenue. The said centre line of the route hereby adopted shall thence run easterly and southeasterly, curving under Fourth avenue and private property, Thirty-ninth street and private property again, to a point in Fortieth street near the intersection of Fortieth street with the westerly line of Fifth avenue; running thence easterly under Fortieth street to a point at or near the intersection of Fortieth street with the easterly side of Ninth avenue; curving thence southeasterly and southerly under Fortieth street and private property to a point near the intersection of the westerly side of New Utrecht avenue with the northerly side of Forty-first street; thence running under and along New Utrecht avenue in a southerly direction to a point immediately south of its intersection with Eighty-first street; thence curving southeasterly and easterly under private property, Eighty-fourth street, private property again, Eighteenth avenue, Eighty-fifth street and private property again, to a point in Eighty-sixth street between Eighteenth and Nineteenth avenues; running thence southeasterly under and along Eighty-sixth street to a point about half way between Bay Thirty-fourth street and Bay Thirty-fifth street, where the said route will emerge from the surface and continue thence upon a viaduct structure; and from the said point running southeasterly along and over Eighty-sixth street to a point at or near the intersection of Eighty-sixth street with Bay Forty-first street; and then crossing southeasterly over private property, Twenty-sixth avenue and private property to a point in Stillwell avenue between its intersection with Eighty-sixth street and its intersection with Bay Forty-third street; and thence running southerly over and along Stillwell avenue and crossing the Gravesend Ship Canal on a bridge and continuing along Stillwell avenue to a point in Coney Island about half way between Neptune avenue and Mermaid avenue where the tracks will diverge so as to form a loop. From the said point of divergence the centre line of the said loop will run southerly over and along Stillwell avenue to Surf avenue; thence curving westerly and running over and along Surf avenue to West Fifteenth street; thence curving northerly and running over and along West Fifteenth street to a point in the easterly side thereof about half way between Surf avenue and Mermaid avenue; thence curving northeasterly and running over private property and over and across Mermaid avenue to a point at or near the intersection of the northerly line of Mermaid avenue with the westerly line of Stillwell avenue; and thence running northerly over and along Stillwell avenue to the point or place of beginning of the said loop.

PLAN OF CONSTRUCTION.

The general plan of construction hereby adopted is as follows:

For the whole of the route above described there shall be four tracks, except in the above-described loop where there shall be two tracks.

All the above-mentioned tracks shall be substantially parallel with each other and on substantially the same level except that between the easterly side of Fifth avenue and the point of connection with the subway or subways to be constructed in Fourth avenue the tracks shall be at such levels and on such alignments as to permit of proper connections; and except, also, that wherever else required by special necessities of surface or subsurface structures or other special or local necessities or for the purpose of avoiding grade crossings, any one or more of the tracks may be elevated above or depressed below the other track or tracks so far as necessary.

The tracks shall be placed in tunnels or subways, except that easterly and southerly from the point where the said route as above described emerges to the surface in Eighty-sixth street the tracks shall be carried upon a viaduct over and along the above-described route on Eighty-sixth street and Stillwell avenue. Near the said point of emergence the said railroad will be constructed partly in open cut and partly on an embankment. If and when all the four tracks herein provided for are constructed, the said open cut and embankment will occupy a space in Eighty-sixth street about sixty feet in width, extending from Twenty-third avenue to Twenty-fourth avenue. The open cut portion will extend southeasterly from Twenty-third avenue to about half way between Bay Thirty-fourth street and Bay Thirty-fifth street; and the embankment will extend southeasterly from the end of the open cut to Twenty-fourth avenue. The said open cut and embankment will therefore occupy all but about forty feet in width of said Eighty-sixth street, between Twenty-third avenue and Twenty-fourth avenue, leaving only about twenty feet on each side for a roadway and sidewalk and probably necessitating a widening of the said street between the said avenues by the legally constituted authorities of The City of New York.

The tracks shall be placed in general under or over the central part of the longitudinal streets and avenues forming a portion of the route above described so far as may be practicable and convenient, but wherever required by special or local necessities or for curves, the tracks or any one or more of them may be diverted as far as necessary to one side or the other of such streets or avenues, or any of them, and any part of said streets or avenues may be occupied so far as the purposes of this general plan require.

Wherever the tracks change from tunnel to viaduct or from viaduct to tunnel, the change shall be made so as to involve the use of the surface to the least possible extent consistent with the proper gradient for the tracks.

Wherever necessary for the proper support of the surface of a street, the roof of the tunnels shall be of iron or steel with brick or concrete arches supported when necessary by iron or steel or masonry columns and resting upon masonry walls; or the roof shall be a masonry structure; or the whole of the lining may be of metal.

The roof of the tunnels when under a street shall in general be as near the street surface as street conditions and grades will conveniently permit, the base of the rail under Sixth avenue being, however, about one hundred feet below the surface, at Seventh avenue about ninety-five feet below the surface, at Eighth avenue about sixty feet below the surface and at Ninth avenue about forty feet below the surface.

The tunnels shall in no case be less than thirteen feet in height in the clear.

There shall be a width in the tunnels not exceeding fifteen feet for each track in addition to the thickness of the supporting walls, except that at stations, switches, turnouts, curves and crossovers the width may be increased. Viaducts shall be built with a width of twelve and a half feet for each track except on curves or where greater width is required for special construction, and with an additional width of three feet on each side for outside footways. Viaducts may be built of metal or of masonry or of both.

The tracks shall be of standard gauge, that is to say, of the width of four feet and eight and one-half inches between the rails.

Adjacent tracks shall be connected by necessary and suitable switches and connections, and an additional track for siding accommodations may be constructed not to exceed in length one-quarter of a mile for each mile of roadway.

The tracks wherever constructed below the surface may at any point of the route be placed in the same tunnel; or there may be separate tunnels for one or more tracks, as shall be most convenient.

Stations and station approaches shall in general be at the intersection of streets and shall be built under or, if the positions of the tracks so require, over the streets and immediately adjoining private abutting property or through private property to be acquired for the purpose, or both under or over streets and through private property as aforesaid. The streets under which stations or station approaches shall be built may include cross streets, but no part of any cross street shall be used for a station approach at a distance greater than seventy-five feet from the exterior line or side of the longitudinal street or avenue of the route.

Wherever along any part of the routes above described it shall be necessary for the proper maintenance or accommodation of pipes, wires, sewers or other subsurface structures, the removal, construction or reconstruction of which shall be rendered necessary by the construction of the railway, the width of any tunnel or subway may be enlarged on either or both sides by an additional width on each side of the route, not to exceed fifteen feet on either side, provided always that the limits hereinbefore provided as to certain longitudinal streets of the route shall be observed. All or any pipes, wires, sewers or other subsurface structures may be placed in suitable galleries to be constructed within the additional widths hereinbefore permitted. At each cross street where accommodation for pipes, wires, sewers and other subsurface structures shall be those provided within the tunnels or subways, such tunnels or subways, in order to provide convenient access to the same, may have, within the limit of the sides or exterior lines of such cross streets or such lines produced, an additional width on each side of the routes not to exceed fifteen feet.

Pipes, wires, sewers, street railway tracks, poles for electric wires and other surface and subsurface structures at any part of the said routes shall be removed or disturbed only when necessary for the construction and operation of the railway above referred to, and if removed or disturbed shall be placed upon, over or under the several streets in such manner and in such location that the use and service thereof shall not be impaired. Pipes, wires, sewers and other subsurface structures shall be left or shall be so arranged as to give free access for their repair or alteration, or for the placing with them, so far as there may be space, of new pipes, wires, sewers and other like structures, and for making connections between the same and abutting buildings at any time.

The manner of construction of subways shall be by tunneling or open excavation.

In parks, parkways and public places under the jurisdiction of the Department of Parks all trees injured or destroyed in the course of construction shall be replaced, under the direction and to the satisfaction of said Department.

MODE OF OPERATION.

The general mode of operation of the route or routes above described shall be by electricity or some other power not requiring combustion within the tunnels, and the motors shall be capable of moving trains at a speed of not less than forty miles per hour for long distances, exclusive of stops.

DEFINITIONS.

The word "streets," wherever used herein, shall include an avenue or public place.

The words "Rapid Transit Act," wherever used herein, shall be taken and held to mean chapter 4 of the Laws of 1891, entitled "An Act to provide for rapid transit railroads in cities of over one million inhabitants," as amended by chapter 752 of the Laws of 1894 and other acts of the Legislature.

MAPS AND DRAWINGS.

It is further

Resolved, That the maps and drawings entitled "Board of Rapid Transit Railroad Commissioners of The City of New York —Routes and General Plan—Bensonhurst Route," one of the said drawings being marked "Key Map No. 4, Borough of Brooklyn, revised May 31, 1906," and the other drawings being marked "Brooklyn No. 4, Sheet No. 1," "Brooklyn No. 4, Sheet No. 2, revised April 4, 1906," "Brooklyn No. 4, Sheet No. 3," "Brooklyn No. 4, Sheet No. 4, revised May 31, 1906," be and they are hereby adopted as showing the foregoing route and general plan for convenience merely, and that said maps and drawings are not to be deemed a part of the description of the routes or a part of the general plans for any purpose whatever.

UNIVERSITY OF MICHIGAN
3 9015 02092 8605

ARTES
VERITAS
SCIENTIA
LIBRARY OF THE
UNIVERSITY OF MICHIGAN
TUEBOR
CIRCUMSPICE
TRANSPORTATION
LIBRARY

www.ingramcontent.com/pod-product-compliance
Lightning Source LLC
LaVergne TN
LVHW011259110826
845149LV00001B/186

* 9 7 8 1 4 1 8 1 8 8 6 7 2 *